Tobacco companies spend tens of billions of dollars each year on tobacco advertising, promotion and sponsorship.

One third of youth experimentation with tobacco occurs as a result of exposure to tobacco advertising, promotion and sponsorship.

mpower

Monitor	Monitor tobacco use and prevention policies
Protect	Protect people from tobacco smoke
Offer	Offer help to quit tobacco use
Warn	Warn about the dangers of tobacco
Enforce	Enforce bans on tobacco advertising, promotion and sponsorship
Raise	Raise taxes on tobacco

Complete bans on tobacco advertising, promotion and sponsorship decrease tobacco use.

WHO Report on the Global Tobacco Epidemic, 2013: Enforcing bans on tobacco advertising, promotion and sponsorship is the fourth in a series of WHO reports that tracks the status of the tobacco epidemic and the impact of interventions implemented to stop it.

WHO Library Cataloguing-in-Publication Data

WHO report on the global tobacco epidemic, 2013: enforcing bans on tobacco advertising, promotion and sponsorship.

1.Smoking - prevention and control. 2.Advertising as topic – methods. 3.Tobacco industry – legislation. 4.Persuasive communication. 5.Health policy. I.World Health Organization.

ISBN 978 92 4 150587 1 (NLM classification: WM 290)
ISBN 978 92 4 069160 5 (PDF)
ISBN 978 92 4 069161 2 (ePub)

Printed in Luxembourg

World Health Organization

WHO REPORT ON THE GLOBAL TOBACCO EPIDEMIC, 2013

Enforcing bans on tobacco advertising, promotion and sponsorship

Made possible by funding from Bloomberg Philanthropies

Contents

Appendices VI to XII are available online at http://www.who.int/tobacco

ABBREVIATIONS

AFR	**WHO African Region**
AMR	**WHO Region of the Americas**
CDC	**Centers for Disease Control and Prevention**
COP	**Conference of the Parties to the WHO FCTC**
EMR	**WHO Eastern Mediterranean Region**
EUR	**WHO European Region**
NRT	**nicotine replacement therapy**
SEAR	**WHO South-East Asia Region**
STEPS	**WHO's STEPwise approach to Surveillance**
US$	**United States dollar**
WHO	**World Health Organization**
WHO FCTC	**WHO Framework Convention on Tobacco Control**
WPR	**WHO Western Pacific Region**

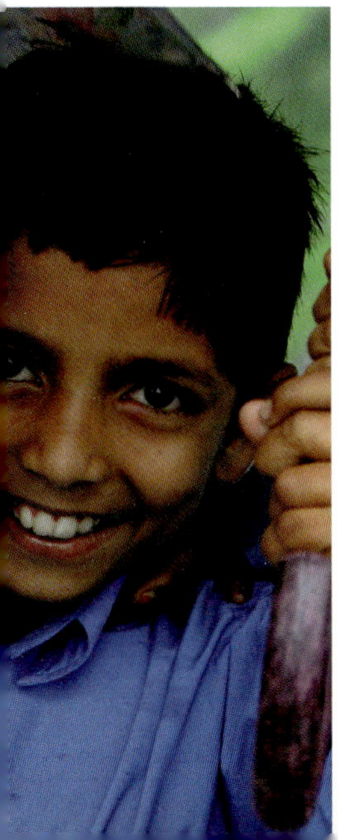
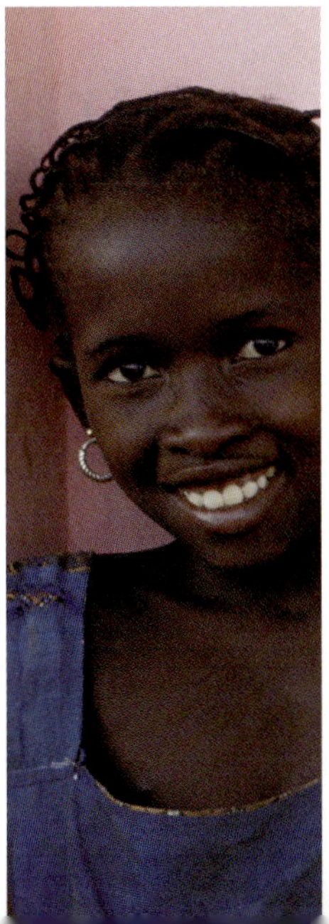
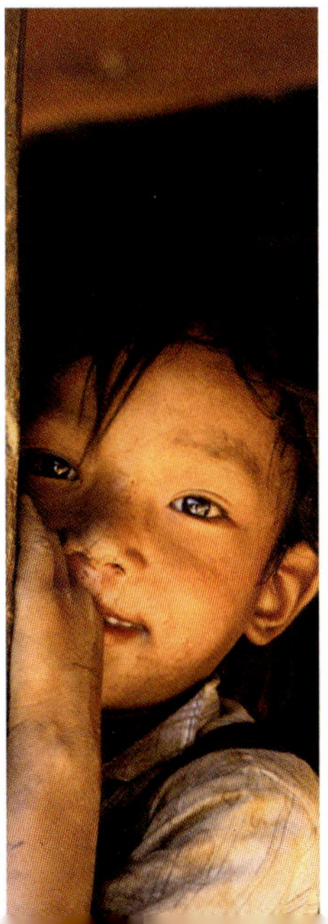
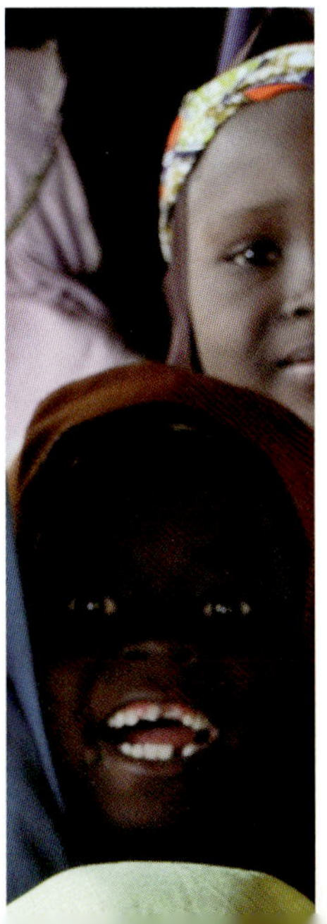

Globally, the population covered by at least one effective tobacco control measure has more than doubled.

We have the tools and we have the will. Millions of lives stand to be saved – we must act together and we must act now.

Dr Oleg Chestnov, Assistant Director-General, World Health Organization

ONE THIRD OF THE WORLD'S POPULATION - 2.3 BILLION PEOPLE - ARE NOW COVERED BY AT LEAST ONE EFFECTIVE TOBACCO CONTROL MEASURE

AN ADDITIONAL 3 BILLION PEOPLE ARE COVERED BY A HARD-HITTING NATIONAL MASS MEDIA CAMPAIGN

When WHO's Member States adopted the WHO Framework Convention on Tobacco Control (WHO FCTC) in 2003, the promise of giving governments real power to combat the deadly effects of tobacco consumption was realized. Ten years later, the tremendous growth in the number of people covered by tobacco control measures is testament to the strength and success of the WHO Framework Convention, and the will of governments to protect their citizens.

This report, WHO's fourth in the series, provides a country-level examination of the global tobacco epidemic and identifies countries that have applied selected measures for reducing tobacco use. Five years ago, WHO introduced the MPOWER measures as a practical, cost-effective way to scale up implementation of specific provisions of the WHO FCTC on the ground. Since then, globally the population covered by at least one effective tobacco control measure has more than doubled from 1 billion to 2.3 billion. This comprises more than a third of the world's population. Mass media campaigns have been shown in 37 countries, covering an additional 3 billion people. As part of a comprehensive tobacco control programme, these measures will, without doubt, save lives.

Advancement such as this is possible because countries, regardless of size or income, are committed to taking the steps necessary to reduce tobacco use and tobacco-related illnesses.

This report focuses on enforcing bans on tobacco advertising, promotion and sponsorship (TAPS). TAPS bans are one of the most powerful tools that countries can put in place to protect their populations. In the past two years, impressive progress has been made. The population covered by a TAPS ban has more than doubled, increasing by almost 400 million people. Demonstrating that such measures are not limited to high-income countries, 99% of the people newly covered live in low- and middle-income countries.

However, the report also serves to show us where there is still work to be done. Only 10% of the world's population is covered by a complete TAPS ban. The tobacco industry spares no expense when it comes to marketing their products – estimates indicate that it spends tens of billions of dollars each year on advertising, marketing and promotion. This is an industry eager to target women and children, and to forward their broad, overt ambition to open new markets in developing countries.

Countries that have implemented TAPS bans have demonstrably and assuredly saved lives. These countries can be held up as models of action for the many countries that need to do more to protect their people from the harms of tobacco use. With populations ageing and noncommunicable diseases (NCDs) on the rise, tackling a huge and entirely preventable cause of disease and death becomes all the more imperative. The global community has embraced this reality, as reflected by the Political Declaration of the High-level Meeting of the United Nations General Assembly on the Prevention and Control of Noncommunicable Diseases, in which heads of state and government acknowledged that NCDs constitute one of the major challenges to development in the 21st century.

NCDs – primarily cancers, diabetes and cardiovascular and chronic lung diseases – account for 63% of all deaths worldwide, killing an astounding 36 million people each year. The vast majority (86%) of premature deaths from NCDs occur in developing countries. Tobacco use is one of the biggest contributing agents and therefore tobacco control must continue to be given the high priority it deserves.

In May 2013, the World Health Assembly adopted the WHO global action plan for the prevention and control of noncommunicable diseases 2013–2020, in which reducing tobacco use is identified as one of the critical elements of effective NCD control. The global action plan comprises a set of actions which – when performed collectively by Member States, WHO and international partners – will set the world on a new course to achieve nine globally agreed targets for NCDs; these include a reduction in premature mortality from NCDs by 25% in 2025 and a 30% relative reduction in prevalence of current tobacco use in persons aged 15 years and older.

Since 2010, 18 new countries have implemented at least one effective tobacco control measure at the highest level. There are now 92 countries that have achieved this commendable goal, which puts them on track to achieve the adopted target on time. With the support of WHO and our intergovernmental and civil society partners, countries will continue to use a whole-of-government approach to scale up the evidence-based tobacco control measures that we know save lives, leading to full implementation of the WHO FCTC.

Dr Margaret Chan, Director-General of WHO, has been a tireless champion of tobacco control and has been forthright in speaking against the tobacco industry, which continues to profit from its deadly products. This and future editions of this report are key components of the global tobacco control fight, measuring how much has been achieved and identifying places where more work must be done. We have the tools and we have the will. Millions of lives stand to be saved – we must act together and we must act now.

Dr Oleg Chestnov

Summary

The WHO Framework Convention on Tobacco Control (WHO FCTC) recognizes the substantial harm caused by tobacco use and the critical need to prevent it. Tobacco kills approximately 6 million people and causes more than half a trillion dollars of economic damage each year. Tobacco will kill as many as 1 billion people this century if the WHO FCTC is not implemented rapidly.

Although tobacco use continues to be the leading global cause of preventable death, there are proven, cost-effective means to combat this deadly epidemic. In 2008, WHO identified six evidence-based tobacco control measures that are the most effective in reducing tobacco use. Known as "MPOWER", these measures correspond to one or more of the demand reduction provisions included in the WHO FCTC: Monitor tobacco use and prevention policies, Protect people from tobacco smoke, Offer help to quit tobacco use, Warn people about the dangers of tobacco, Enforce bans on tobacco advertising, promotion and sponsorship, and Raise taxes on tobacco. These measures provide countries with practical assistance to reduce demand for tobacco in line with the WHO FCTC, thereby reducing related illness, disability and death. The continued success in global tobacco control is detailed in this year's *WHO Report on the Global Tobacco Epidemic, 2013*, the fourth in a series of WHO reports. Country-specific data are updated and aggregated in the report.

To ensure ongoing improvement in data analysis and reporting, the various levels of achievement in the MPOWER measures have been refined and, to the extent possible, made consistent with updated WHO FCTC guidelines. Data from earlier reports have also been reanalysed so that they better reflect these new definitions and allow for more direct comparisons of the data across years. As in past years, a streamlined summary version of this year's report has been printed, with online-only publication of more detailed country-specific data (http://www.who.int/tobacco).

There continues to be substantial progress in many countries. More than 2.3 billion people living in 92 countries – a third of the world's

More than 2.3 billion people are now covered by at least one of the MPOWER measures at the highest level of achievement.

population – are now covered by at least one measure at the highest level of achievement (not including Monitoring, which is assessed separately). This represents an increase of nearly 1.3 billion people (and 48 countries) in the past five years since the first report was released, with gains in all areas. Nearly 1 billion people living in 39 countries are now covered by two or more measures at the highest level, an increase of about 480 million people (and 26 countries) since 2007.

In 2007, no country protected its population with all five or even four of the measures. Today, one country, Turkey, now protects its entire population of 75 million people with all MPOWER measures at the highest level.

Three countries with 278 million people have put in place four measures at the highest level. All four of these countries are low- or middle-income.

Most of the progress in establishing the MPOWER measures over the past five years since the first report was launched, has been achieved in low- and middle-income countries and in countries with relatively small populations. More high-income and high-population countries need to take similar actions to fully cover their people by completely establishing these measures at the highest achievement level.

This year's report focuses on complete bans on tobacco advertising, promotion and sponsorship (TAPS), which is a highly effective way to reduce or eliminate exposure to cues for tobacco use. The report provides a comprehensive overview of the evidence base for establishing TAPS bans, as well as country-specific information on the status of complete bans and bans on individual TAPS components.

While there has been a steady increase in the number of countries that have established a complete TAPS ban and the number of people worldwide protected by this type of ban, this measure has yet to be widely adopted. Only 24 countries (with

SHARE OF THE WORLD POPULATION COVERED BY SELECTED TOBACCO CONTROL POLICIES, 2012

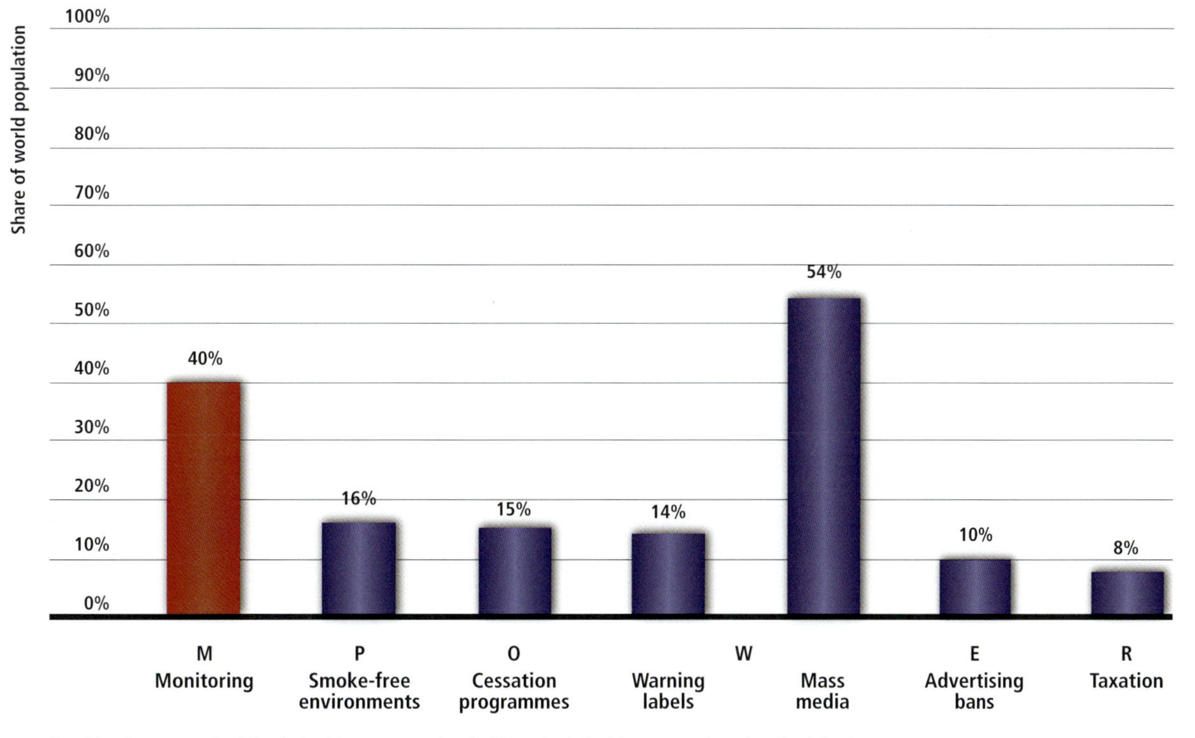

Note: The tobacco control policies depicted here correspond to the highest level of achievement at the national level; for the definitions of these highest categories refer to Technical Note I.

694 million people, or just under 10% of the world's population) have put in place a complete ban on direct and indirect TAPS activities, although this trend has accelerated since 2010. More than 100 countries are close to having a complete TAPS ban, needing to strengthen existing laws to ban additional types of TAPS activities to attain the highest level. However, 67 countries currently do not ban any TAPS activities, or have a ban that does not cover advertising in national broadcast and print media.

The WHO FCTC demonstrates sustained global political will to strengthen tobacco control and save lives. As countries continue to make progress in tobacco control, more people are being protected from the harms of second-hand tobacco smoke, provided with help to quit tobacco use, exposed to effective health warnings through tobacco package labelling and mass media campaigns, protected against tobacco industry marketing tactics, and covered by taxation policies designed to decrease tobacco use and fund tobacco control and other health programmes.

However, more countries need to take the necessary steps to reduce tobacco use and save the lives of the billion people who may otherwise die from tobacco-related illness worldwide during this century.

24 countries have a complete ban on direct and indirect TAPS activities.

THE STATE OF SELECTED TOBACCO CONTROL POLICIES IN THE WORLD, 2012

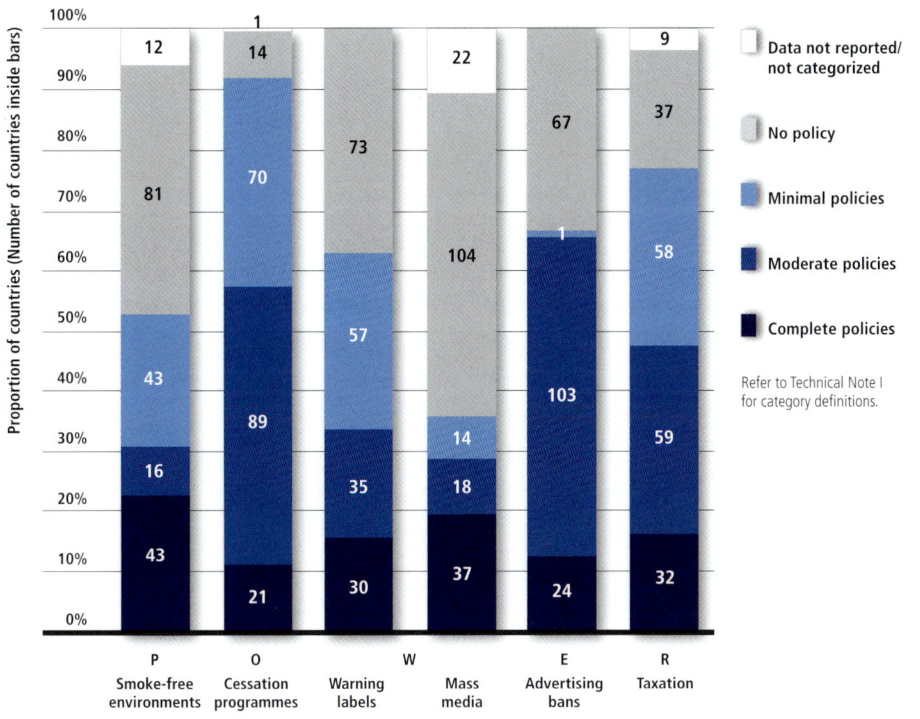

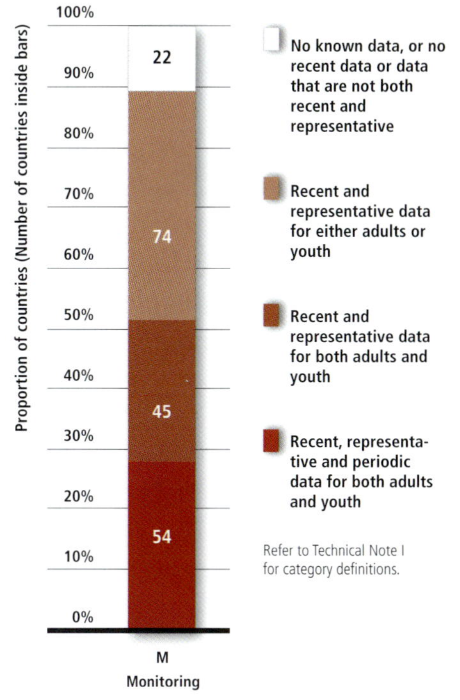

INCREASE IN THE SHARE OF THE WORLD POPULATION COVERED BY SELECTED TOBACCO CONTROL POLICIES, 2010 TO 2012

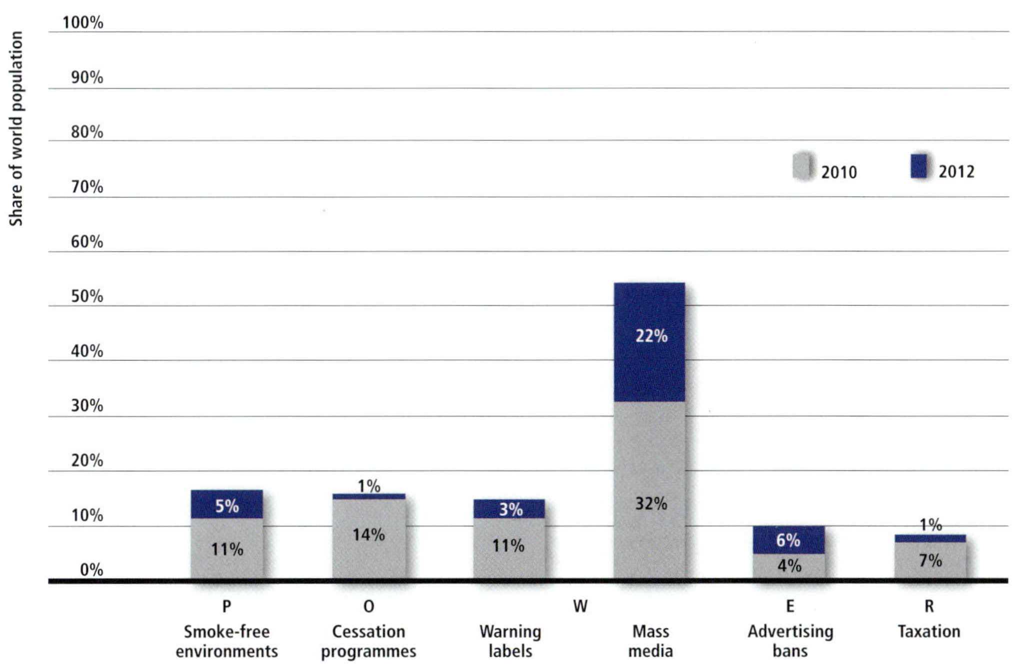

Note: Data on Monitoring are not shown in this graph because they are not comparable between 2010 and 2012. The tobacco control policies depicted here correspond to the highest level of achievement at the national level; for the definitions of these highest categories refer to Technical Note I.

WHO Framework Convention on Tobacco Control

Two decades ago, the global tobacco epidemic was threatening to become uncontrollable. Annual tobacco-related mortality and tobacco use were rising rapidly in some countries – particularly among women *(1)* – while the tobacco industry continued to develop and perfect techniques to increase its customer base and undermine government tobacco control efforts. In the intervening years, predictions that the problem would continue to worsen were unfortunately realized.

Recognizing the critical nature of the crisis, Member States of the World Health Organization (WHO) took concerted action, passing Resolution 49.17 in May 1996, which initiated development of a "framework convention on tobacco control" *(2)*. Applying WHO's power to conclude treaties for the first time in its history, an intergovernmental negotiating body comprised of all WHO Member States was established in 1999 and the treaty – the WHO Framework Convention on Tobacco Control (WHO FCTC) *(3)* – was finalized and adopted in 2003.

Tobacco remains a serious threat to global health, killing nearly 6 million people each year and causing hundreds of billions of dollars of economic harm annually in the form of excess health-care costs and lost productivity. However, countries changed the paradigm for combating this epidemic when they adopted the WHO FCTC. One of the most successful treaties in United Nations history, with 176 Parties (as of 15 June 2013), the WHO FCTC is an evidence-based set of legally binding provisions that establish a roadmap for successful global tobacco control.

Provisions of the WHO Framework Convention

Mindful of the importance of addressing each stage in the production of tobacco, its distribution and consumption, and with awareness of the financial and political power of the tobacco industry, Member States innovatively included substantive provisions focusing on both demand- and supply-side concerns.

Demand reduction

Article 6. Price and tax measures to reduce the demand for tobacco.
Article 8. Protection from exposure to tobacco smoke.
Article 9. Regulation of the contents of tobacco products.
Article 10. Regulation of tobacco product disclosures.
Article 11. Packaging and labelling of tobacco products.
Article 12. Education, communication, training and public awareness.
Article 13. Tobacco advertising, promotion and sponsorship.
Article 14. Reduction measures concerning tobacco dependence and cessation.

Supply reduction

Article 15. Illicit trade in tobacco products.
Article 16. Sales to and by minors.
Article 17. Provision of support for economically viable alternative activities.

The WHO FCTC also contains provisions for collaboration between and among Parties, including Article 5 delineating

general obligations and specifying the need to protect public health policies from commercial and other vested interests of the tobacco industry; Article 20 on technical cooperation and communicating information; and Articles 25 and 26 on international information and resource sharing. The WHO FCTC requires each Party to submit to the Conference of the Parties (COP), through the Convention Secretariat, periodic reports on its implementation of the Convention. The objective of reporting is to enable Parties to learn from each others' experience in implementing the WHO FCTC. In this way, the treaty itself provides support mechanisms that assist Parties to fully implement its provisions, share best practice and present a united, cohesive front against the tobacco industry.

The power of the WHO FCTC lies not in its content alone, but also in the global momentum and solidarity that has developed around the shared goal of reducing the harms caused by tobacco use.

The importance of the Convention was emphasized in the political declaration of the High-level Meeting of the General Assembly on the Prevention and Control of Noncommunicable Diseases in September 2011, in which the assembled countries declared their commitment to "[a]ccelerate implementation of the WHO Framework Convention on Tobacco Control" *(4)*. This shared commitment helps bolster countries in their efforts to prevent tobacco-related illness and death by knowing that they are part of a broad international community, and that their collective work is supported by international law. This is particularly important in light of the increased aggressiveness with which the tobacco industry is selling and promoting its products, and attempting to capture new users.

The Conference of the Parties (COP), an intergovernmental entity comprised of all Parties that serves as the governing body for the WHO FCTC, oversees and guides treaty implementation and interpretation. The COP meets every two years to discuss progress, examine challenges and opportunities, and follow up ongoing business. The Convention Secretariat supports the Parties and the COP in their respective individual and collective work. Official reports from the WHO FCTC Parties to the COP and accompanying documentation have been used as sources for this report.

In accordance with WHO FCTC Article 7 (Non-price measures to reduce the demand for tobacco), the COP has been mandated with the task of proposing appropriate guidelines for the implementation of the provisions of Articles 8 to 13 *(3)*. Accordingly, the COP has developed and adopted a number of guidelines; most relevant to this Report, in November 2008, the COP unanimously adopted guidelines for Article 13 (Tobacco advertising, promotion and sponsorship), which provide clear purpose, objectives and recommendations for implementing the provisions of Article 13 to their best effect *(5)*.

The WHO FCTC is an evidence-based set of legally binding provisions that establish a roadmap for successful global tobacco control.

Article 13 – Tobacco advertising, promotion and sponsorship

Advertising, promotion and sponsorship form the front line of the tobacco industry's efforts to maintain and increase its customer base and normalize tobacco use. Against a landscape of robust supporting data and evidence, the WHO FCTC recognizes that meaningful tobacco control must include the elimination of all forms of tobacco advertising, promotion and sponsorship (TAPS). This goal is so critical that Article 13 (Tobacco advertising, promotion and sponsorship) is one of only two provisions in the treaty that includes a mandatory timeframe for implementation. All Parties must implement a comprehensive TAPS ban (or restrictions in accordance with its constitution if a comprehensive ban would violate its constitutional principles) within five years after the entry into force of the treaty for that Party. The requirement includes domestic TAPS activities, as well as all cross-border TAPS activities that originate within a Party's territory.

Article 1 (Use of terms) of the WHO FCTC provides a very broad definition of TAPS. Tobacco advertising and promotion means "any form of commercial communication, recommendation or action with the aim, effect or likely effect of promoting a tobacco product or tobacco use either directly or indirectly" *(3)*. Tobacco sponsorship as defined in the Article 13 guidelines means "any form of contribution to any event, activity or individual with the aim, effect or likely effect of promoting a tobacco product or tobacco use either directly or indirectly" *(5)*.

In addition to requiring a ban on TAPS (or restrictions within constitutional mandates), Article 13 further requires that, at a minimum, Parties shall:

- prohibit all TAPS activities that promote a tobacco product by any means that are false, misleading or deceptive (e.g. use of terms such as "light" or "mild");
- require that health or other appropriate warnings accompany all tobacco advertising and, as appropriate, promotion and sponsorship;
- restrict the use of direct or indirect incentives that encourage tobacco product purchases;
- require, if it does not have a comprehensive ban, the disclosure to relevant governmental authorities of expenditures by the tobacco industry on those TAPS activities not yet prohibited;
- prohibit (or restrict as constitutionally appropriate) tobacco sponsorship of international events, activities and/or participants therein.

Parties are encouraged to go beyond these measures as well as to cooperate with each other to facilitate eliminating cross-border TAPS activities. Additionally, Article 13 calls for Parties to consider elaborating a protocol, or new treaty, to specifically address cross-border TAPS activities. In 2006, the COP convened a working group in this regard, which submitted its report and proposal for consideration in 2007 *(6)*.

The WHO FCTC recognizes that meaningful tobacco control must include the elimination of all forms of tobacco advertising, promotion and sponsorship.

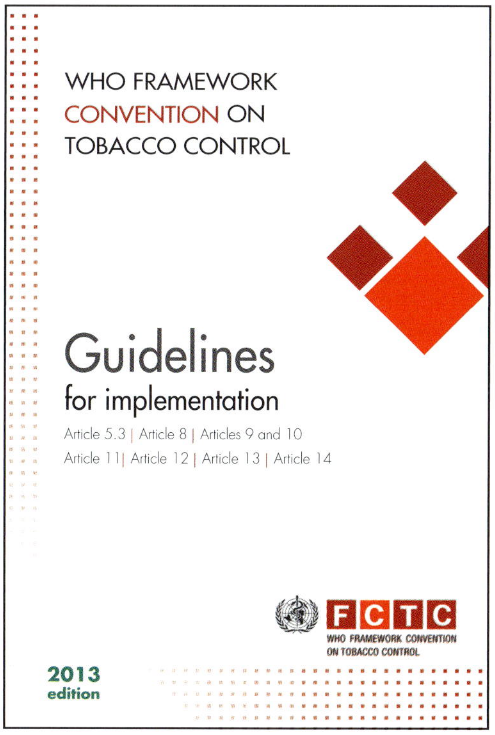

Guidelines for implementation of Article 13

Guidelines for Article 13 are intended to assist Parties in meeting their WHO FCTC obligations by drawing on the best available evidence as well as Parties' experiences. The guidelines provide clear direction on "the best ways to implement Article 13 of the Convention in order to eliminate tobacco advertising, promotion and sponsorship effectively at both domestic and international levels" *(5)*. The substance of the Article 13 guidelines is separated into seven sections.

Scope of a comprehensive ban

The guidelines provide recommendations in eight separate areas regarding the scope of a comprehensive TAPS ban.

A comprehensive TAPS ban should cover:

- all advertising and promotion, as well as sponsorship, without exemption;
- direct and indirect advertising, promotion and sponsorship;
- acts that aim at promotion and acts that have or are likely to have a promotional effect;
- promotion of tobacco products and the use of tobacco;
- commercial communications and commercial recommendations and actions;
- contributions of any kind to any event, activity or individual;
- advertising and promotion of tobacco brand names and all corporate promotion;
- traditional media (print, television and radio) and all media platforms, including Internet, mobile telephones and other new technologies, as well as films.

Retail sale and display

Display and visibility of tobacco products at points of sale constitutes advertising and promotion and should be banned. Vending machines should also be banned because they constitute, by their very presence, a means of advertising and promotion.

Packaging and product features

Packaging and product design are important elements of advertising and promotion. Parties should consider adopting plain (or generic) packaging requirements to eliminate the advertising and promotional effects of packaging. Product packaging, individual cigarettes or other tobacco products should carry no advertising or promotion, including design features that make products more attractive to consumers.

Internet sales

Internet sales of tobacco should be banned as they inherently involve tobacco advertising and promotion. Given the often covert nature of tobacco advertising and promotion on the Internet and the difficulty of identifying and reaching violators, special domestic resources will be needed to make these measures operational.

Brand stretching and brand sharing

"Brand stretching" occurs when a tobacco brand name, emblem, trademark, logo or trade insignia or any other distinctive feature is connected with a non-tobacco product or service to link the two. "Brand sharing" similarly links non-tobacco products or services with a tobacco product or tobacco company by sharing a brand name, emblem, trademark, logo or trade insignia or any other distinctive feature. Both brand stretching and brand sharing should be regarded as TAPS activities and should be part of a comprehensive TAPS ban.

Corporate social responsibility

It is increasingly common for tobacco companies to seek to portray themselves as good corporate citizens by making contributions to deserving causes or by otherwise promoting "socially responsible" elements of their business practices. Parties should ban contributions from tobacco companies to any other entity for "socially responsible causes", as this is a form of sponsorship. Publicity given to "socially responsible" business practices of the tobacco industry should also be banned, as it constitutes a form of advertising and promotion.

Depictions of tobacco in entertainment media

Parties should implement particular measures concerning the depiction of tobacco in entertainment media, including requiring certification that no benefits have been received for any tobacco depictions, prohibiting the use of identifiable tobacco brands or imagery, requiring anti-tobacco advertisements either directly within or immediately adjacent to the entertainment programming, and implementing a ratings or classification system that takes tobacco depictions into account.

Legitimate expression

Implementation of a comprehensive ban on TAPS activities does not need to interfere with legitimate types of expression, such as journalistic, artistic or academic expression, or legitimate social or political commentary. Parties should, however, take measures to prevent the use of journalistic, artistic or academic expression or social or political commentary for the promotion of tobacco use or tobacco products.

Communications within the tobacco trade

The objective of banning TAPS can usually be achieved without banning communications within the tobacco trade. Any exception to a comprehensive ban on TAPS activities for the purpose of providing product information to business entities participating in the tobacco trade should be defined and strictly applied.

Constitutional principles in relation to a comprehensive ban

Insofar as Article 13 provides that countries with constitutional constraints on implementing a comprehensive TAPS ban may instead undertake restrictions to the extent that constitutional principles permit, the guidelines clearly and strongly remind Parties that such restrictions must be as comprehensive as possible within those constraints. This is in light of the treaty's overall objective "to protect present and future generations from the devastating health, social, environmental and economic consequences of tobacco consumption and exposure to tobacco smoke" *(3)*.

Consistency

Domestic bans and their effective enforcement are the cornerstones of any meaningful comprehensive ban on TAPS activities at the global level. Any Party with a comprehensive domestic TAPS ban (or restrictions) should ensure that any cross-border TAPS originating from its territory are banned or restricted in the same manner. Moreover, the ban should also apply to any person or entity that broadcasts or transmits TAPS that could be received in another state. Parties should make use of their sovereign right to take effective actions to limit or prevent any cross-border TAPS entering their territory, whether from Parties that have implemented restrictions or those that have not.

Responsible entities

The entities responsible for TAPS should be defined widely, and the manner and extent to which they are held responsible for complying with the ban should depend on their role.

- Primary responsibility should lie with the initiator of TAPS activities, usually tobacco manufacturers, wholesale distributors, importers, retailers, and their agents and associations.
- Persons or entities that produce or publish content in any type of media, including print, broadcast and online, should be banned from including TAPS in the content they produce or publish.
- Persons or entities (such as event organizers and celebrities, including athletes, actors and musicians) should be banned from engaging in TAPS activities.
- Particular obligations, for example, to remove content, should be applied to other entities involved in production or distribution of analogue and/or digital media after they have been made aware of the presence of TAPS in their media.

Domestic enforcement of laws on tobacco advertising, promotion and sponsorship

The guidelines provide recommendations on both appropriate and effective sanctions as well as monitoring, enforcement and access to justice. Specifically, Parties should apply effective, proportionate and dissuasive penalties, and should designate a competent, independent authority with appropriate powers and resources to monitor and enforce laws that ban (or restrict) TAPS activities. Civil society also plays a key role in monitoring and enforcement of these laws.

Public education and community awareness

The guidelines state clearly that Parties should promote and strengthen, in all sectors of society, public awareness of the need to eliminate TAPS and of existing laws against TAPS activities. Engaging the support of civil society sectors within communities to monitor compliance and report violations of laws against TAPS activities is an essential element of effective enforcement.

International collaboration

The guidelines note the importance of international collaboration to eliminate cross-border TAPS. Additionally, it is explicitly recognized that Parties benefit from sharing information, experience and expertise with regard to all TAPS activities, in that "[e]ffective international cooperation will be essential to the elimination of both domestic and cross-border" TAPS *(5)*.

Enforce bans on tobacco advertising, promotion and sponsorship

Tobacco companies spend billions of US dollars on advertising, promotion and sponsorship every year

Although precise calculations have not been made, the best estimate is that the tobacco industry spends tens of billions of US dollars worldwide each year on tobacco advertising, promotion and sponsorship (TAPS) *(7)*. In the United States alone, the tobacco industry spends more than US$ 10 billion annually on TAPS activities *(8)*. To sell a product that kills up to half of its users requires extraordinary marketing savvy, and tobacco companies are some of the most manipulative product sellers and promoters in the world. They are increasingly aggressive in circumventing prohibitions on TAPS that are designed to curb tobacco use. The requirements of the WHO Framework Convention on Tobacco Control (WHO FCTC) for a comprehensive ban on TAPS are intended to counter this. WHO introduced the MPOWER measures to support countries in building capacity to implement these bans.

Tobacco advertising, promotion and sponsorship increase the likelihood that people will start or continue to smoke

Although TAPS activities are designed to have broad appeal to consumers in all demographic groups, and especially among current smokers, specific efforts are made to persuade non-smokers to start. As a result, key target populations for TAPS include youth, who are at the age when people are most likely to start regular smoking *(9, 10)*, and women, who in most countries are less likely to be current smokers than men *(10)*.

Young people are especially vulnerable to becoming tobacco users and, once addicted, will likely be steady customers for many years. Adolescents are at a critical transitional phase in their lives, and TAPS activities communicate messages that using tobacco products will satisfy their social and psychological needs (e.g. popularity, peer acceptance and positive self-image) *(10, 11)*. People who smoke are generally extremely loyal to their chosen brand of cigarettes, so their choice of brand during their smoking initiation period is especially important *(12)*, and becomes crucial to the ability of tobacco companies to maintain them as life-long customers *(10)*.

Exposure to TAPS, which usually occurs at very young ages (before age 11 and often earlier), increases positive perceptions of tobacco and curiosity about tobacco use. It also makes tobacco use seem less harmful than it actually is, and influences beliefs and perceptions of tobacco use prevalence *(13, 14, 15)*, which increase the likelihood that adolescents will start to smoke *(10, 16, 17)*.

To sell a product that kills up to half of its users requires extraordinary marketing savvy, and tobacco companies are some of the most manipulative product sellers and promoters in the world.

Women, who in many countries have traditionally not used tobacco, are viewed by the tobacco industry as an enormous potential emerging market because of their increasing financial and social independence, and have been targeted accordingly *(1)*. As a result, smoking among women is expected to double worldwide from 2005 to 2025 *(18)*. Many niche cigarette brands have been developed to appeal specifically to women (e.g. Virginia Slims, Eve), and existing brands have been restyled to increase their appeal among women (e.g. Doral). In South Korea, these strategies increased smoking rates among women from 1.6% to 13% between 1988 and 1998 *(19)*.

Tobacco companies target low- and middle-income countries

The tobacco industry is also increasingly targeting people in low- and middle-income countries, especially youth and women *(20)*. Tobacco use is stable or declining slightly in most higher-income countries, but is increasing in many lower-income countries – in some cases rapidly – as they continue to develop economically *(21)*. To capture the many potential new users in lower-income countries, the tobacco industry is rapidly expanding TAPS activities in these countries, using tactics refined and perfected over decades in high-income countries *(20)*.

The tobacco industry has become adept at tailoring these advertising and promotion tactics to the specific market environments of low- and middle-income countries *(20)*. Examples of country-specific targeting abound.

- In Guinea, attractive young women are hired by tobacco companies as marketing executives, but in reality serve as so-called "cigarette girls" whose duty is to promote cigarettes at nightclubs, in front of retail shops and in other public places *(22)*. A similar strategy is used in Thailand, where young women are hired as "ambassadors of smoking" to conduct tobacco company promotions *(23)*.
- In both Indonesia and Senegal, most of the public basketball courts in these countries' cities are painted with the logos of cigarette brands *(22)*.
- In Indonesia, which has yet to become a Party to the WHO FCTC, several youth-friendly international music stars have performed in concerts sponsored by tobacco companies *(24)*.
- Tobacco sales and promotions continue to be popular in bars, cafés and nightclubs in all WHO regions, with larger establishments more likely to display tobacco advertising and participate in tobacco company promotions *(25)*.
- In Brazil, an interactive gaming machine in many clubs, bars and other locations popular with young people have players capture an on-screen moving Marlboro logo to win prizes; the machine also gathers players' email addresses to enable the sending of promotional information *(26)*.

Although Marlboro had been the world's top-selling cigarette brand since the early 1970s, Philip Morris began conducting sophisticated market research in different countries and regions in the 1990s to develop advertising and promotional strategies that focused on the youth market. These targeted efforts further intensified Marlboro's brand appeal among young adults worldwide, solidifying its position as the most widely recognized, most popular and largest selling cigarette brand globally *(27)*.

Advertising, promotion and sponsorship activities normalize and glamourize tobacco use

TAPS falsely associates tobacco use with desirable qualities such as youth, energy, glamour and sex appeal *(28)*. To attract new users, the industry designs marketing campaigns featuring active and attractive young people enjoying life with tobacco *(10, 29)*.

TAPS also creates additional obstacles that blunt tobacco control efforts. Widespread TAPS activities "normalize" tobacco by depicting it as being no different from any other consumer product. This increases the social acceptability of tobacco use and makes it more difficult to educate people about tobacco's harms *(10)*. It also strengthens the tobacco industry's influence over the media, as well as sporting and entertainment businesses, through tens of billions of dollars in annual spending on TAPS activities.

To capture new users in lower-income countries, the tobacco industry is rapidly expanding TAPS activities, using tactics perfected in high-income countries.

TEENAGERS ARE EXPOSED TO BILLBOARD TOBACCO ADVERTISING AT AN ALARMING MAGNITUDE (DATA FROM THE GLOBAL YOUTH TOBACCO SURVEY)

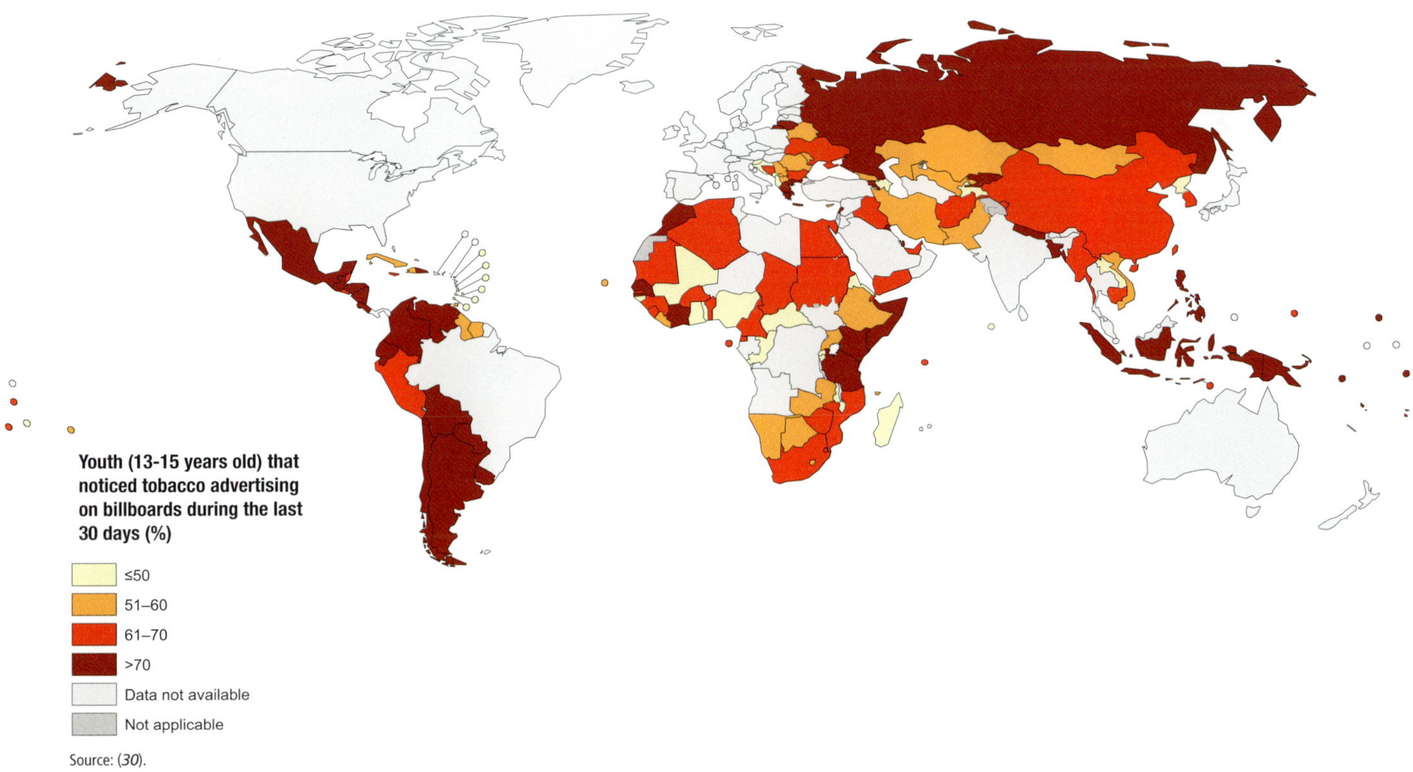

Source: *(30)*.

Notes: The range of survey years (data year) used for producing these maps is 2004-2011.
The following countries and territories have conducted subnational or regional level GYTS: Afghanistan, Algeria, Benin, Bolivia (Plurinational State of), Brazil, Burkina Faso, Cameroon, Central African Republic, Chile, China, Colombia, Democratic Republic of the Congo, Ecuador, Ethiopia, Gambia, Guinea-Bissau, Honduras, Iraq, Liberia, Mozambique, Nicaragua, Nigeria, Pakistan, Poland, Somalia, United Republic of Tanzania, Uzbekistan, Zimbabwe, and West Bank and Gaza Strip.

Complete bans are needed to counteract the effects of tobacco advertising, promotion and sponsorship

Tobacco companies rely heavily on advertising and other promotional techniques to attract new users, who are critical to maintaining demand for tobacco products because they replace smokers who quit or who die prematurely from tobacco-related illness. In countries whose populations are growing more rapidly than rates of tobacco use are declining, advertising will increase the market for tobacco even further. To counteract the tens of billions of dollars spent worldwide each year by the tobacco industry on advertising, promotion and sponsorship *(7)*, prohibiting all forms of TAPS activities is a key tobacco control strategy. To assist countries in achieving this goal, the Conference of the Parties to the WHO FCTC has adopted guidelines for implementing Article 13 of the Convention *(5)*.

Exposure to TAPS is associated with higher smoking prevalence rates *(31, 32)*, and in particular with initiation and continuation of smoking among youth *(9, 33)*. The goal of bans on TAPS is therefore to completely eliminate exposure to tobacco industry advertising and promotional messages *(34)*.

Bans on tobacco advertising, promotion and sponsorship are effective at reducing smoking

A comprehensive ban on all TAPS activities significantly reduces exposure to smoking cues resulting from tobacco advertising and promotion *(35)*. This in turn significantly reduces the industry's ability to continue promoting and selling its products, both to young people who have not yet started to use tobacco as well as to adult tobacco users who want to quit *(36)*. About a third of youth experimentation with tobacco occurs as a result of exposure to TAPS *(37)*. Protecting people from TAPS activities can substantially reduce tobacco consumption *(38)*, and the more channels in which tobacco advertising and promotion are prohibited, the less likely that people will be exposed to TAPS *(39)*.

Comprehensive bans on TAPS reduce cigarette consumption in all countries regardless of income level *(31)*. In high-income countries, a comprehensive ban that covers tobacco advertising in all media and also includes bans on all promotions or displays using tobacco brand names and logos has been documented to

decrease tobacco consumption by about 7%, independent of other tobacco control interventions *(40, 41, 42)*.

One of the strongest arguments to support bans on TAPS is the effect that they have on youth smoking initiation and prevalence rates *(43)*. Tobacco companies know that most people do not initiate smoking after they reach adulthood and develop the capacity to make informed decisions *(29, 44)*, and reductions in youth smoking rates may lead to lower adult smoking prevalence in future years *(45)*.

Partial bans and voluntary restrictions are ineffective

Partial TAPS bans have little or no effect on smoking prevalence *(31)*, and enable the industry to maintain its ability to promote and sell its products to young people who have not yet started using tobacco as well as to adult tobacco users who want to quit *(46)*. Partial bans also generally do not include indirect or alternative forms of marketing such as promotions and sponsorships *(39, 47)*.

When faced with a ban that does not completely cover all TAPS activities, the tobacco industry will maintain its total amount of advertising and promotional expenditures by simply diverting resources to other permitted types of TAPS activities to compensate *(10, 40)*. In places where partial bans prohibit direct advertising of tobacco products in traditional media, for example, tobacco companies will invariably attempt to circumvent these restrictions by employing a variety of indirect advertising and promotional tactics *(10, 48)*.

Each type of TAPS activity works in a specific way to reach smokers and potential smokers but any will suffice as a substitute when bans are enacted. If only television and radio advertising is banned, for example, the tobacco industry will reallocate its advertising budgets to other media such as newspapers, magazines, billboards and the Internet *(10)*. If all traditional advertising channels are blocked, the industry will

Partial TAPS bans have little or no effect on smoking prevalence, and enable the industry to promote and sell its products to young people who have not yet started using tobacco.

convert advertising expenditures to other TAPS activities, including sponsorship of events popular among youth, such as sports and music events, and to tobacco promotions in bars and nightclubs *(10)*.

Examples of this type of substitution by the tobacco industry include the immediate increase in expenditures for print media advertising in the United States in 1971 to compensate for a complete ban on television and radio tobacco advertising *(49)*. In Singapore, the first country to restrict tobacco advertising, tobacco companies increased their spending on television advertising in neighbouring Malaysia that could be received by consumers in Singapore, and Philip Morris introduced a new cigarette brand by first promoting a wine cooler with the same name (a tactic known as "brand stretching") *(50)*.

Voluntary restrictions on TAPS activities are also ineffective *(10, 51)*, as ultimately there is no law compelling the industry to comply with its own voluntary regulations *(52, 53)*. In addition, voluntary restrictions usually do not cover activities by tobacco retailers, distributors and importers, which in most cases not are under direct control and supervision of tobacco companies, and consequently fail to prevent point-of-sale advertising or displays, which are among the most pervasive forms of tobacco advertising.

ADOLESCENTS IN NORTHERN AFRICA ARE MORE LIKELY TO SMOKE IF EXPOSED TO TOBACCO PROMOTION

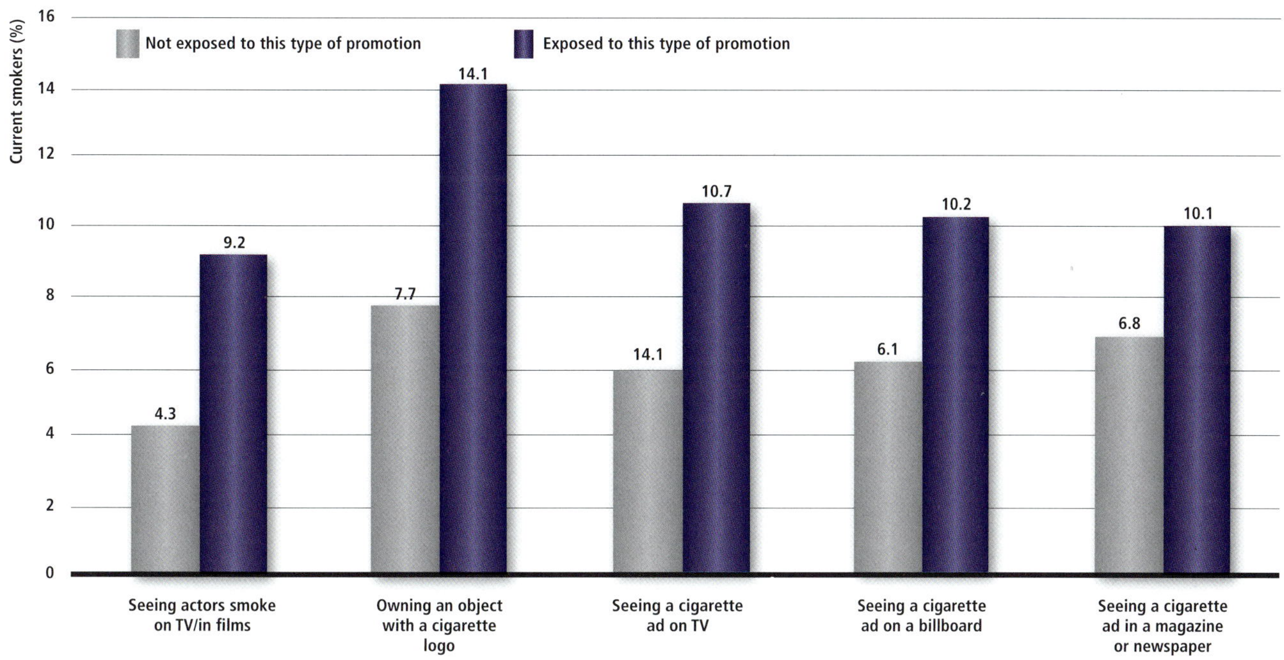

Source: (*54*).
Notes: all differences statistically significant at p<0.001.
Data from Egypt, Libya, Morocco, Sudan and Tunisia.

TOBACCO COMPANIES TARGET TEENAGERS BY OFFERING FREE CIGARETTES (DATA FROM THE GLOBAL YOUTH TOBACCO SURVEY)

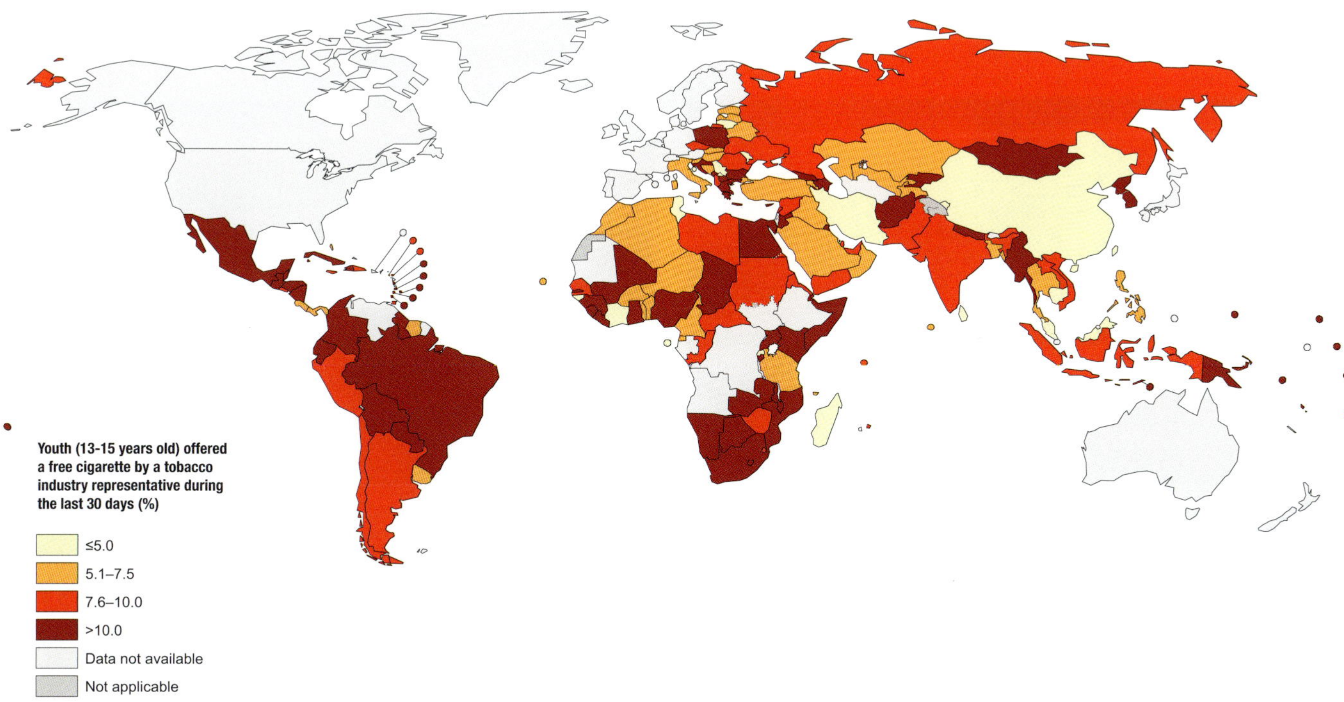

Source: (*30*).

Notes: The range of survey years (data year) used for producing these maps is 2004-2011.
The following countries and territories have conducted subnational or regional level GYTS: Afghanistan, Algeria, Benin, Bolivia (Plurinational State of), Brazil, Burkina Faso, Cameroon, Central African Republic, Chile, China, Colombia, Democratic Republic of the Congo, Ecuador, Ethiopia, Gambia, Guinea-Bissau, Honduras, Iraq, Liberia, Mozambique, Nicaragua, Nigeria, Pakistan, Poland, Somalia, United Republic of Tanzania, Uzbekistan, Zimbabwe, and West Bank and Gaza Strip.

Bans must completely cover all types of tobacco advertising, promotion and sponsorship

To be effective in reducing tobacco consumption, bans must be complete and apply to all types of advertising in all media, as well as to all promotion and sponsorship activities, both direct and indirect *(31, 46, 55)*. Legislation should be written in uncomplicated language and include clear definitions, as outlined in the WHO FCTC and the guidelines for implementing Article 13, to maximize the effectiveness of the ban *(5)*.

Direct advertising is only one component of the integrated set of marketing strategies that tobacco companies use to promote their products *(10, 44)*. If advertising is prohibited in one particular medium, the tobacco industry merely redirects expenditures to alternative advertising, promotion and sponsorship vehicles to carry their message to target populations *(10, 40, 42, 56)*.

Bans on direct advertising

Bans on direct advertising should cover all types of media, including:

- print (newspapers, magazines);
- broadcast, cable and satellite (radio, television);
- cinemas (on-screen advertisements shown before feature films);
- outdoor displays (billboards, transit vehicles and stations);
- point-of-sale (advertising, signage and product displays in retail stores);
- Internet.

Bans on indirect advertising, promotion and sponsorship

A complete TAPS ban should also prohibit all forms of indirect tobacco advertising, including promotion and sponsorship activities such as:

- free distribution of tobacco and related products in the mail or through other means;
- promotional discounts;
- non-tobacco goods and services identified with tobacco brand names (brand stretching);
- brand names of non-tobacco products used for tobacco products (brand sharing);

Display of tobacco products in Norway before display ban

Since the ban entered into force, tobacco products are no longer visible at the point of sale in Norway

- appearance of tobacco products and tobacco brand names in television, films and other audiovisual entertainment products, including on the Internet;
- sponsored events;
- so-called "corporate social responsibility" initiatives.

Tobacco companies invest in sophisticated branding to promote their products *(10)*. Promotion and sponsorship activities associate tobacco use with desirable situations or environments and include showing tobacco use in films and television, sponsoring music and sporting events, using fashionable non-tobacco products or popular celebrities to promote tobacco, and brand stretching that allows consumers to make statements of identity (e.g. tobacco brand logos printed on clothing). Indirect advertising can also serve to improve the public image of tobacco and tobacco companies *(57)*.

Tobacco packaging itself is among the most prominent and important forms of tobacco advertising and promotion *(58)*. The tobacco industry exploits all packaging elements, including pack construction, in addition to graphic design and use of colour, to increase the appeal of smoking *(29)*. Brightly coloured cigarette packages are attractive to children, who are drawn to the images and associate them with positive attributes such as "fun" and "happiness", and tobacco packaging can be designed in a manner specifically intended to attract both male and female young adults *(59)*. Many youth consider plain packaging to be unattractive and that it enforces negative attitudes toward smoking *(59)*.

Point-of-sale bans are a key policy intervention

Point-of-sale retail settings have become increasingly important for TAPS activities *(10)*, and in many countries people are more aware of tobacco advertising in stores than via any other advertising channel *(39)*. Therefore, it is important to ban point-of-sale advertising, including product displays and signage, in retail stores *(60)*. Currently,

YOUTH EXPOSED TO DISPLAY OF TOBACCO PRODUCTS IN SHOPS ARE MORE SUSCEPTIBLE TO STARTING SMOKING (DATA FROM THE UK)

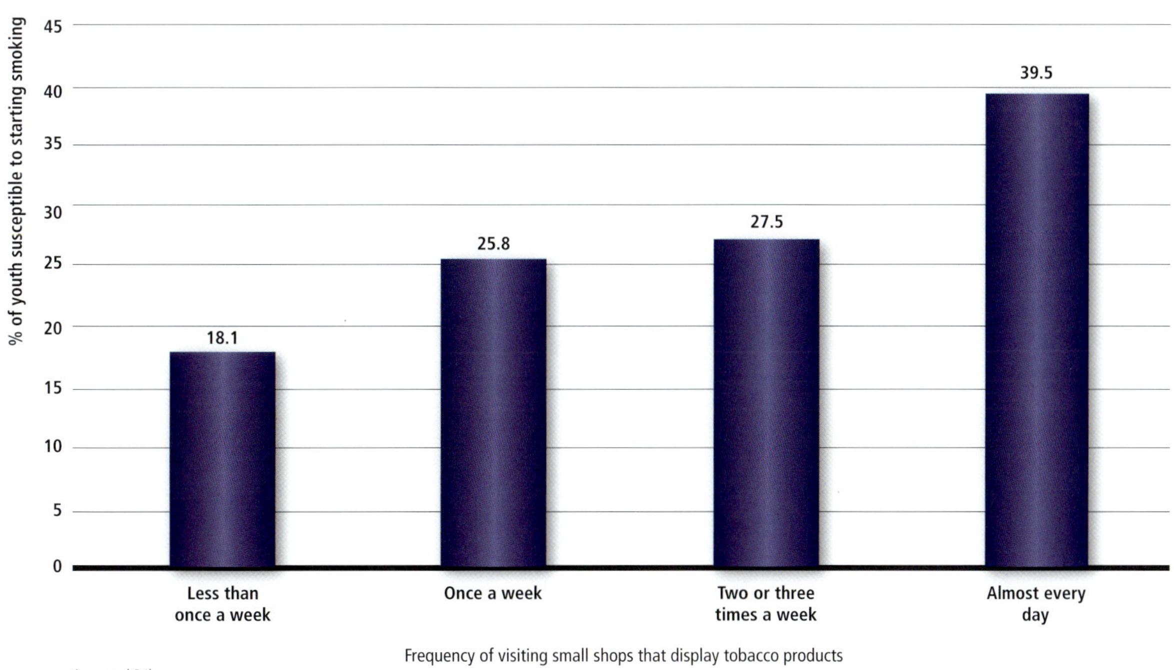

Source: *(61)*.

very few countries restrict point-of-sale cigarette package displays, which have the same effect as media advertising and similarly influence smoking behaviour *(62)*.

Point-of-sale promotion, including price discounts and product giveaways, may account for the majority of TAPS expenditures in some countries *(7)*. A ban on these activities limits the ability of marketing to cue tobacco users to make a purchase, which appears to lead to reductions in youth smoking as well as reduce impulse purchases among adults wanting to quit *(63)*.

In Ireland, which eliminated point-of-sale tobacco displays in 2009, the lack of visual smoking cues in shops caused youth to be less likely to believe their peers were smokers, thus helping to denormalize tobacco use and reduce the likelihood of smoking initiation *(64)*. In Norway, which enacted a ban in 2010, removal of point-of-sale tobacco displays was perceived as a barrier for youth purchases of tobacco and diminished the value of branding in purchasing choices *(65)*. In the UK, cigarette sales declined by 3% in retail stores that had covered up or removed product displays in advance of an announced ban *(66)*.

This intervention can be further strengthened by keeping tobacco products behind the counter and out of public view, so that customers must ask specifically if the store sells them. The small extra effort required to ask a retailer for tobacco products may deter some purchases and assist with cessation efforts. Youths are less likely to attempt a purchase in stores where tobacco products are hidden from view *(67)*.

"Corporate social responsibility" initiatives should be prohibited

Tobacco companies frequently engage in so-called "corporate social responsibility" activities, such as sponsorship of research, charities, educational programmes, community projects and other "socially responsible" activities, to improve their image as socially acceptable economic contributors and good corporate citizens *(10)*. Many such activities focus on health philanthropy, but there is a clear conflict of interest between the health harms caused by tobacco use and tobacco industry spending on initiatives that address health issues *(68)*. Other examples of this strategy include tobacco companies providing economic support to countries and communities suffering from natural disasters or other crises, which helps improve public perceptions of the industry, creates goodwill among influential groups such as journalists and policy-makers, and serves as brand promotion *(69)*.

However, these activities are actually intended as corporate political activity to broker access to public officials, influence policy development, and counteract opposing political coalitions *(70)*, with the ultimate goal of persuading governments not to implement policies that may restrict tobacco use and reduce sales *(71)*. In the case of disaster relief, the intent is to persuade "beneficiaries" to side with their tobacco industry benefactors to oppose tobacco control measures. Ultimately, "corporate social responsibility" activities

YOUTH EXPOSED TO SMOKING IN FILMS ARE MORE LIKELY TO TRY SMOKING (DATA FROM SIX EUROPEAN COUNTRIES)

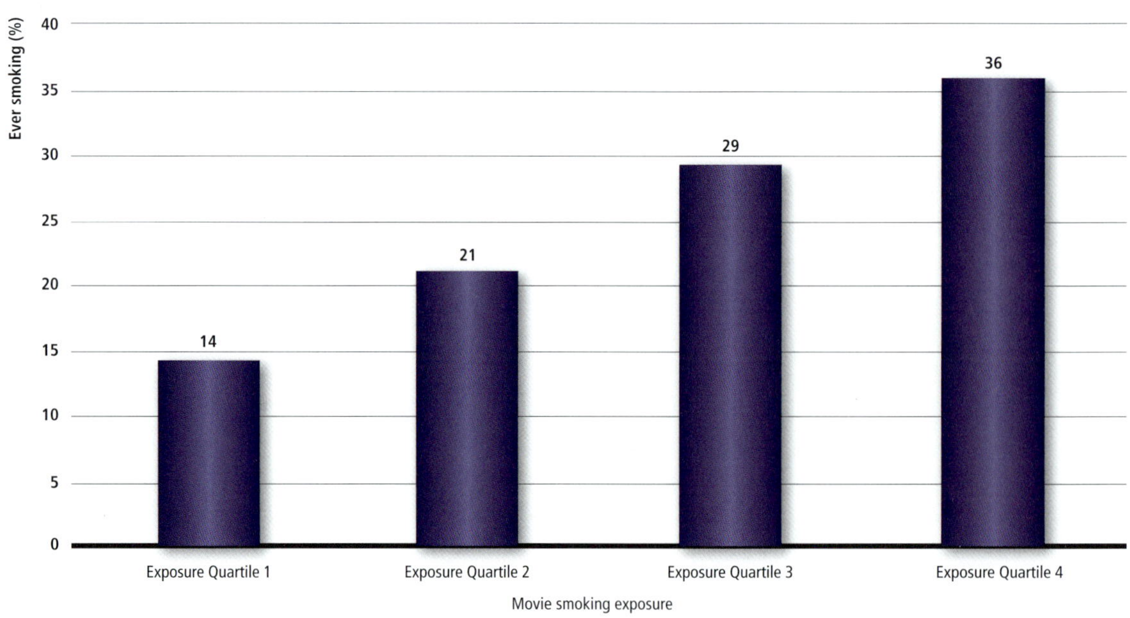

Source: *(72)*.

do little to address the health and economic impacts of tobacco use *(73)*. Bans on this form of promotional activity would be another important component of a comprehensive tobacco control programme.

The tobacco industry will strongly oppose bans on its advertising, promotion and sponsorship activities

The tobacco industry strongly opposes bans on TAPS because they are highly effective in reducing tobacco use and initiation, and the industry will lobby heavily against even the most minimal restrictions. The industry often argues that legislative bans on TAPS are not necessary and that voluntary codes and self-regulation are sufficient. The industry will claim that bans restrict free enterprise, prevent consumers from making their own choices and impede free speech, including the right to promote a legal product.

The tobacco industry also claims that TAPS activities are not intended to expand sales or attract new users, but are simply a means of influencing brand choice and fostering market competition among brands for current tobacco users *(31)*. However, the primary purpose of TAPS is to increase tobacco sales *(10)*, which contributes towards killing more people by encouraging current smokers to smoke more and decreasing their motivation to quit. TAPS activities also lead potential users – and young people specifically – to try tobacco and become long-term customers *(46)*. TAPS that targets youth and specific demographic subgroups is particularly effective *(10,74,75)*.

Tobacco importers and retailers are typically business entities that in most countries are separate from manufacturers, but because they are still part of the tobacco industry, they have a direct interest in avoiding any restrictions on TAPS activities. Media, entertainment and sporting businesses, which benefit from tobacco industry marketing expenditures, will act as proxies for the tobacco industry to fight bans on TAPS and other tobacco control policies because they fear losing customers or advertising, promotion and sponsorship revenues.

Industry arguments can be effectively countered

Several points can be raised to effectively counter tobacco industry arguments against bans on TAPS activities.

- Tobacco use kills people and damages their health.
- Governments have the authority and obligation to protect the health and rights of their people.
- TAPS leads to increased tobacco consumption and smoking initiation, and is not intended merely to influence brand choice among current smokers.
- Tobacco use causes economic harm to individuals and families, as well as to communities and countries.
- Many governments ban or restrict advertising and promotion of other legal products (e.g. alcohol, firearms, medications) as part of consumer protection laws.
- Tobacco advertising is deceptive and misleading *(76)*.
- The tobacco industry has a demonstrated pattern of targeting youth *(10)*.
- The right of people to live a healthy life free of addiction is more important than the financial interests of the tobacco industry.

Effective legislation must be enforced and monitored

Government intervention through well-drafted and well-enforced legislation is required because the tobacco industry has substantial expertise in circumventing bans on TAPS activities *(10)*. Despite industry opposition to such laws and regulations, they are easy to maintain and enforce if written carefully so that they are clear and unambiguous. Comprehensive bans on TAPS can be achieved by following the international best practice standards outlined in the guidelines for implementation of Article 13 of the WHO FCTC (see chapter "WHO Framework Convention on Tobacco Control") *(5)*.

Political will and public support are necessary

Political will at the highest levels of government is necessary to enact and enforce effective legislation, as well as to counter the inevitable opposition from the tobacco industry and the related groups and businesses that benefit from TAPS expenditures. Enlisting the support of civil society and the public in favour of a ban can put pressure on the government to act. Support can be built by effectively countering claims by the tobacco industry, questioning the motives of tobacco sponsorship, and showing the impact of TAPS activities on tobacco consumption and health.

Bans should be announced in advance of implementation

Policy-makers should announce bans on TAPS well in advance of implementation. This provides sufficient time for media outlets, event promoters and other businesses that benefit from TAPS expenditures to find new advertisers and sponsors. A complete ban is also more equitable, as it will not advantage one type of media or business over another.

International and cross-border bans can be enforced

Legislation should include bans on incoming and outgoing cross-border advertising, such as tobacco advertising on international television and Internet sites, and sponsorship of international sporting and cultural events. Although bans on advertising in international media may be challenging under traditional regulatory models, it is feasible to prevent TAPS from crossing international borders *(77)*. Many countries publish national editions of international newspapers and magazines that respect the laws of the countries in which they operate. Local Internet servers can block objectionable advertising provided by web sites located in other countries through geolocation and filtering technologies, as is currently done with other content deemed to be objectionable (e.g. pornography, online gambling). International satellite broadcasts can be

Monitoring tobacco industry strategies that attempt to circumvent the law is important for establishing effective countermeasures.

edited at a centralized downlink before being transmitted within a country, and telecommunications licensing provisions can require that TAPS activities be prohibited as a condition of issuance. International bans can also be achieved when culturally close countries simultaneously ban tobacco marketing, as is the case among many European Union countries *(78)*.

Legislation should be updated to address new products and industry tactics

Comprehensive bans on TAPS must be periodically updated to address innovations in industry tactics and media technology, as well as new types of tobacco products or cigarette substitutes (e.g. a type of oral tobacco known as "snus", and electronic cigarettes, which deliver nicotine through aerosol vapour rather than via smoke caused by ignition of tobacco).

Legislation should not include exhaustive lists of prohibited activities or product types, which can limit application of the law to new products not on the list. Instead, legislation should include the flexibility to allow for coverage of new products and future developments in communications technology and tactics without the necessity of passing revised legislation. Examples of prohibited TAPS activities are useful in legislation, provided it is clear that they are examples only.

Although the commercial Internet is now a quarter of a century old, it is still developing as a communications medium, and many tobacco companies have taken innovative approaches to using web sites to advertise and promote their products *(79)*. The current explosion in social networking media is being exploited by the tobacco industry to promote its products to users of these emergent communications channels *(80)*, who are generally younger and are often still children or adolescents. For example, employees of British American Tobacco have aggressively promoted the company's products and brands on Facebook (the world's largest social media web site) by starting and administrating groups, joining pages as fans, and posting photographs of company events, products and promotional items, all of which undermine provisions of the WHO FCTC *(81)*.

Penalties for violations must be high to be effective

Financial penalties for violations of bans on TAPS activities must be high to be effective. Tobacco companies have large amounts of money, and are often willing to pay fines that are small in comparison to the additional business gained from TAPS. Substantial punitive fines and other sanctions are thus necessary to deter efforts to circumvent the law.

Potential new areas for legislation

The WHO FCTC encourages countries to implement measures beyond the treaty obligations, a call that is reiterated in the text of Article 13 itself *(5)*. Examples of other legislation to block TAPS activities under consideration by some countries include:

- *eliminating tax incentives.* TAPS activities can be reduced if companies are not allowed to take business tax deductions for these expenses, including price discounting and product giveaways, thus reducing financial incentives for these expenditures. Although this action has been proposed in the past *(82)*, most recently by the US state of California *(83)*, it has not yet been implemented.
- *requiring plain packaging.* Australia is, as of 1 December 2012, the first country to require plain (or standardized) packaging of tobacco products; other countries including Ireland and New Zealand are considering similar legislation. Package design serves an increasingly critical role in promoting tobacco use as other TAPS activities are restricted or prohibited *(84)*. Requiring plain packaging – without colour, pictures or distinctive typefaces, other than required health warnings – minimizes the ability to promote brands and can neutralize the value of individual brands *(85)*.

Monitoring of tobacco advertising, promotion and sponsorship activities is essential

TAPS activities should be monitored to ensure compliance with bans. Monitoring tobacco industry strategies that attempt to circumvent the law is also important for establishing effective countermeasures. Monitoring and enforcement programmes should cover traditional media and marketing channels, as well as new and emerging advertising and promotional strategies, technologies and social trends (e.g. social networking). Ongoing monitoring can identify new types of TAPS activities that circumvent even the most clearly written comprehensive bans.

Coordination with other government ministries and civil society organizations is important

To maximize the effectiveness of legislation or regulations enacted by legislatures and/or justice ministries or implemented

by executive order, coordination with a variety of government ministries, NGOs and civil society organizations is necessary. Examples of areas within government where coordination of activities is needed include:

- Health ministry (or other appropriate ministry/institution), to oversee the national tobacco control programme, including bans on TAPS; the government should designate an organization or public institution to monitor TAPS activities and the impact of bans, and report regularly to the health ministry and other government mechanisms that coordinate tobacco control activities.
- Justice ministry (or other appropriate law enforcement agency according to national law, e.g. agency for consumer protection), to enforce bans on TAPS.
- Finance ministry, to make reports on TAPS expenditures as required by the WHO FCTC (in countries where TAPS activities are not banned completely).
- Commerce ministry, to monitor and enforce bans on TAPS.
- Communications ministry, to monitor and enforce broadcast and Internet advertising bans.

Enlisting the support of civil society organizations is also important in successfully enacting and enforcing bans on TAPS activities. These include:

- media businesses;
- other business organizations, especially in industries targeted by the tobacco industry (e.g. sport, music, bars/nightclubs);
- retail organizations (especially for point-of-sale TAPS activities);
- youth organizations;
- NGOs involved with health, education, child protection, women's issues, human rights and other relevant social areas.

To maximize the effectiveness of legislation, coordination with government ministries, NGOs and civil society organizations is necessary.

Combatting tobacco industry interference

Tobacco industry interference with tobacco control can be neutralized

Parties to the WHO FCTC have committed to overcoming tobacco industry interference by implementing Article 5.3 of the treaty, which states: "In setting and implementing their public health policies with respect to tobacco control, Parties shall act to protect these policies from commercial and other vested interests of the tobacco industry in accordance with national law" *(3)*.

Tobacco control historically has been opposed by the tobacco industry, which has systematically employed a wide range of tactics to interfere with tobacco control efforts. Tobacco companies attempted to prevent, delay or derail the process of negotiation of the WHO FCTC. After failing to prevent its adoption by the World Health Assembly in 2003 and ratification by most WHO Member States, the tobacco industry is now concentrating its efforts to prevent comprehensive implementation of the treaty by its Parties. Because the tobacco industry has massive resources, it spends substantial amounts of money on sophisticated product marketing, political lobbying and campaign contributions, financing research favourable to its interests, so-called "social responsibility" and other philanthropic initiatives, and media manipulation to discredit scientific research and influence governments.

Tobacco industry interference takes many forms, but all have the goal of weakening or obstructing strong tobacco control policies. Some activities are conducted openly, while others are more covert. However, all of these attempts at interference can be successfully countered to ensure that tobacco control policies and programmes remain effective at reducing the epidemic of tobacco use.

The tobacco industry has been particularly aggressive in blocking bans on tobacco advertising, promotion and sponsorship (TAPS). TAPS remain essential to attract new tobacco users, who are vital to the industry's ability to continue generating revenues and profits. Consequently, the industry views bans on TAPS activities as one of the biggest

threats to its interests and will strongly oppose even the most minimal restrictions (see chapter "Enforce bans on tobacco advertising, promotion and sponsorship" for more detail).

Countering industry tactics

In 2008, the Conference of the Parties of the WHO FCTC adopted guidelines for implementation of Article 5.3 of the Convention. These guidelines aim to assist Parties in meeting their legal obligations under Article 5.3 of the Convention and draw on the best available scientific evidence and the experience of Parties in addressing tobacco industry interference. They provide a set of recommendations on how Parties can best address efforts of the industry to interfere with tobacco control policy development (*5*). In addition to the obligations under Article 5.3, the WHO FCTC contains several provisions that address protection of tobacco control from tobacco industry interference. The preamble to the treaty recognizes "the need to be alert to any efforts by the tobacco industry to undermine or subvert tobacco control efforts and the need to be informed of activities of the tobacco industry that have a negative impact on tobacco control efforts" *(3)*.

Understanding tobacco industry practices is critical to success in tobacco control. Although the industry attempts to position itself as a legitimate partner and stakeholder in tobacco control, it cannot be allowed to be involved in any way in tobacco control efforts. To prevent such involvement, some countries that recently adopted new tobacco control legislations (Burkina Faso, Djibouti and Namibia) included specific references to measures under Article 5.3 of the WHO FCTC and its respective guidelines.

Research, surveillance and exchange of information are key components of the WHO FCTC (*3*). Surveillance of tobacco industry activities and strategies allows us to know more about tactics used to interfere with tobacco control and provides information about who represents the tobacco industry, including the identity of front groups.

Tobacco industry interference can be successfully countered to ensure that tobacco policies and programmes remain effective.

Tobacco industry tactics to interfere with tobacco control efforts

There are several tactics used by the tobacco industry to interfere with tobacco control efforts *(86)*.

- *Influencing the political and legislative process.* The industry has been highly resourceful in undermining governments' efforts to protect health by creating and exploiting legal loopholes and hiring lobbyists to influence decision makers and weaken normative texts.
- *Exaggerating the economic importance of the industry.* The industry often uses economic arguments to suggest that effective tobacco control would nullify the alleged economic benefits of their business to local communities and national economies, but its data exaggerate the economic importance.
- *Manipulating public opinion to improve the industry's image.* The industry uses a wide range of public relations tactics to manipulate public opinion and improve its image, including so-called "social responsibility" initiatives.
- *Fabricating support through front groups.* The industry uses affiliated businesses in its own and other industries to create seemingly independent "grassroots" groups that support its interests, but which commonly receive direct tobacco industry funding.
- *Discrediting proven science.* In order to weaken tobacco control efforts, the industry creates false controversies about the scientific evidence of the harms of tobacco by manipulating standards of scientific proof and distorting evidence.
- *Intimidating governments with litigation.* Legal action, or even the threat of action, is a popular industry tactic to intimidate governments and dissuade them from introducing effective tobacco control policies.

Legal mechanisms must be in place to support monitoring as well as to set up firewalls between government and the tobacco industry.

WHO and other organizations monitor tobacco industry efforts to undermine global tobacco control, and disseminate this information through reports and databases of tobacco industry activities. This involves monitoring the tobacco industry at national as well as local levels, including review of industry publications and market analyses, monitoring media coverage of industry-related issues, and reviewing communications by legislators and other policy-makers to ascertain their views on tobacco control. Also, the reporting instrument of the WHO FCTC requires Parties to provide information on their progress made in implementation of Article 5.3 and its guidelines (*87*).

With this information it is possible to implement legislation and regulations that neutralize tobacco industry interference and increase the likelihood of success in tobacco control. Informing and involving the public and civil society will also help counter interference with tobacco control programmes.

Further, legal mechanisms must be in place to support monitoring as well as to set up firewalls between government and the tobacco industry. This helps prevent collaboration and avoid conflicts of interest, especially since some government officials and elected representatives will support tobacco industry positions. A code of conduct for public officials that prescribes standards with which they should comply in their dealings with the tobacco industry would also help avoid conflicts of interest for government officials and employees working in tobacco control.

Transparency and disclosure of tobacco industry conduct and finances, including lobbying activities, campaign contributions and TAPS expenditures, are also important.

A strong tobacco control programme is one of the best defences against tobacco industry interference. Enacting and strictly enforcing comprehensive tobacco control measures, communicating effectively about tobacco control policies and regulations, building strong anti-tobacco coalitions within government and civil society, applying lessons learned from the successes of other countries, and using evidence and enlisting tobacco control "champions" to tell the truth about the harms of tobacco use and refute industry arguments will all serve to counter tobacco industry attempts to interfere with tobacco control.

Five years of progress in global tobacco control

One third of the world's people are protected by at least one effective tobacco control measure

In the five years since publication of the first *WHO Report on the Global Tobacco Epidemic* in 2008, one third of all countries have successfully implemented one or more of the MPOWER measures at the highest level of achievement (Monitoring of tobacco use is reported separately and is not included in this grouped analysis; see Technical Note I for definitions).

More than 2.3 billion people living in 92 countries – a third of the world's population – are now covered by at least one of the five MPOWER measures (not including Monitoring) at the highest level, an increase of nearly 1.3 billion people (and 48 countries) since 2007. Nearly 1 billion people living in 39 countries are now covered by two or more of the MPOWER measures at the highest level, an increase of about 480 million people (and 26 countries) since 2007.

In 2007, no country protected its population with all five – or even four – of the MPOWER measures. Today, one country, Turkey, now protects its entire population of 75 million people with all five tobacco control measures at the highest level. Three countries (Brazil, the Islamic Republic of Iran and Panama), with 278 million people have put in place four of the five MPOWER measures at the highest level. All of these countries are low- or middle-income countries.

Most progress has been in low- and middle-income countries

Almost all progress in the MPOWER measures over the past five years has been achieved in low- and middle-income countries. This is critically important, as tobacco use has increased in many low- and middle-income countries even as it has stabilized or declined slightly in some high-income countries. However, high-income countries cannot afford to fall behind in protecting their people against the harms of tobacco use.

Of the 48 countries that newly implemented at least one MPOWER measure at the highest level since 2007, most (80%) are low- or middle-income, with 18% of the world's population newly protected by

FIVE YEARS OF PROGRESS IN SELECTED TOBACCO CONTROL MEASURES (2007–2012)

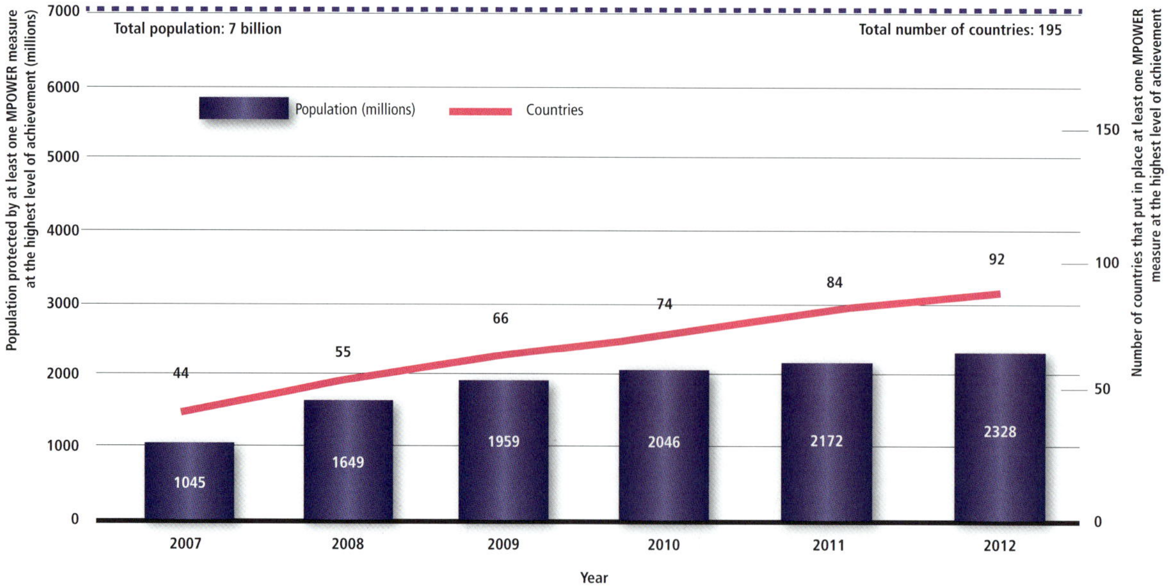

Note: 2009 and 2011 data include some estimation where the year of complete O and R policies was not known.
Data on Monitoring of tobacco use and Mass media campaigns are not included.

at least one measure. An additional 16 countries that already had one MPOWER measure in place at the highest level in 2007 or earlier added at least one more by 2012.

Covering 5% of the world's population, 19 of the 26 countries that have reached the highest level of achievement on at least two MPOWER measures since 2007 are low- or middle-income. Of the eight countries that have achieved the highest level on at least three MPOWER measures, five are low- or middle-income. No high-income country has yet implemented more than three of the MPOWER measures at the highest level, compared with four low- or middle-income countries that have done so.

Although the number of countries that have put each of the five MPOWER measures in place increased sharply between 2007 and 2012, the growth in population covered by each individual measure has been less pronounced. Many countries with newly implemented MPOWER measures have relatively small populations, and have surpassed some high-population countries in the levels of protection they provide against the harms of tobacco use. More populous countries need to take similar action to fully cover their people with complete implementation of MPOWER measures.

Some tobacco control measures have become more established than others

Although many countries have made a great deal of progress over the past five years in the MPOWER measures, some countries have made little to no headway against the epidemic of tobacco use. Additionally, some MPOWER measures are far more likely to be put in place than others. While all of these measures are important on their own, and each will help reduce tobacco use, countries that establish a coordinated tobacco control programme that incorporates all these measures will have a far greater likelihood of success in reducing tobacco use.

Monitoring tobacco use and prevention policies. More than a quarter of countries, with 40% of the world's population, regularly monitor tobacco use among adults and youth using nationally representative surveys, an increase of 14 countries (5% of world population) since 2007. It takes time to establish a surveillance system that regularly surveys both adults and youth at least once every five years. In 2007, 32 countries had no recent data for adults

or youth. By 2012, only 22 countries (8% of world population) still had no recent adult or youth surveys. Six of these countries are middle-income countries, and three are high-income countries.

Protecting people from the harms of tobacco smoke. In terms of both countries and population covered, the measure with the greatest progress since 2007 has been protecting people from the dangers of tobacco smoke by enacting laws that create smoke-free workplaces and public places. There are 32 countries (including 26 low- and middle-income counties) that adopted complete smoking bans between 2007 and 2012. Since 2007, the population protected by a comprehensive smoke-free law more than quadrupled, with 1.1 billion people (16% of world population) now protected from the dangers of second-hand smoke. Almost all of these newly protected people live in middle-income countries, which have taken the lead in passing complete smoke-free laws.

Offering help to quit tobacco use. Twice as many people now have access to appropriate cessation services than did five years ago, when only 502 million people (7% of world population) in 12 countries were offered sufficient assistance to quit. Now, more than 1 billion people (15% of world population) in 21 countries are receiving this critical help to stop tobacco use. Middle- and high-income countries continue to be more likely to provide their people with appropriate cessation support; no low-income country yet provides cessation support at the highest level, and few are close to doing so.

Warning about the dangers of tobacco. The number of people worldwide who are exposed to strong, graphic health warning labels on cigarette packs has nearly tripled in the past five years, from 356 million (5% of world population) in 10 countries in 2007 to more than 1 billion people (14% of world population) in 30 countries by 2012. Middle-income countries are more likely to have established strong warning label requirements over the past five years, although most high-income countries mandate warning labels with at least some of the defined characteristics.

Enforcing bans on tobacco advertising, promotion and sponsorship. In 2007, a mere 2.4% of people worldwide (170 million people in 8 countries) were protected by complete bans on tobacco advertising, promotion and sponsorship. Five years later, this has more than quadrupled to 694 million people (10% of world population) in 24 countries. Low-income countries have taken greater action to put this MPOWER measure in place at the highest level than have either high- or middle-income countries.

Raising taxes on tobacco. The most cost-effective tobacco control strategy is increasing the price of tobacco products by raising tobacco tax. However, this is the MPOWER measure with the least progress since data were first collected. In 2008, 7% of people worldwide (490 million people in 22 countries) were subject to tax rates sufficiently high to represent 75% of the retail price of cigarettes. In 2012, that had increased to only 530 million people (8% of world population) in 32 countries. Low-income countries, which are in greater need of government funding for tobacco control programmes, are the least likely to have sufficiently high tax rates.

There has been great progress over the past five years, with both the number of countries and the number of people worldwide protected by effective tobacco control measures more than doubling since 2007.

More progress is needed in all countries

There has been great progress in global tobacco control efforts over the past five years, with both the number of countries protecting their people and the number of people worldwide protected by effective tobacco control measures more than doubling since 2007. However, far more work is needed in almost every country, especially to pass and enforce effective tobacco control legislation and take other actions that incorporate all elements of the WHO Framework Convention on Tobacco Control.

The successes of the majority of countries in applying the MPOWER measures demonstrate that it is possible to tackle the tobacco epidemic regardless of size or income. Most progress in protecting people with these measures has been made by low- and middle-income countries, which remain at greatest risk from tobacco industry efforts to increase tobacco use. Despite the achievements in some countries to establish effective tobacco control measures, only one country so far has reached the highest level of achievement in all MPOWER measures. Efforts must be accelerated in all countries to save even more lives.

FIVE YEARS OF PROGRESS IN SELECTED TOBACCO CONTROL MEASURES (2007–2012)

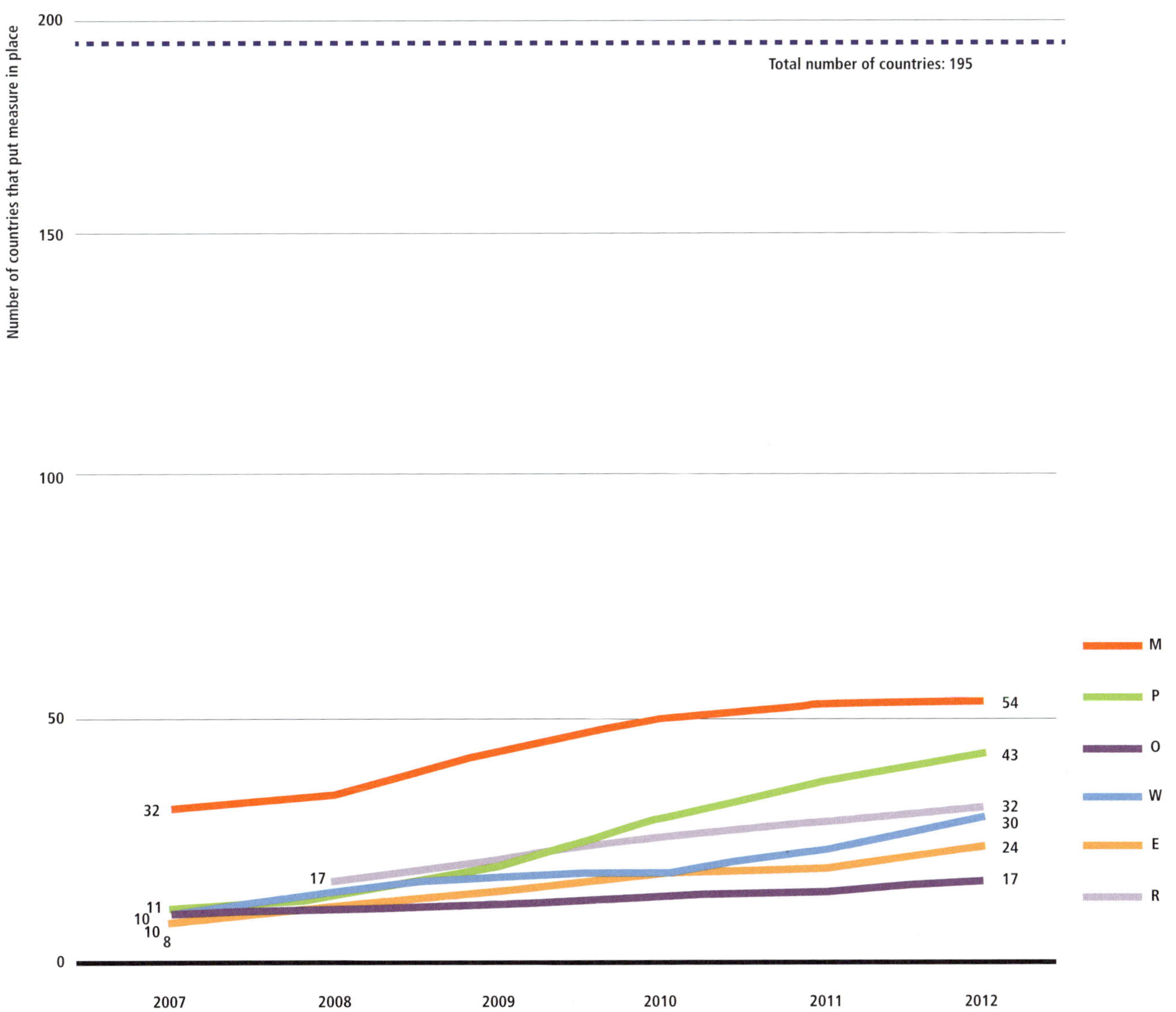

Notes: for M and R measures, a value was imputed for 2009 and 2011. Year of complete O measure unknown for four countries.

Turkey marks singular achievement in tobacco control

History of tobacco control in Turkey

- The first organized anti-tobacco civil society movement started in Turkey in 1991.
- Turkey's first tobacco control bill was vetoed in 1991. Parliament tabled a 1992 bill.
- In 1996, tobacco control legislation was enacted. Implementation was successful despite tobacco industry opposition, but enforcement was uneven.
- In 2002, Turkey established the Tobacco and Alcohol Market Regulatory Authority (TAPDK).
- Turkey signed the WHO FCTC on 28 April 2004 and ratified it on 30 November 2004, one of the first countries to do so.
- Following ratification, the Ministry of Health (MoH) formed a National Tobacco Control Committee to prepare a national tobacco control programme and implementation plan.
- The tobacco control law was substantially strengthened in 2008, with clearly established enforcement mechanisms instituted by the MoH and TAPDK that include inspection teams in each province.

MPOWER measures in Turkey

MORE THAN 13% DECLINE IN SMOKING PREVALENCE IN TURKEY AFTER COMPREHENSIVE TOBACCO CONTROL IS PUT IN PLACE

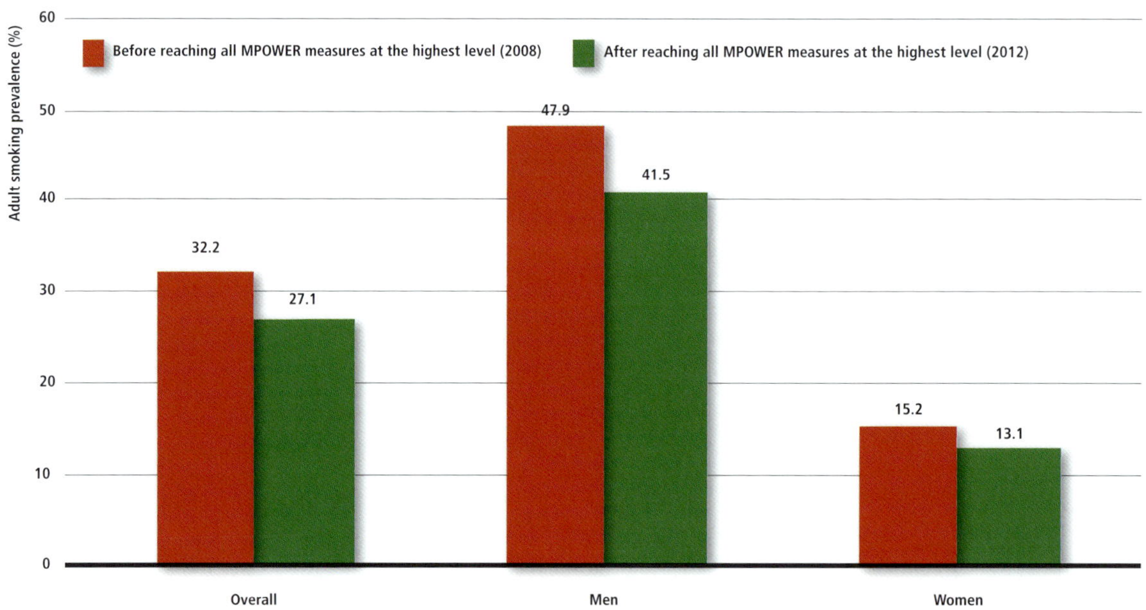

Source: (*89*).

Monitoring of tobacco use and prevention policies

- Turkey was the first country to complete data collection for the Global Adult Tobacco Survey (GATS) in 2008, and was one of two countries to repeat GATS in 2012.
- Turkey conducted the Global Youth Tobacco Survey (GYTS) in 2003, 2009 and 2012.
- A study of smoking and health-care professionals was conducted in 2007 and repeated in 2011.
- In addition to these systematic surveys, other surveys show strong public support for the law, increased compliance, and improvements in indoor air quality and health benefits.

Protecting people from tobacco smoke

- Turkey's first smoke-free law was enacted in 1996 and substantially strengthened in 2008 to cover the hospitality industry, most importantly adding restaurants, bars and cafés.
- In addition, the MoH and TAPDK issued regulations to ensure compliance. However, a few exceptions are still in place.

Offering help to quit tobacco use

- The 2008 legislation charged the MoH to develop programmes to help people stop using tobacco and ensure accessibility of cessation medications.
- The government established a national quit line service in 2010, and began to cover costs of nicotine replacement therapy and other cessation services.

Warning about the dangers of tobacco

Health warning labels

- The 1996 law mandated warning labels, but they were only small text warnings and did not appear on the main package display areas.
- In 2005, the TAPDK required larger text warnings covering 30-40% of the front and back of packages.
- In 2012 the TAPDK mandated pictorial warnings covering 65% of both the package front and back, and prohibited misleading and deceptive terms such as "mild" or "light".

Anti-tobacco mass media campaigns

- The 1996 law directed all television stations to broadcast anti-tobacco programmes, but many were aired late at night and viewership was low.
- The 2008 revision required that programming be aired during prime viewing hours to reach more people.
- Media campaigns featured anti-tobacco advertisements pretested for effectiveness, including the hard-hitting "Sponge" ads.
- Campaigns were also launched to publicize provisions of the new law, in particular the smoke-free requirements and the national quit line service.

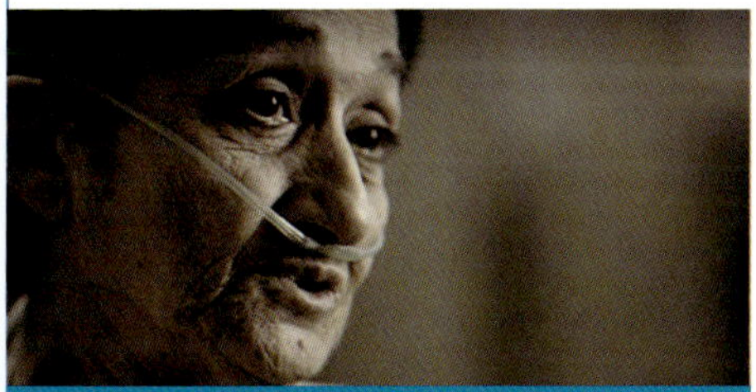

Testimonial anti-tobacco TV campaign showing health effects of tobacco use.

Enforcing of bans on tobacco advertising, promotion and sponsorship

- The 1996 law banned virtually all tobacco advertisement and promotion, but not sponsorships.
- The 2008 revision expanded the ban to include all sponsorships, and added retail display restrictions.
- In 2012, Turkey implemented a total TAPS ban (including brand sharing and brand stretching).

Raising taxes on tobacco

- Tobacco taxes in Turkey represented 65-70% of the retail price for many years.
- Since passage of the revised law in 2008, taxes were gradually increased, and now represent 80.3% of the retail price.

Tobacco use in Turkey is declining

Although Turkey has had a long tradition of tobacco use and high smoking prevalence, particularly among men, tobacco use is now declining at unprecedented rates.

- Among adults, data from GATS show that smoking prevalence significantly decreased from 31.2% (16 million) in 2008 to 27.1% (14.8 million) in 2012.
- This represents a 13.4% relative decline (13.5% for males; 13.7% for females).
- Despite this sharp decline, however, more than a quarter of Turkey's adults continue to use tobacco.

Turkey: an example for other countries

Turkey is the first country to attain the highest level of achievement in all six MPOWER measures. This progress is a testament to the Turkish government's sustained political commitment to tobacco control, and is an excellent example of collaboration between government, WHO and other international health organizations, and civil society.

The need for other countries to follow Turkey's example and apply all six MPOWER measures at the strongest level is urgent. Even more progress is possible in Turkey and elsewhere if we continue doing what works.

- Subsidized cessation assistance can be offered to more people, and access made easier.
- Health warning labels can be made even larger with more impactful images, and anti-tobacco advertising campaigns can be expanded.
- Bans on TAPS can be strengthened to include all point-of-sale and promotional activities.
- Taxes can be raised further, with revenues specifically earmarked for tobacco control.
- Enforcement of all measures can be strengthened.

Achievement continues but much work remains

mpower — **M**onitor tobacco use and prevention policies

mpower — **P**rotect from tobacco smoke

mpower — **O**ffer help to quit tobacco use

mpower — **W**arn about the dangers of tobacco

mpower — **E**nforce bans on tobacco advertising, promotion and sponsorship

mpower — **R**aise taxes on tobacco

Monitor tobacco use and prevention policies

Article 20 of the **WHO Framework Convention on Tobacco Control** states: "… Parties shall establish … surveillance of the magnitude, patterns, determinants and consequences of tobacco consumption and exposure to tobacco smoke … Parties should integrate tobacco surveillance programmes into national, regional and global health surveillance programmes so that data are comparable and can be analysed at the regional and international levels …" (*3*).

RECENT ACHIEVEMENTS AND DEVELOPMENTS

Standardized Tobacco Questions for Surveys incorporated into monitoring programmes worldwide

Tobacco Questions for Surveys (TQS) form a set of 22 key standardized questions used in the Global Adult Tobacco Survey (GATS) to measure tobacco use and progress of the MPOWER measures. TQS, released in 2011 and available in seven languages, are now being used in surveys in a number of countries to ensure reporting of internationally comparable data, e.g. in the WHO STEPS NCD Risk Factor Survey, the Demographic and Health Survey (DHS) and the Behavioral Risk Factor Surveillance System (BRFSS).

GATS repeated in Turkey and Thailand

Both Turkey and Thailand, which conducted their initial GATS in 2008 and 2009 respectively, have conducted follow-up surveys. Turkey, which conducted its follow-up GATS in 2012, released the following findings in May 2013 (*88*):

- Tobacco use prevalence decreased from 31.2% in 2008 to 27.1% in 2012 – representing 1.2 million fewer adult smokers – with larger declines among men than among women.
- Second-hand smoke exposure declined, with the largest drop occurring in restaurants (a 12.9% exposure rate in 2012 compared to 55.9% in 2008).
- More tobacco users plan to quit smoking, with women more likely to make an attempt to quit than men.

Thailand conducted its follow-up GATS in 2011, releasing a full report in May 2012 with the following key findings (*89*):

- Overall tobacco use was essentially unchanged from 27.2% in 2009 to 26.9% in 2011.
- Quit attempts among current smokers in the past 12 months declined from 49.8% in 2009 to 36.7% in 2011.
- The proportion of adults who noticed cigarette advertising in stores increased from 6.7% in 2009 to 18.2% in 2011.
- Among current smokers of manufactured cigarettes, 10% purchased new, inexpensive brands introduced following a 2009 tobacco tax increase.

Monitoring is critical to tobacco control efforts

Monitoring tobacco use and tobacco control measures is critical to effectively addressing the epidemic and assessing the effects of global tobacco control. Monitoring systems should not only track tobacco use indicators, including use of alternative forms of smoked tobacco (e.g. water pipe), smokeless tobacco products (e.g. snus) and new types of cigarette substitutes (e.g. electronic cigarettes), but also the impact of tobacco control policy interventions (*90*) and tobacco industry activities (*91*). Timely and accurate data facilitate appropriate policy implementation, accurate measurement of policy impact and adjustment of strategies as indicated, all of which greatly improve the likelihood of success (*92*).

Monitoring tobacco use and tobacco control measures is critical to effectively addressing the epidemic and assessing the effects of global tobacco control.

MONITORING

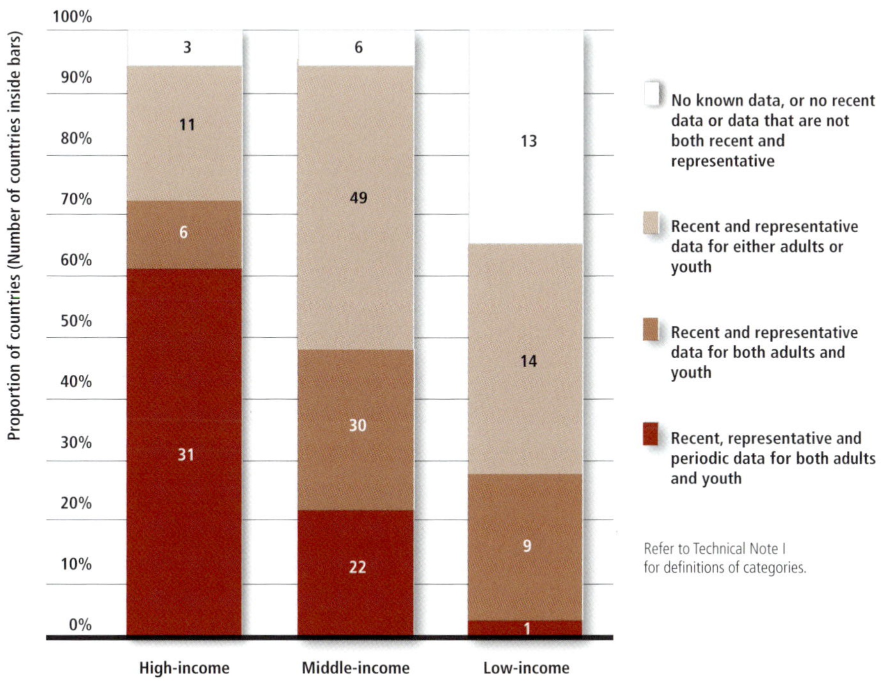

Refer to Technical Note I for definitions of categories.

Tobacco use monitoring has become weaker globally

Despite the success of the Global Adult Tobacco Survey as a tool to strengthen high-quality monitoring in the 18 countries in which it has been implemented, overall global monitoring of tobacco use has regressed over the past two years. Only three countries (Hungary, Malaysia and Togo) strengthened their tobacco use monitoring to implement ongoing, periodic surveys for both adults and youth at least every five years. At the same time, 10 countries at the highest level of achievement in 2010 did not maintain ongoing surveys; eight of these are low- and middle-income countries, which are in greatest need of accurate, up-to-date monitoring.

As a result, only 2.8 billion people in 54 countries (or 40% of the world's population) are now covered by effective tobacco use surveillance – down from the 2.9 billion covered in 2010. There are 96 countries (with almost 3 billion people) that did not collect representative data for both adults and youth, or that collected no data at all in the previous five years.

There are 45 countries that conducted recent adult and youth surveys but have not done so periodically, making it more difficult to detect trends in tobacco use. An additional 1.2 billion people could be covered by high-level monitoring if these 45 countries were to repeat the surveys they have previously run every five years. Thirty-nine of these countries are low- and middle-income countries. Tobacco Questions for Surveys can be inserted into existing national surveys to minimize surveillance system and survey costs.

2.8 billion people in 54 countries are covered by effective tobacco use surveillance.

MONITOR THE PREVALENCE OF TOBACCO USE – HIGHEST ACHIEVING COUNTRIES, 2012

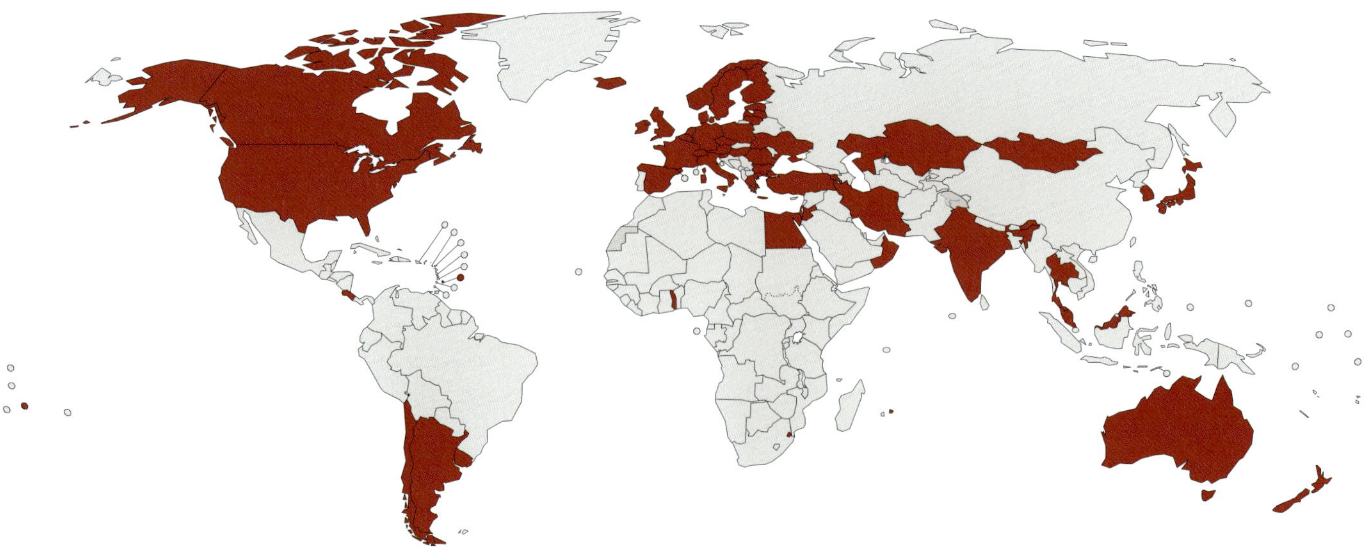

Countries with the highest level of achievement: Argentina, Armenia, Australia, Austria, Barbados, Belgium, Bulgaria, Canada, Chile, Costa Rica, Czech Republic, Denmark, Egypt, Estonia, Finland, France, Germany, Greece, Hungary*, Iceland, India, Iran (Islamic Republic of), Ireland, Israel, Italy, Japan, Jordan, Kazakhstan, Latvia, Lithuania, Luxembourg, Malaysia*, Mauritius, Mongolia, Netherlands, New Zealand, Niue, Norway, Oman, Poland, Republic of Korea, Romania, Slovenia, Spain, Swaziland, Sweden, Switzerland, Thailand, Togo*, Turkey, Ukraine, United Kingdom of Great Britain and Northern Ireland, United States of America and Uruguay.

*Country newly at the highest level since 31 December 2010.

Qatar conducts initial Global Adult Tobacco Survey

To accurately measure tobacco use in this rapidly growing and economically developing country, Qatar conducted its first Global Adult Tobacco Survey (GATS) survey. The Supreme Council of Health (SCH) in Qatar worked with WHO and its Regional Office for the Eastern Mediterranean (EMRO) to implement GATS using government-allocated funds for tobacco control activities and research, without need for international financial support. All SCH tobacco control team members were involved in adapting the GATS protocol to suit Qatar's country-specific situation, under supervision of and with technical support from EMRO and the Centers for Disease Control and Prevention (CDC). An assessment of technical capacity was conducted to ensure that GATS could be implemented according to the required global standard. The Qatar Statistics Authority was selected to conduct sampling and fieldwork because of its well-trained staff and knowledge of and experience with electronic data collection in similar household surveys, including the 2010 national census, the first electronically conducted census in the Arab region. About 8000 household surveys were completed in early 2013, with GATS data analysis and reporting to follow later in the year.

Panama demonstrates an ongoing commitment to robust tobacco use surveillance

Panama has conducted numerous national surveys on tobacco use over the past decade, including the Global Youth Tobacco Survey (GYTS) of students aged 13–15 years in 2002, 2008 and 2012; the Encuesta Nacional de Salud y Calidad de Vida (National Survey of Health and Quality of Life), which included several questions on tobacco use, in 2007; and the Global Health Professions Student Survey, a standardized school-based survey of third-year students pursuing advanced degrees in medicine and related fields, which also includes questions on tobacco use, in 2008. Panama conducted its first Global Adult Tobacco Survey (GATS) earlier in 2013, which was funded using revenues from the country's tobacco tax (half of total tobacco tax revenue is earmarked for tobacco control), making it the first country in the region of the Americas to fund GATS exclusively with national resources. Prior to conducting the survey, Panama adapted the questionnaire for national use, completed quality assurance processes and trained its data collection teams, and is now in the process of analysing and reporting the data collected.

Protect from tobacco smoke

Article 8 of the **WHO Framework Convention on Tobacco Control** states: " … scientific evidence has unequivocally established that exposure to tobacco smoke causes death, disease and disability … [Parties] shall adopt and implement … measures providing for protection from exposure to tobacco smoke in indoor workplaces, public transport, indoor public places and, as appropriate, other public places" (*3*). WHO FCTC Article 8 guidelines (*5*) are intended to assist Parties in meeting their obligations under Article 8 of the Convention and provide a clear timeline for Parties to adopt appropriate measures (within five years after entry into force of the WHO FCTC for a given Party).

RECENT ACHIEVEMENTS AND DEVELOPMENTS

European Football Championship organized as a 100% tobacco-free event

The Union of European Football Associations (UEFA) organized the 14th UEFA European Football Championship (Euro 2012) in Poland and Ukraine as a completely tobacco-free event. This entailed a complete ban on the use, sale and promotion of tobacco in all spaces in all stadia involved in the tournament, both indoors and outdoors, with no exceptions. The Euro 2012 Organizing Committees in the host countries of Poland and Ukraine developed this policy with assistance from its official collaborating partner WHO, as well as from the World Heart Federation, European Healthy Stadia Network, and local organizing committees and health advocacy groups. The policy was publicly supported by the two host governments and clearly communicated in the event's fan guide. Four workshops in each of the four host cities were conducted to train 3000 event volunteers on the tobacco-free policy, and local authorities collaborated with other city partners and institutions to enforce the policy. Despite the many challenges faced by the two host countries in relation to tobacco control, UEFA's decision to ban tobacco from the world's third largest sporting event sends a strong message to football fans everywhere, reaffirming the link between sport and good health.

2014 Sochi Winter Olympics to be smoke-free

During the 2014 Winter Olympic Games in Sochi, Russian Federation, smoking will be forbidden in all Olympic and Paralympic venues, including all bars and restaurants in the Olympic park. This will be the 14th consecutive smoke-free Olympic Games. No tobacco products will be sold in any of the Olympic venues, and the no-smoking policy will be publicized during all events on scoreboards and radio broadcasts. This policy is intended to protect more than 155 000 athletes, sports delegation representatives and volunteers, as well as potentially a million or more spectators, from exposure to second-hand smoke. The Olympic Organizing Committee and local government authorities are also working with WHO on commitments to make Sochi a smoke-free city by the time the Games begin in February 2014, including developing effective enforcement and compliance mechanisms.

Second-hand smoke kills

Scientific evidence has proven that there is no safe level of exposure to second-hand smoke (*90*). WHO and other leading global health organizations concur that second-hand smoke exposure leads to serious and often fatal diseases, including cardiovascular and respiratory disease as well as lung and other cancers (*90*). Children, including fetuses and newborns, can also suffer harm from exposure to second-hand smoke (*91*).

Smoke-free laws save lives

Environments that are completely smoke-free and do not allow for any exceptions are the only proven way to fully protect people from the harms of second-hand tobacco smoke (*91*). Accommodations such as separate smoking rooms and ventilation systems are not effective in preventing second-hand smoke exposure (*91*). Governments must enact comprehensive smoke-free laws and maintain support for them through proactive, uniform enforcement that achieves high compliance (*91*).

Smoke-free laws are popular, do not hurt business and improve health

The ever-increasing number of countries and subnational areas with comprehensive smoke-free legislation shows that effective laws are relatively easy to pass and

Comprehensive smoke-free legislation is the most widely adopted measure, with 1.1 billion people covered.

SMOKE-FREE LEGISLATION

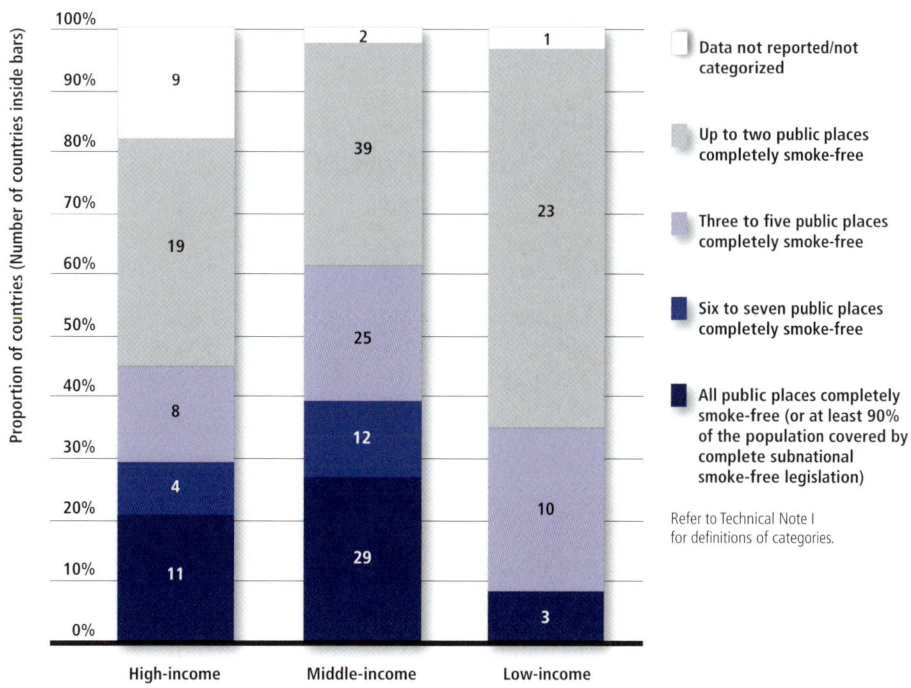

Refer to Technical Note I for definitions of categories.

enforce, and that doing so generally has overwhelming popular support, causes no financial harm to businesses, and improves the health of both non-smokers and smokers (*91*). Smoke-free environments also reduce tobacco use by smokers and help those who want to quit succeed over the long term (*91*). In addition, they can encourage people to protect children and other non-smokers by making their homes smoke-free, which also reduces both adult and youth smoking (*91*).

Comprehensive smoke-free legislation is the most widely adopted policy measure

Strong smoke-free legislation is the most widely adopted policy measure, with 1.1 billion people (16% of the world's population) covered – an increase of 350 million people since 2010. There are 12 countries (Argentina, Brazil, Brunei Darussalam, Bulgaria, Congo, Costa Rica, Ecuador, Lebanon, Mongolia, Nepal, Papua New Guinea and Venezuela) and one territory (West Bank and Gaza Strip) that have newly passed strong smoke-free laws on a nationwide level; all but one are low- or middle-income.

There are 16 countries (with 4% of the world's population) that could attain the highest level of achievement through further strengthening of existing smoke-free laws. Six of these countries (1% of the world's population) are missing only one single public place to be completely smoke-free; for most of these the missing place is indoor private offices and workplaces; the other 10 countries (3% of the world's population) would attain the highest level if they implemented smoking bans in two additional places: the most frequently missing public places to be smoke-free are restaurants and cafés, pubs and bars. Nearly half of all countries, including nearly two thirds of low-income countries, have weak or no smoke-free laws, leaving their populations vulnerable to the dangers of second-hand smoke.

Of the 445 million people (6.3% of the world's population) who live in one of the world's 100 largest cities, only 112 million (in 21 cities) are protected by a comprehensive smoke-free law. Two large cities (Hong Kong Special Administrative Region of China and Houston) and six states/provinces containing a large city (Mexico City, New York City, Chicago, Jakarta, Sydney and Melbourne) have introduced comprehensive smoke-free laws independently of national authorities to protect their citizens from second-hand smoke; people in the other 13 largest cities are covered by national legislation.

SMOKE-FREE ENVIRONMENTS – HIGHEST ACHIEVING COUNTRIES, 2012

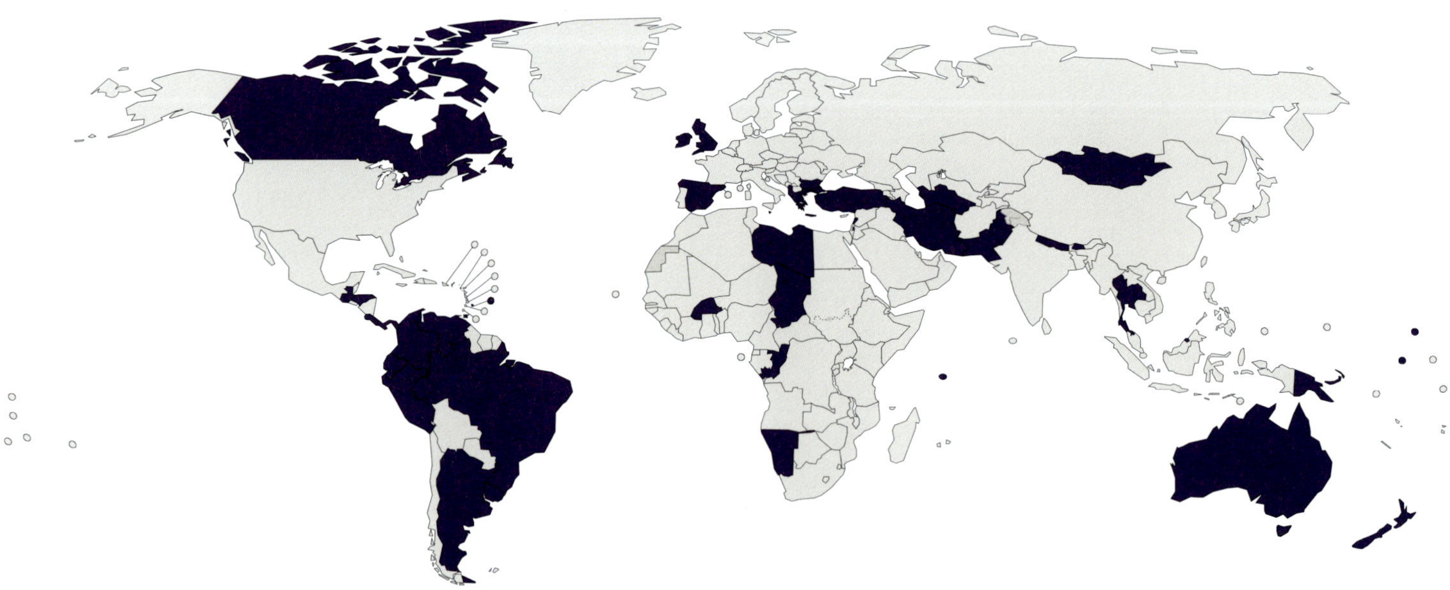

Countries and territories with the highest level of achievement: Albania, Argentina*, Australia, Barbados, Bhutan, Brazil*, Brunei Darussalam*, Bulgaria*, Burkina Faso, Canada, Chad, Colombia, Congo*, Costa Rica*, Ecuador*, Greece, Guatemala, Honduras, Iran (Islamic Republic of), Ireland, Lebanon*, Libya, Malta, Marshall Islands, Mongolia*, Namibia, Nauru, Nepal*, New Zealand, Pakistan, Panama, Papua New Guinea*, Peru, Seychelles, Spain, Thailand, Trinidad and Tobago, Turkey, Turkmenistan, United Kingdom of Great Britain and Northern Ireland, Uruguay, Venezuela* and West Bank and Gaza Strip*.

* Country or territory newly at the highest level since 31 December 2010.

Harbin, China enacts comprehensive subnational smoke-free law

Harbin, a city of over 10 million people, is a major metropolitan area in northern China. There have historically been high rates of tobacco use in Harbin, with more than half of men current smokers, and more than 70% of the population regularly exposed to second-hand tobacco smoke. A law making all indoor workplaces and public places in Harbin 100% smoke-free became effective on 31 May 2012. Even the name of the law – "The Act on the Prevention of the Harms Caused by Second-hand Tobacco Smoke in Harbin" – highlights the aim of the law to protect health and brings it closer to the concepts of the WHO FCTC. The title also helped achieve public understanding and support for the law which, combined with public education about the harms of tobacco use and second-hand smoke exposure, facilitated its passing. An implementation mechanism led by the municipal government and organized, coordinated and monitored by the health department is carried out by 12 government agencies. Enforcement focuses on premises owners and managers rather than on individual smokers, with fines of up to 30 000 Yuan (US$ 4800) for serious, repeated violations.

"Harbin city ordinance to prevent exposure to second-hand tobacco smoke"
Banning smoking in indoor public places, workplaces and inside public transport
Smoking ban complaint hotline: 12320
The leading group for preventing exposure to second-hand tobacco smoke in Harbin.

Lebanon passes comprehensive law making entire country 100% smoke-free

After a five-year legislative effort that saw a number of delays, including continuing interference from the tobacco industry to weaken and postpone consideration of any laws, Lebanon's parliament passed a comprehensive tobacco control law making Lebanon 100% smoke-free as of September 2012. The law, drafted with international assistance to incorporate best practices from around the world, as well as advocacy to increase public support, also bans all forms of tobacco advertising and mandates health warnings covering 40% of all tobacco product packaging. According to a nationwide public opinion poll conducted before the legislation was passed, 94% agreed that banning indoor smoking in public places would benefit people's health, and 82% believed that a ban on indoor smoking would be fair.

Minister of Public Works and Transportation announces smoke-free public transport.

Offer help to quit tobacco use

Article 14 of the **WHO Framework Convention on Tobacco Control** states: "Each Party shall ... take effective measures to promote cessation of tobacco use and adequate treatment for tobacco dependence ... Each Party shall ... design and implement effective programmes aimed at promoting the cessation of tobacco use" *(3)*. WHO FCTC Article 14 guidelines *(5)* are intended to assist Parties in meeting their obligations under Article 14 of the Convention.

RECENT ACHIEVEMENTS AND DEVELOPMENTS

WHO publishes tobacco quit line manual

Guidelines for implementation of Article 14 of the WHO FCTC recognize that offering quit lines is an effective population-level approach to help tobacco users quit, and that easily accessible and toll-free telephone quit lines should be included in any comprehensive tobacco control programme. WHO's manual, *Developing and improving national toll-free tobacco quit line services*, provides technical advice and case examples for establishing and operating a national quit line service, drawing on experiences from quit lines around the world. The manual, currently available in English and Arabic, is primarily intended to help low- and middle-income countries in the early stages of quit line development, and focuses on choosing appropriate service delivery options, optimizing population coverage and utilization, and developing partnerships with health-care systems to provide cessation support, including medications. It can also be useful to managers of existing quit lines to improve services.

Clinical cessation interventions are effective, and also extremely cost-effective compared to other health-care interventions.

Most smokers want to quit

Most tobacco users who understand the full range of harms caused by tobacco use want to quit, but it is difficult for many to do so unaided because of the extreme addictiveness of nicotine (*90*). Most smokers who quit are able to do so without assistance, but cessation interventions greatly increase quit rates (*91*). People who quit tobacco use experience immediate and significant health benefits, and reduce most of their excess health risk within a few years (*91*).

Tobacco cessation interventions are effective

Clinical cessation interventions are effective, and also extremely cost-effective compared to other health-care interventions (*92*). At least three types of clinical treatment should be included in any tobacco control programme (*91*).

- *Cessation advice in primary health-care systems.* Brief advice from doctors and other health-care workers increases quit rates (*91*).
- *Quit lines*. Cessation advice and counselling can also be provided through free telephone help lines (known as quit lines) (*91*).
- *Pharmacological therapy*. Clinical cessation treatment can at least include nicotine replacement therapy (NRT), which is available over the counter in most countries (*91*). Pharmacological therapy with NRT alone or in combination with other prescription cessation medications can double or triple quit rates (*91*).

TOBACCO DEPENDENCE TREATMENT

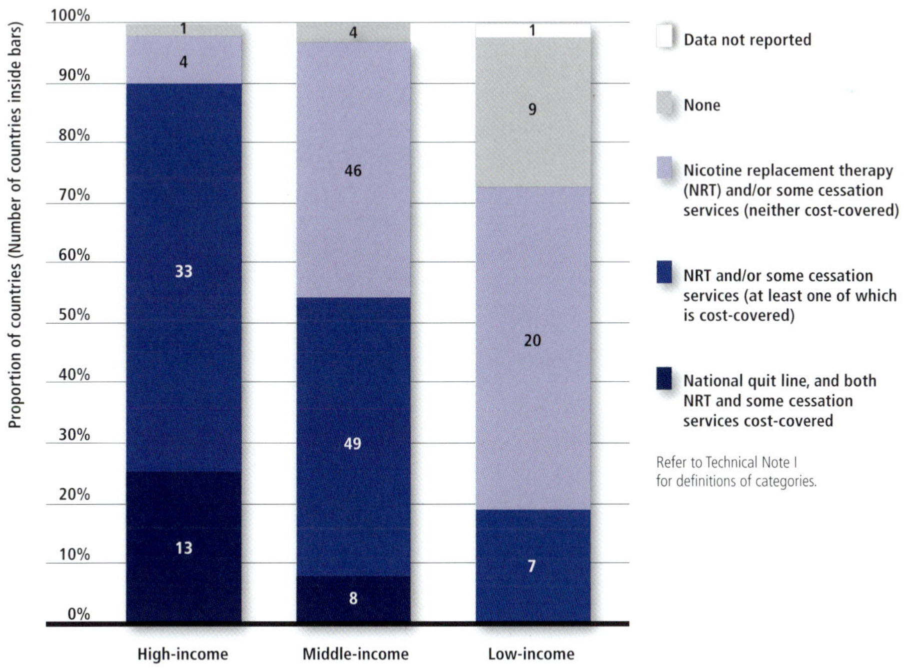

Government must support cessation treatment

Each country's health-care system should have primary responsibility for smoking cessation programmes (*91*). Cessation services are most effective when incorporated into a coordinated national tobacco control programme (*91*). It is also recommended that each country's Essential Medicines list should include NRT.

There has been little progress in providing access to essential help to quit smoking

Very little has been achieved to make tobacco cessation services readily available since 2010. Just over 1 billion people (15% of the world's population) live in the 21 countries that provide appropriate cessation support. Since 2010, four additional countries (Denmark, El Salvador, Kuwait and Thailand) with a population of 85 million people, all of which are middle- or high-income countries, have provided access to cost-covered services including a toll-free national quit line.

There are 89 countries (with 40% of the world's population) that come close to attaining the highest level of achievement. Of these, 43 countries (34% of the world's population) are missing only one criterion to attain the highest level (16 need only establish a national toll-free quit line and 27 need only at least partially cover costs of NRT). Nearly half of all countries, including more than 80% of low-income countries, have minimal or no programmes to provide appropriate help to people who want to quit tobacco use.

Of the 445 million people (6.3% of the world's population) who live in the world's 100 largest cities, only about 96 million (in 21 cities) have access to appropriate cessation support. All but one city is located in a nation that provides such access to its entire population. Only one city (Hong Kong Special Administrative Region of China) has established a strong cessation programme ahead of the national policy.

TOBACCO DEPENDENCE TREATMENT – HIGHEST ACHIEVING COUNTRIES, 2012

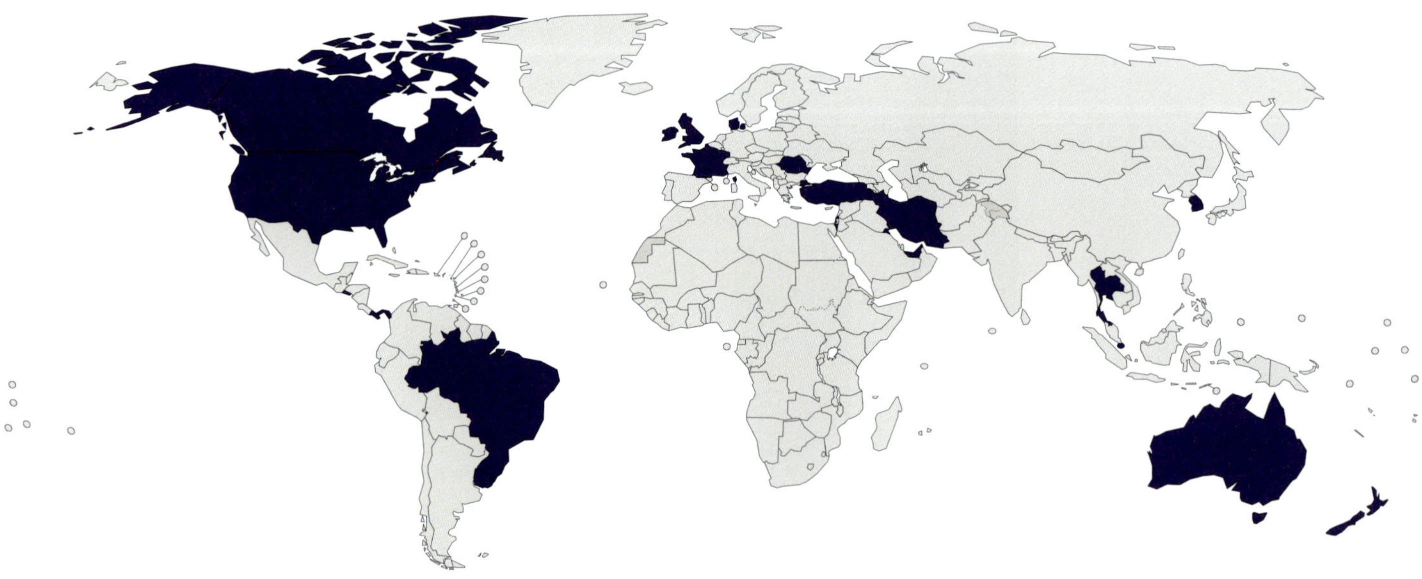

Countries with the highest level of achievement: Australia, Brazil, Canada, Denmark*, El Salvador*, France, Iran (Islamic Republic of), Ireland, Israel, Kuwait*, New Zealand, Panama, Republic of Korea, Romania, Singapore, Thailand*, Turkey, United Arab Emirates, United Kingdom of Great Britain and Northern Ireland, United States of America and Uruguay.

* Country newly at the highest level since 31 December 2010.

Thailand's national quit line helps increase smoking cessation rates

"Quit smoking, call Quitline 1600."

Thailand set up its national quit line in 2009 (named Quitline 1600, after the telephone access number) following a full year of preparation and training. Since then, Quitline 1600 has been in operation 12.5 hours a day, five days a week, with people who call out of hours being given the option to leave a message for a call-back. The service expanded from 10 lines in January 2009 to 30 lines in June 2011, and as of February 2012, calls to Quitline 1600 incurred no telecommunications charges. More than 11 000 incoming calls are logged each month, with more than 2000 people enrolling in a smoking cessation programme and about 1200 setting a quit date per month. Each person calling Quitline 1600 is provided with information and counselling, and those who enroll in a cessation programme are contacted six times over the course of the following year for follow-up and relapse prevention. A quality monitoring system implemented in August 2011 provides Quitline 1600 counsellors with ongoing feedback to improve their competencies. About 30% of those who quit remain abstinent after six months – about three times the rate of those receiving no assistance – which translates to more than 4000 people a year nationwide who stop smoking because of Quitline 1600 programmes.

Since 2010, four additional countries with a population of 85 million people have provided access to cost-covered services including a toll-free national quit line.

Warn about the dangers of tobacco

Health warning labels

Article 11 of the **WHO Framework Convention on Tobacco Control** states: "Each Party shall … adopt and implement … effective measures to ensure that … tobacco product packaging and labelling do not promote a tobacco product by any means that are false, misleading, deceptive or likely to create an erroneous impression about its characteristics, health effects, hazards or emissions … [Parties shall adopt and implement effective measures to ensure that] each unit packet and package of tobacco products and any outside packaging and labelling of such products also carry health warnings describing the harmful effects of tobacco use … These warnings and messages … should be 50% or more of the principal display areas but shall be no less than 30% of the principal display areas, … [they] may be in the form of or include pictures or pictograms" (*3*). WHO FCTC Article 11 guidelines (*5*) are intended to assist Parties in meeting their obligations under Article 11 of the Convention, which provides a clear timeline for Parties to adopt appropriate measures (within three years after entry into force of the WHO FCTC for a given Party).

"Smoking increases risk of more than 25 diseases including cancer and cardiovascular disease."

RECENT ACHIEVEMENTS AND DEVELOPMENTS

Regulations for Gulf Cooperation Council (GCC) warning labels directive put into force

After a five-year process, in August 2012 countries of the Gulf Cooperation Council (GCC) adopted and put into force a unified regulation for implementing pictorial health warnings. These pictorial warnings were designed to meet the cultural and population needs of the Arab region and include the following provisions:

- Pictorial and text warnings are to cover not less than 50% of both the package front and back.
- Text areas are not to exceed 40% of the total warning label.
- Warning text is to appear in Arabic on the front and in English on the back.
- Images of both cigarettes and shisha (water pipes) are to be used.
- New images and appropriate text warnings may be developed and updated.

Health warnings change social norms about tobacco, which will reduce tobacco use and increase support for tobacco control measures.

Health warnings provide needed information about the dangers of smoking

People have a fundamental right to information about the harms of tobacco use (*93*). Despite clear evidence about its dangers, many smokers do not fully understand the risk to their health or that of others (*93*). Accurate warnings about the harms of tobacco use and second-hand smoke exposure influence people's decisions about tobacco (*93*). Ultimately, health warnings are intended to change social norms about tobacco use, which will reduce tobacco use and increase support for tobacco control measures (*93*).

Warning labels on tobacco packaging are effective

Effective health warning labels provide direct health messages to smokers to raise awareness of health risks, which increases the likelihood they will reduce or quit tobacco use (*93*). Large and graphic pictorial warnings that cover at least half of both the front and back of tobacco packages are more effective than smaller or text-only warnings (*93*).

Warning labels have greater public support than most other tobacco control interventions, and can be implemented at virtually no cost to government (*93*). They should describe specific health effects of tobacco use and be periodically rotated to maintain their impact (*93*). Deceptive terms suggesting that some products are less harmful (e.g. "light" or "mild") should be banned (*93*). Plain (standardized) packaging enhances the impact of health warnings and other packaging and labelling measures.

WARNING LABELS

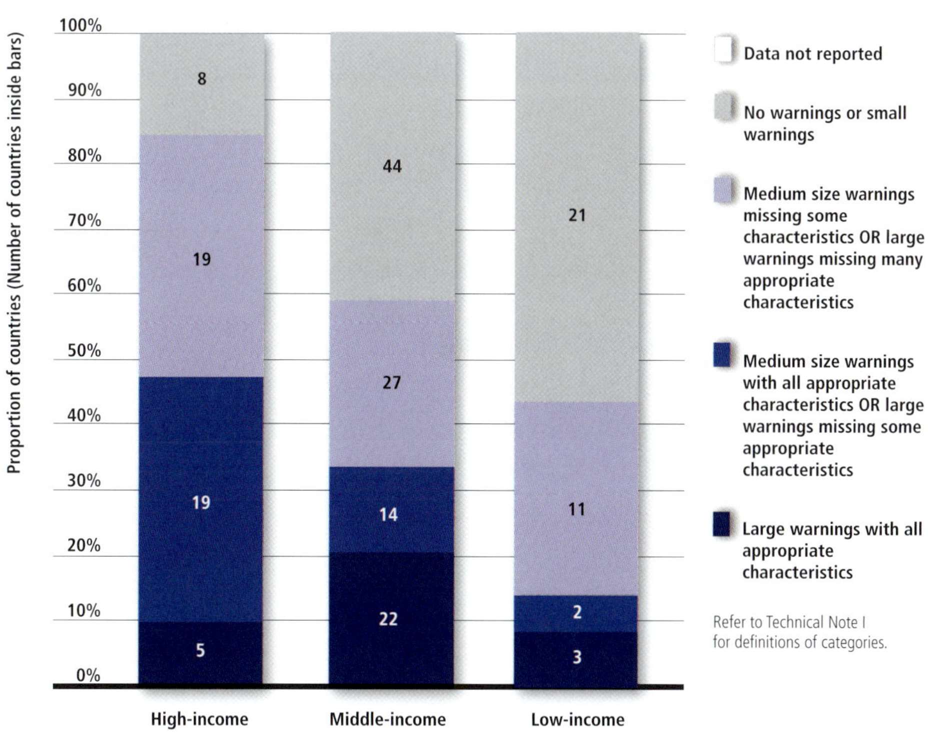

Refer to Technical Note I for definitions of categories.

Use of graphic pack warnings is increasing

Use of graphic pack warnings has increased since 2010. There are 265 million people living in 11 countries (Argentina, Canada, Ecuador, El Salvador, Madagascar, Mongolia, Nepal, Niger, Seychelles, Sri Lanka and Turkey) with new requirements since 2010 for warning labels that are sufficiently large, use pictures, and include all other appropriate characteristics, bringing the global total to just over 1 billion people (14% of the world's population). Middle-income countries have shown leadership in this area – 22 of the 30 countries with highest-category warning labels are middle-income countries.

Of the 445 million people (6.3% of the world's population) who live in one of the world's 100 largest cities, almost 99 million (in 20 cities) are exposed to graphic pack warnings. All but one city is located in a country with national legislation stipulating strong pack warnings; only one city (Hong Kong Special Administrative Region of China) has established graphic pack warnings ahead of the national policy.

There are 35 countries (18% of the world's population) that would reach the highest level of achievement by further strengthening existing warning label requirements. Of these, 19 countries (mostly in the EU) need only to increase the size of warnings to cover 50% of primary package display surfaces to meet criteria for the highest level. An additional 10 countries that already have large warnings need to add only one additional characteristic to attain the highest level of achievement. Together, these 29 countries represent 16% of the world's population that could be protected at the highest level with minor strengthening of existing requirements. However, about 40% of countries, including nearly 60% of low-income countries, still have not implemented any warning label policies or require only small warnings that cover less than 30% of the package.

1 billion people live in countries that have large, graphic warning labels.

HEALTH WARNING LABELS ABOUT THE DANGERS OF TOBACCO – HIGHEST ACHIEVING COUNTRIES, 2012

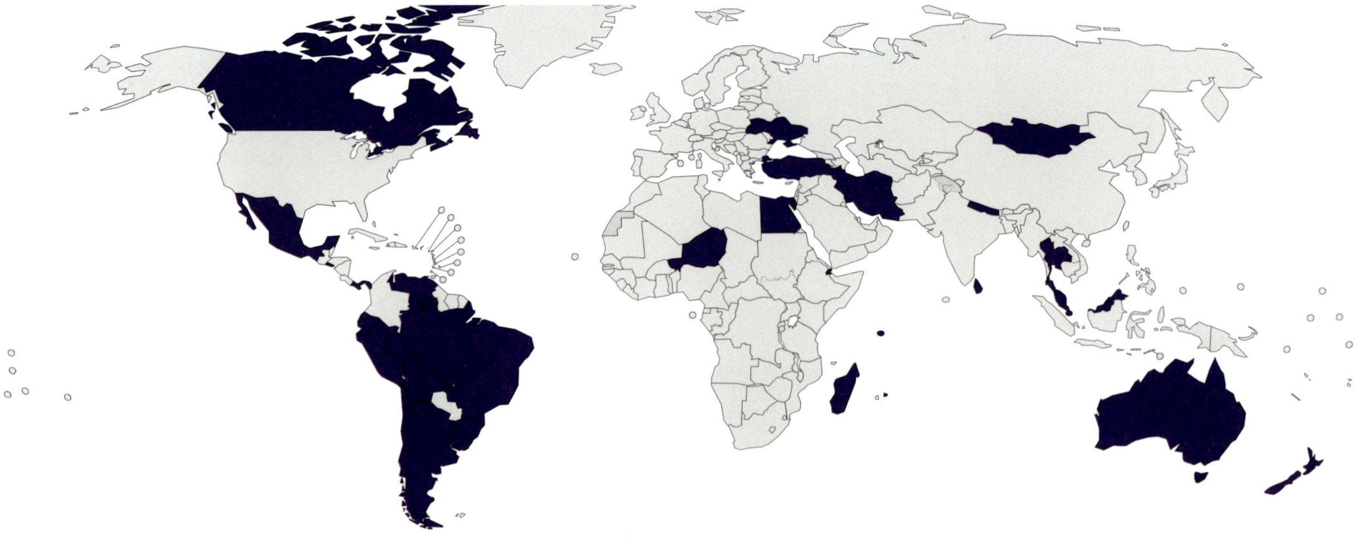

Countries with the highest level of achievement: Argentina*, Australia, Bolivia (Plurinational State of), Brazil, Brunei Darussalam, Canada*, Chile, Djibouti, Ecuador*, Egypt, El Salvador*, Iran (Islamic Republic of), Madagascar*, Malaysia, Mauritius, Mexico, Mongolia*, Nepal*, New Zealand, Niger*, Panama, Peru, Seychelles*, Singapore, Sri Lanka*, Thailand, Turkey*, Ukraine, Uruguay and Venezuela.

* Country newly at the highest level since 31 December 2010.

Madagascar implements pictorial warning labels

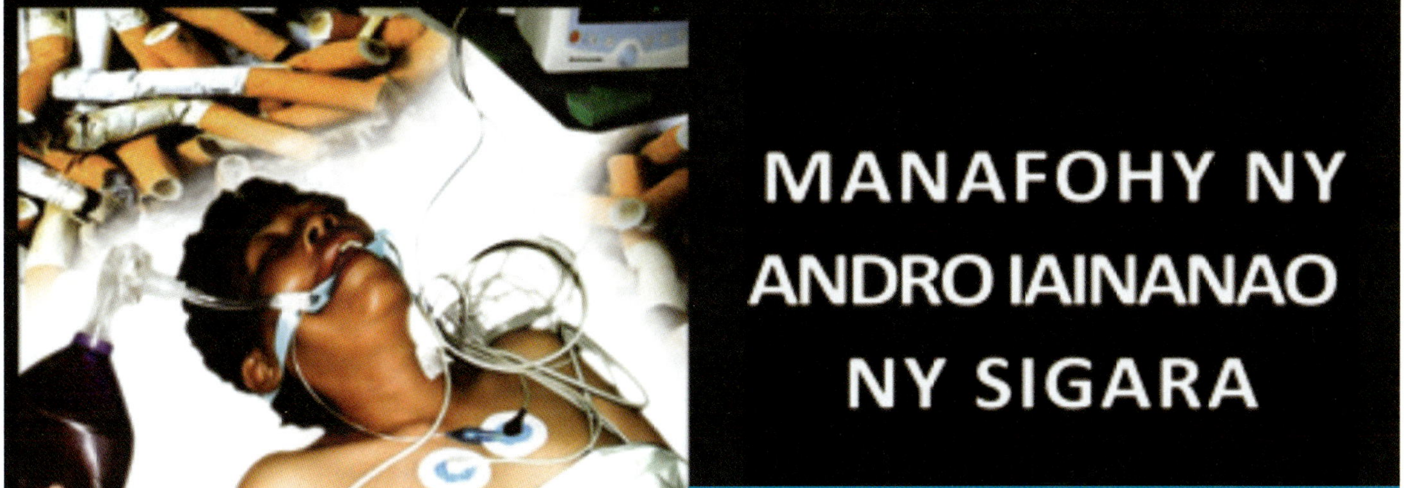

"Tobacco use shortens your life."

The government of Madagascar finalized regulations that require pictorial health warnings on tobacco packages on 17 July 2012. All cigarette, chewing tobacco and snuff tobacco packages now contain required health warnings that cover 50% of both the front and back of the package, with a pictorial warning on the front and a text warning in the Malagasy language on the back. A total of eight different health warning messages were approved for use, each with an image and accompanying text, which will be rotated in two batches. The first four messages appeared for 12 months beginning in October 2012, and will be replaced in October 2013 by the second set of four messages. Additionally, misleading and deceptive terms such as "light", "ultra-light", "mild" and "flavoured" are prohibited on tobacco packages, whether in Malagasy or any other language, and sales of cigarette cases intended to block the warnings are also prohibited.

Australia now requires plain (standardized) packaging for all tobacco products

As of 1 December 2012, Australia is the first country to require plain (or generic) packaging of all tobacco products. Use of all brand logos and colours have been replaced with generic drab brown colour and identical plain text fonts noting only the brand and product type. Additionally, the law also increased the size of required graphic pictorial health warning labels, which now must cover 75% of the front and 90% of the back of the package with additional text warnings on the package sides, and also include the national quit line number. Misleading and deceptive product descriptors such as "light" and "mild" are also prohibited. The plain packaging law was passed by the Australian Parliament in 2011, and came into effect on 1 December 2012. The tobacco industry launched a challenge to the law in Australia's High Court, arguing that the legislation infringed its intellectual property rights by "unjustly acquiring" tobacco company trademarks. The Australian High Court ruled against these claims in August 2012, but tobacco companies are continuing litigation in international trade courts. Many other countries including Ireland and New Zealand are now considering similar legislation.

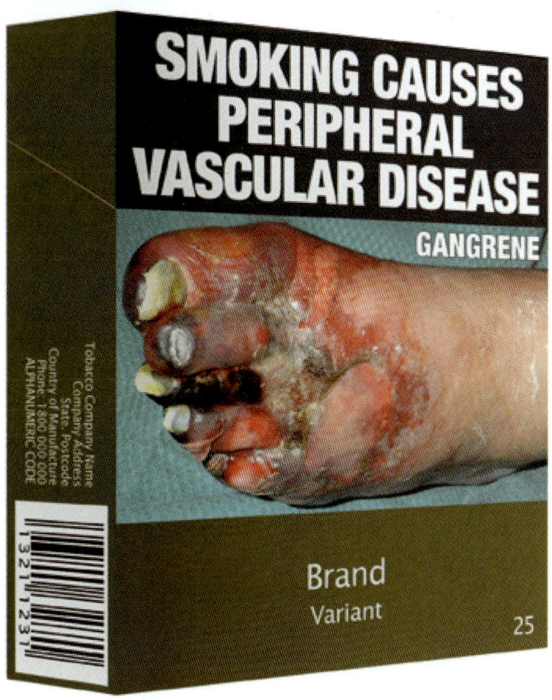

© Commonwealth of Australia

Anti-tobacco mass media campaigns

Article 12 of the **WHO Framework Convention on Tobacco Control** states: "Each Party shall promote and strengthen public awareness of tobacco control issues, using all available communication tools, as appropriate. ... each Party shall ... promote ... broad access to effective and comprehensive educational and public awareness programmes on the health risks including the addictive characteristic of tobacco consumption and exposure to tobacco smoke; ... [Each party shall promote] public awareness about the risks of tbacco consumption and exposure to tobacco smoke, and about the benefits of the cessation of tobacco use and tobacco-free lifestyles;... [each party shall promote] public awareness of and access to information regarding the adverse health, economic, and environmental consequences of tobacco production and consumption" (*3*). WHO FCTC Article 12 guidelines (*5*) are intended to assist Parties in meeting their obligations under Article 12 of the Convention.

RECENT ACHIEVEMENTS AND DEVELOPMENTS

Research shows that graphic TV ads are effective in countries of all income levels

While it has long been established that anti-tobacco television advertisements that graphically show the harms of smoking are effective in high-income countries, new research published in January 2013 shows that they are also effective in low- and middle-income countries (*94*). Existing ads that are proven effective can be readily translated and adapted for use in other countries, but should be pretested to ensure that they are effective when adapted to a different country or culture. Ads using images that graphically demonstrate the health harms of tobacco use are shown to be easily understood and consistently effective in all countries, regardless of income level. Ads containing complex medical terms or personal testimonials require more careful translation and pretesting to maximize their effectiveness.

Anti-tobacco mass media campaigns can reduce tobacco use

Hard-hitting anti-tobacco mass media campaigns increase awareness of the harms of tobacco use, reduce tobacco use, increase quit attempts, and reduce second-hand smoke exposures (*93*). Campaigns should be sustained over long periods to have a lasting effect, although more limited campaigns can have some impact if run for at least a few weeks (*93*).

Despite the expense involved, mass media campaigns are very effective at reaching large populations quickly and efficiently (*93*). Television advertising with graphic imagery is especially effective in convincing tobacco users to quit (*93*).

Airing of anti-tobacco mass media campaigns is increasing

Nearly 3.8 billion people (54% of the world's population) live in countries that have aired at least one national anti-tobacco mass media campaign on TV and/or radio for a duration of a least three weeks in the past two years. However, about half of countries in each income group have not used any national mass media campaigns in the past two years to inform people about the harms of tobacco use, or encourage them to quit.

Hard-hitting anti-tobacco mass media campaigns increase awareness of the harms of tobacco use reduce tobacco use, increase quit attempts and reduce second-hand smoke exposures.

MASS MEDIA CAMPAIGNS

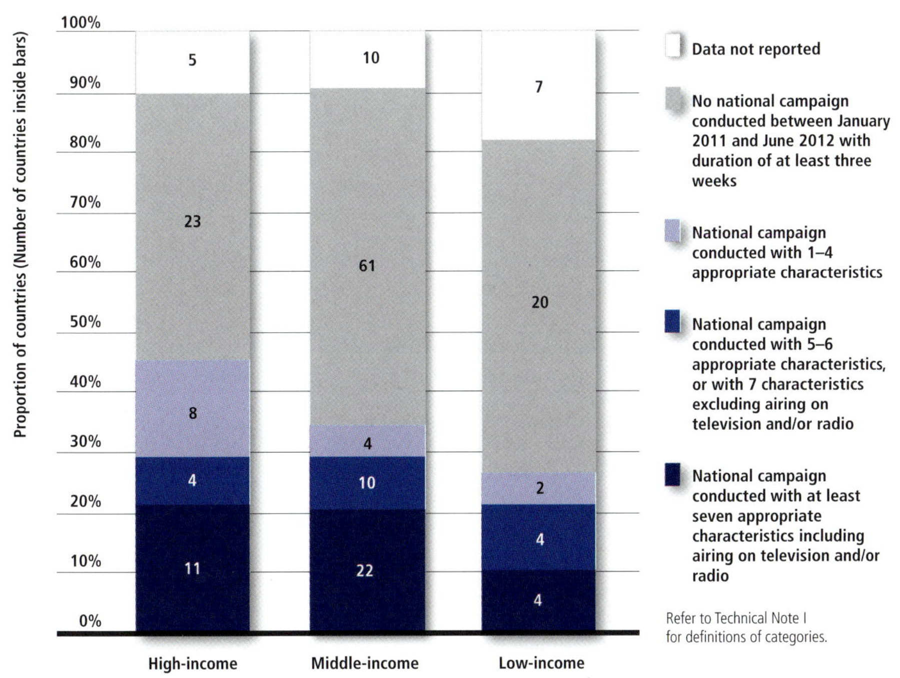

Refer to Technical Note I for definitions of categories.

Bangladesh anti-tobacco mass media campaign increases quit attempts

About 43% of adults in Bangladesh use some form of tobacco, with the annual cost of tobacco-related illness and death estimated at US$ 653 million. Additionally, 30% of the country's deforestation is connected to tobacco manufacturing (95). To assist with tobacco control efforts in Bangladesh, international tobacco control partners offered to conduct a mass media campaign demonstration project. Five best-practice anti-tobacco television advertisements were identified and adapted into the local language following discussions with local stakeholders, and a media plan was developed to run the ads over a four-week period, commencing on World No Tobacco Day 2011. The "Sponge" advertisement, used successfully in a dozen other countries, was selected for the first campaign. This campaign achieved more than 70% recall among smokers, with 40% of smokers who recalled the campaign making a quit attempt, compared to only 10% who did not recall it.

ANTI-TOBACCO MASS MEDIA CAMPAIGNS – HIGHEST ACHIEVING COUNTRIES, 2012

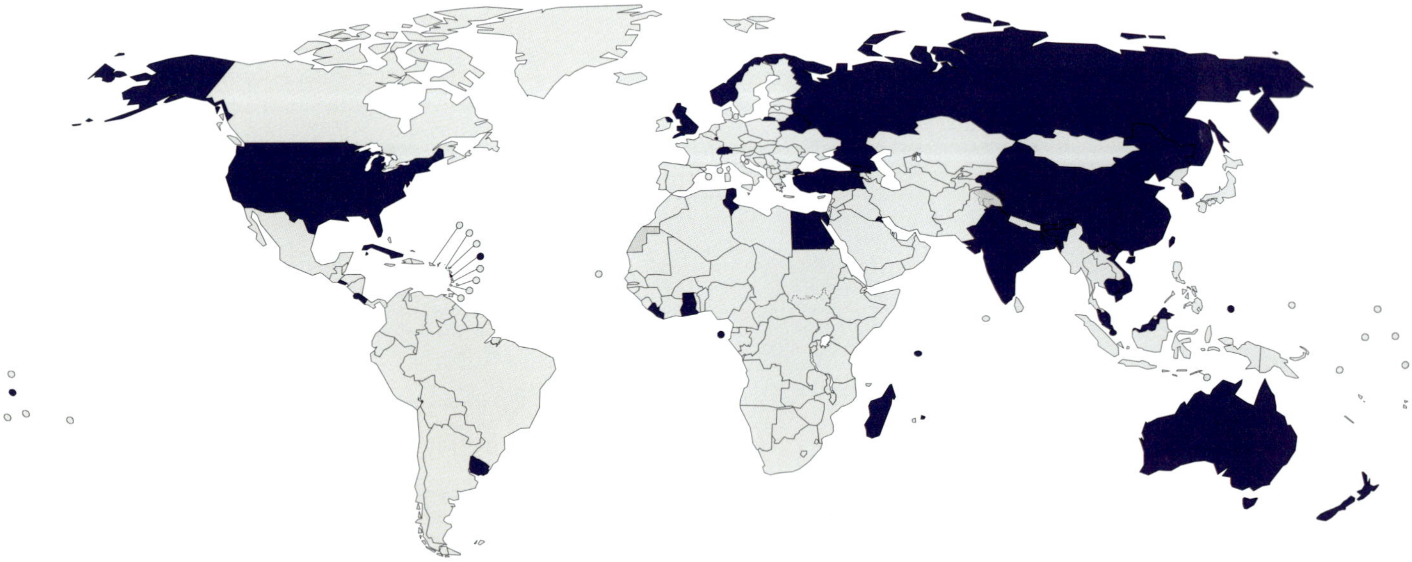

Countries with the highest level of achievement: Australia, Bahrain*, Bangladesh*, Belarus*, Bhutan, Cambodia*, China*, Costa Rica*, Cuba, Dominica*, Egypt, El Salvador*, Georgia*, Ghana*, India, Kuwait*, Liberia*, Luxembourg*, Madagascar, Malaysia, Mauritius*, New Zealand*, Norway*, Palau*, Republic of Korea*, Russian Federation, Samoa, Sao Tome and Principe*, Seychelles*, Singapore, Switzerland, Tunisia*, Turkey, United Kingdom of Great Britain and Northern Ireland, United States of America*, Uruguay* and Viet Nam.

* Country newly at the highest level since 31 December 2010.

Norway reactivates anti-tobacco mass media campaigns

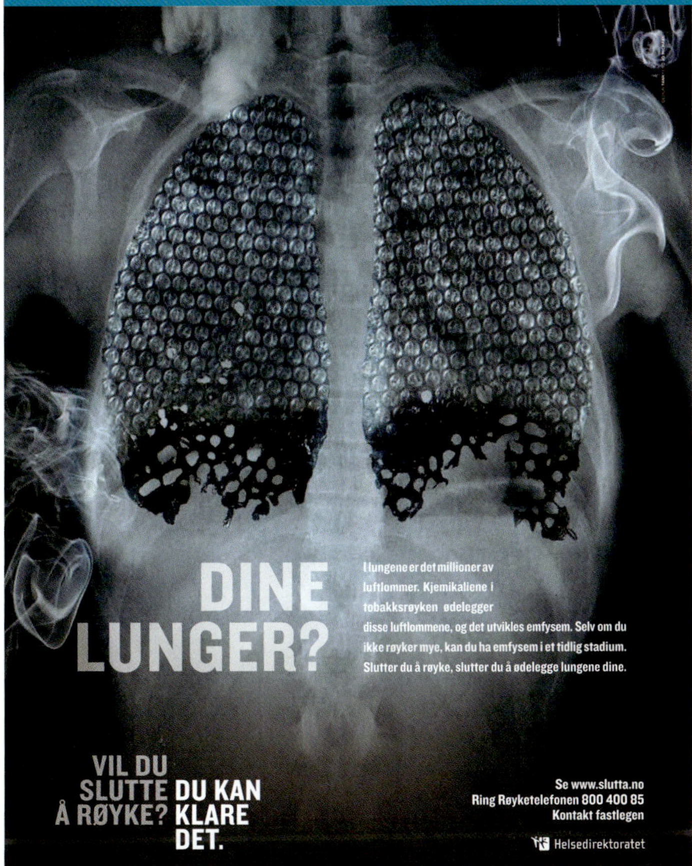

"Your lungs?
Do you want to stop smoking? You can do it."

After some years without using mass media for anti-tobacco advertising campaigns and a concurrent stagnation in declines in tobacco use prevalence, the Norwegian government launched a two-month anti-tobacco mass media campaign in January 2012 that featured four television advertisements as well as print media ads. The materials were adapted from Australian campaigns that have proven highly successful in a number of countries of all income levels and in most WHO Regions. Among the ads selected was "Sponge", originally created in Australia in 1979 and updated in 2007, and which has been used to warn people about the harms of smoking in a dozen countries. Approximately 70 news stories that provided free publicity for the campaign were run in Norwegian print and broadcast media within its first two weeks. A phone survey found 68% of Norwegians recalled being exposed to these anti-tobacco advertisements, and that among smokers who saw the campaign, 59% said it motivated them to make a quit attempt. A new campaign was launched in January 2013 targeting "social" smokers who use tobacco only occasionally.

Nearly 3.8 billion people live in countries that have aired at least one national anti-tobacco mass media campaign during the past two years.

Enforce bans on tobacco advertising, promotion and sponsorship

Bans on TAPS activities are effective, but underused

Banning tobacco advertising, promotion and sponsorship (TAPS), the focus of this report, is an effective way to reduce or eliminate exposure to cues for tobacco use. However, this measure remains under-adopted, as only 24 countries (with 694 million people, or just under 10% of the world's population) have passed a complete ban on direct and indirect TAPS activities. Low- and middle-income countries are more likely to have implemented a complete TAPS ban than high-income countries.

Although overall adoption of complete TAPS bans is low, impressive progress has been made in just the past two years. Since 2010, seven countries (Bahrain, Brazil, Ghana, Guinea, Togo, Turkey and Viet Nam) with about 400 million people, enacted new complete TAPS bans, more than doubling the total population fully protected by a complete ban. One country fell from the top group because it approved a new decree in 2012 that no longer bans point-of-sale advertising.

There are 67 countries that do not currently ban any TAPS activities, or that have a ban that does not cover advertising in national broadcast and print media. Low-income countries are the most likely not to have implemented any TAPS ban.

Rapid progress in establishing complete TAPS bans

In the 10 years since the WHO Framework Convention on Tobacco Control was adopted by the 56th World Health Assembly, there has been a steady increase in the number of countries that have established a complete TAPS ban and the number of people worldwide who are protected by this type of measure.

In 2003, when the WHO Framework Convention was adopted, only two countries (Madagascar and Kuwait) with 25 million people had enacted a complete TAPS ban.

BANS ON ADVERTISING, PROMOTION AND SPONSORSHIP

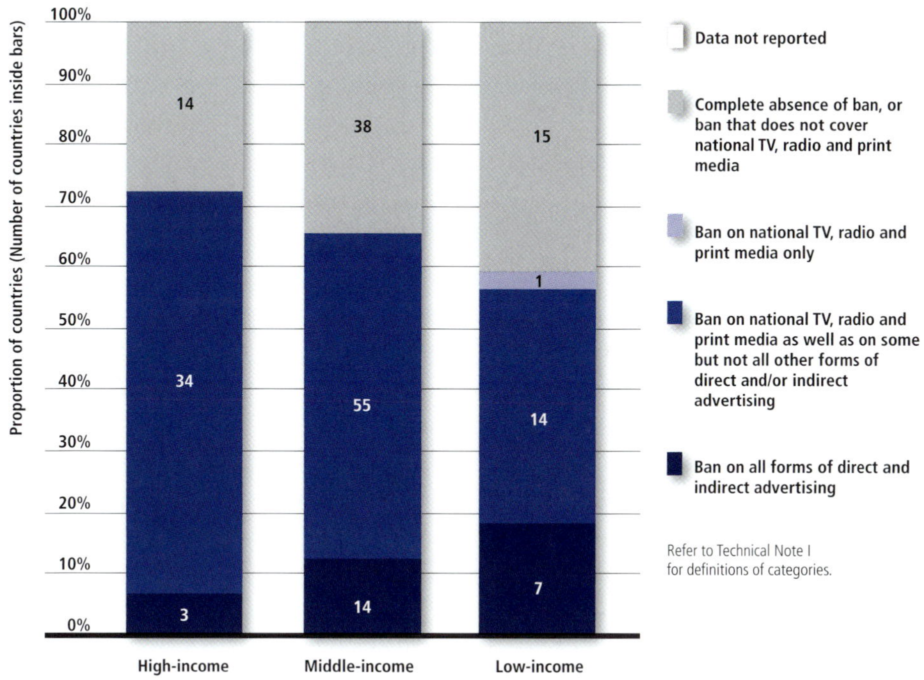

24 countries with 10% of the world's population have passed a complete TAPS ban.

ENFORCE BANS ON TOBACCO ADVERTISING, PROMOTION AND SPONSORSHIP – HIGHEST ACHIEVING COUNTRIES, 2012

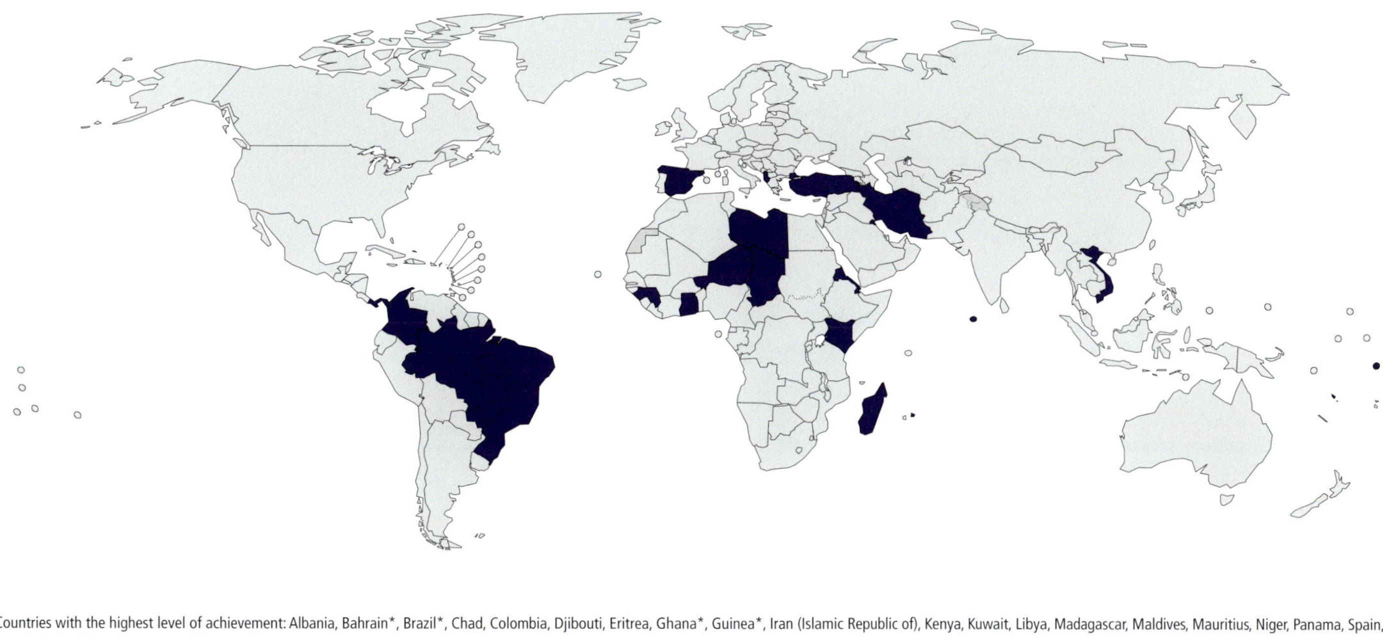

Countries with the highest level of achievement: Albania, Bahrain*, Brazil*, Chad, Colombia, Djibouti, Eritrea, Ghana*, Guinea*, Iran (Islamic Republic of), Kenya, Kuwait, Libya, Madagascar, Maldives, Mauritius, Niger, Panama, Spain, Togo*, Turkey*, Tuvalu, Vanuatu, Viet Nam*.

* Country newly at the highest level since 31 December 2010.

One more country (Eritrea) with 6 million people implemented a complete ban by 2005, when the treaty entered into force. By 2007, when data for the first WHO Report on the Global Tobacco Epidemic were collected, eight countries with 170 million people had passed a complete TAPS ban.

Over the past five years, adoption of complete TAPS bans has accelerated. By 2010, there were 18 countries with 304 million people that had passed a complete ban, and by 2012 there were 24 countries with 694 million people that had done so. Much of this progress took place between 2011 and 2012. Only one other MPOWER measure, protecting people from the harms of tobacco smoke by establishing completely smoke-free public places and workplaces, has been taken up more rapidly by more countries to protect more people. Low-income countries are more likely to have put a complete TAPS ban in place than either high- or middle-income countries.

Many countries are close to having a complete TAPS ban

There are 103 countries (with 64% of the world's population) that ban most but not all forms of TAPS. Of these, 27 countries (23% of the world's population) would reach a complete ban by adding only one additional criterion, 10 of which (20% of the world's population) would attain the highest level of achievement by banning point-of-sale advertising and six of which (2% of the world's population) would attain the highest level by banning sponsorships. Another 13 countries (3% of the world's population) would attain the highest level if they were to add two additional forms of TAPS activities to their existing bans. High-income countries are more likely than low- and middle-income countries to be close to having a complete TAPS ban.

Bans on direct advertising are the most common

The most common form of TAPS ban is a national ban on tobacco advertising in TV and radio broadcasts originating within the country, with 144 countries instituting this type of ban to protect nearly 6 billion people (85% of the world's population).

Also common are bans on tobacco advertising in local magazines and newspapers, and on billboards and other outdoor advertising, with 129 countries (75% of the world's population) having a ban on print advertising and 129 countries (53% of the world's population) having a ban on outdoor display advertising.

Advertising that originates outside a country's borders is also frequently banned. Tobacco advertising in TV and radio programmes originating from other

PROGRESS ON COMPLETE TAPS BANS

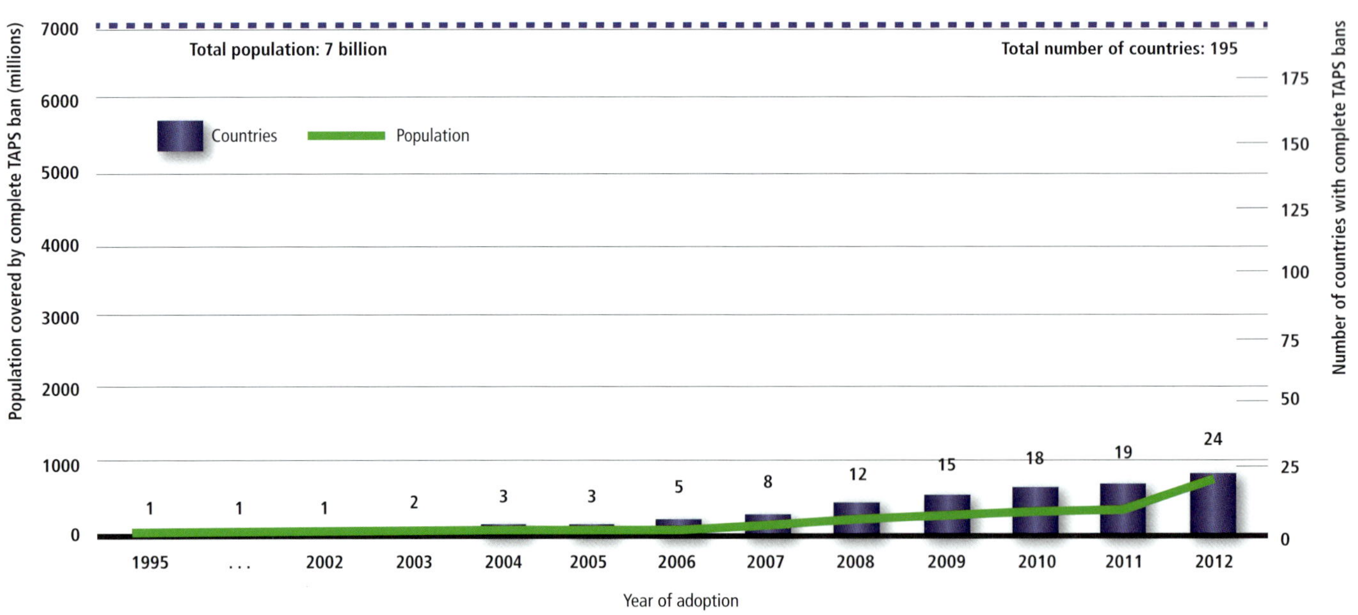

countries, including via satellite, has been banned by 118 countries (75% of the world's population). Countries are about as likely to have banned this type of TAPS regardless of their income classification. Since 2010, 15 countries (8% of the world's population) have introduced this type of ban.

Tobacco advertising in international newspapers and magazines is prohibited by 86 countries (63% of the world's population), and is about twice as likely to be banned by low- and middle-income countries than high-income countries. Since 2010, 17 countries (8% of the world's population) introduced this type of TAPS ban, which is most effective in countries where print publications from other countries circulate heavily.

Other types of TAPS activities are banned less frequently

Point of sale. Only 67 countries (20% of the world's population) have banned tobacco advertising at the point of sale. Middle- and high-income countries are only slightly more likely to have banned advertising at the point-of-sale than are low-income countries.

Brand stretching and brand sharing. Brand stretching (non-tobacco goods and services identified with tobacco brand names) has been banned by 80 countries (45% of world population). Brand sharing (brand names of non-tobacco products used for tobacco products) has been banned by 57 countries (34% of world population). Countries in all income groups have been slow to ban brand sharing and brand stretching, although middle-income countries are more likely to protect their people with these measures.

Promotional price discounting. Bans on promotional price discounting, in which the manufacturer reduces its costs to allow retailers to charge lower prices, has been banned by 84 countries (49% of the world's population).

Event sponsorships. Bans on event sponsorships have been passed by 89 countries (44% of the world's population). High-income countries are more likely to have adopted this type of TAPS ban, although a greater proportion of people in middle-income countries is protected by such a ban.

Tobacco vending machines. There are 89 countries (62% of world population) that ban tobacco vending machine sales. Since 2010, 14 countries (25% of the world's population) have introduced this type of ban. Middle-income countries are about twice as likely to have put this type of ban in place than high- or low-income countries.

Internet advertising. There are now 96 countries (48% of the world's population) that ban tobacco advertising on the Internet. High-income countries are more likely to have adopted this type of TAPS ban. Since 2010, 14 countries (3% of the world's population) introduced this type of ban.

Distribution of free tobacco products. Free tobacco product distribution, either in public or by mail, is prohibited in 102 countries (53% of the world's population). High-income countries are more likely to have banned this type of TAPS activity, although a greater proportion of people in middle-income countries is protected by such a ban.

Tobacco use on TV and in films. Bans on depicting tobacco use or showing tobacco brands and products on TV and in films have been enacted by 106 countries (74% of the world's population). High-income countries are more likely to have introduced this type of TAPS ban, although a greater proportion of people in middle-income countries is protected by such a ban. Since 2010, eight countries (5% of world population) introduced this requirement. Additionally, 11 countries (25% of the the world's population) require that anti-tobacco advertisements be shown before, during or after TV, film, and other visual entertainment media that depicts tobacco products, use or images.

So-called "corporate social responsibility" is also a TAPS activity and is increasingly banned

More countries are recognizing that so-called "corporate social responsibility" initiatives by the tobacco industry are merely thinly disguised TAPS activities, and have taken steps to ban them. Low- and middle-income countries are more likely than high-income countries to have introduced a ban on this type of TAPS activity. There are now 29 countries (8% of the world's population) that prevent the tobacco industry or individual companies from publicizing these types of activities, nine of which (3% of world population) have introduced this type of ban since 2010.

Because the tobacco industry often enlists front groups (i.e. civil society organizations that purport to act independently but that are actually under tobacco industry control), 28 countries (8% of the world's population) prohibit other entities from publicizing tobacco company activities. Since 2010, nine countries (3% of the world's population) have introduced this type of ban. There are 18 countries (5% of the world's population) that prohibit tobacco companies from funding or making contributions (including in-kind contributions) to smoking prevention

TAPS BANS. NUMBER OF COUNTRIES LEGISLATING EACH CHARACTERISTIC

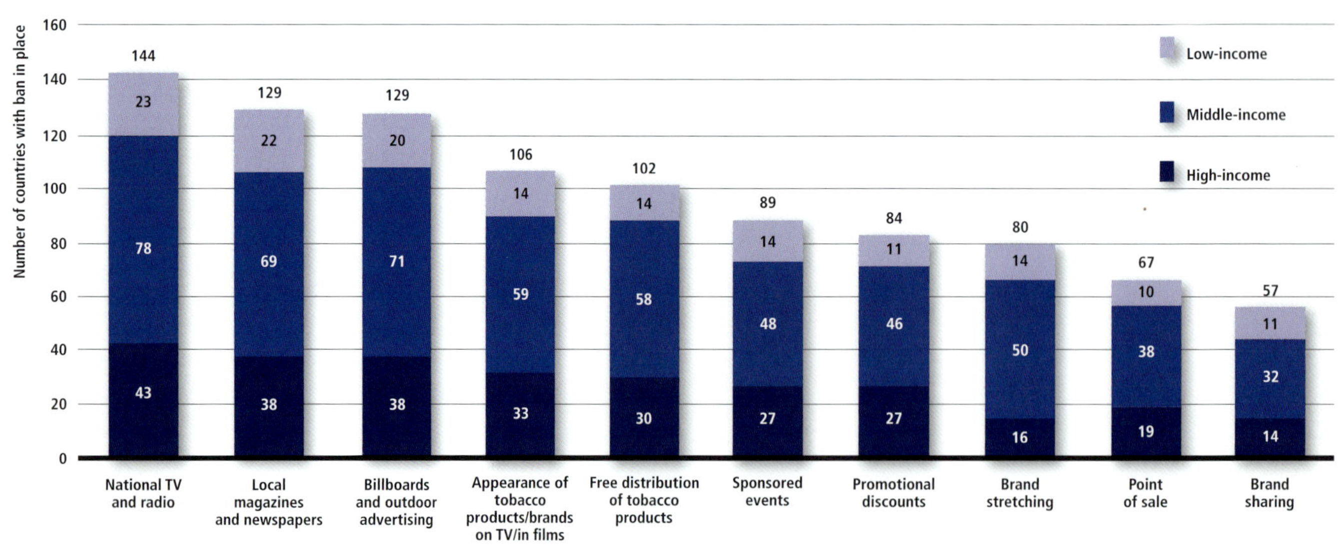

media campaigns, including those directed at youth – an increase of seven countries (3% of the world's population) doing so since 2010.

Subnational TAPS bans are becoming more common

Although relatively few subnational jurisdictions have passed bans on TAPS activities compared to other tobacco control policies such as smoke-free places, it is becoming more common for subnational jurisdictions to take action ahead of their nations. In the 172 countries with an incomplete TAPS ban, only two subnational jurisdictions (Neuquén, Argentina, and Goa, India, with together about 2 million people) have complemented the national law to completely ban all TAPS in these jurisdictions.

An additional 28 jurisdictions in 7 countries (Argentina, Australia, Canada, China, Egypt, India, and the United Kingdom) have TAPS bans that, together with national bans, are close to complete. Ten of these subnational jurisdictions, with a combined population of over 150 million people, are missing just a single criterion to attain the highest level of achievement for TAPS bans: the most common missing criterion is a ban on point of sale advertising. Among the 18 jurisdictions who are just two criteria away from a complete TAPS ban, the most common missing bans are brand sharing and brand stretching.

Of the 445 million people (6.3% of world population) who live in one of the world's 100 largest cities, less than 54 million (in 12 cities) are completely protected from exposure to TAPS. All but one city is located in a country with national legislation banning TAPS throughout the country; only the Hong Kong Special Administrative Region of China has completely banned TAPS ahead of the national legislation.

Compliance with TAPS bans is good but can improve

More than half of the 24 countries with a complete ban on TAPS activities have achieved strong levels of compliance (a score of at least 8 on a scale of 10), with high-income countries more likely to achieve high compliance than low- or middle-income countries. Among countries that have banned at least one specific TAPS activity, compliance is higher for bans on direct advertising in broadcast, print and outdoor media, with close to half of countries in each category achieving a high compliance measure. For other TAPS categories, including all types of indirect promotional activities, only about a quarter or less of the countries with a ban have achieved high levels of compliance.

Ghana's comprehensive tobacco control legislation includes complete TAPS ban

On 11 July 2012, Ghana's Parliament passed the Public Health Act, a consolidation of nine separate laws concerning public health that included a series of tobacco control measures. In addition to a complete ban on all TAPS activities including limits at the point of sale, the law prohibits smoking in many public places, and mandates health warning labels on tobacco packs (though does not require pictorial warnings), public education on the effects of tobacco use and second-hand smoke exposure, and provision of cessation treatment. Ghana's president made a personal commitment that the country would pass tobacco control legislation and was a catalyst in ensuring that the law moved speedily through the legislative process. Tobacco control stakeholders in government and civil society are now working together to develop a strong legislative instrument, which will be needed to fully implement and enforce the law.

India regulates depictions of tobacco products and tobacco use in films and television programmes

Although many countries have enacted bans on TAPS activities, scenes depicting smoking are still common in movies and television programmes, including those rated suitable for youth. India, the world's largest producer of movies, is one of the few countries to take action to reduce tobacco imagery in films and television as part of a comprehensive TAPS ban. Regulations put into effect in 2011 and 2012 now require films and television programmes depicting tobacco use to show a 30-second anti-tobacco spot at the beginning and middle, as well as a prominent static message at the bottom of the screen during scenes with tobacco use. New films and television programmes must justify depictions of tobacco use and include disclaimers at the beginning and middle of the film about the harms of tobacco. No brand names of tobacco products or tobacco product placement may be shown, close-ups of tobacco products and packaging are prohibited, and promotional materials such as movie posters may not depict tobacco use. These rules also assign responsibility for implementation to cinema owners or managers and television broadcasters, with penalties for violations including suspension or cancellation of licenses.

Iran enacts a complete tobacco advertising, promotion and sponsorship ban

Ministry of Health and Medical Education, Tehran

The Islamic Republic of Iran is one of the first countries in the Eastern Mediterranean Region to completely ban all forms of tobacco advertising, promotion and sponsorship. Iran introduced its Comprehensive National Tobacco Control Act 2006, which among other provisions forbids all forms of direct and indirect TAPS activities, with financial penalties for violations that are revised periodically to keep pace with inflation. To further strengthen the legislation, bylaws were implemented to specifically ban various forms of indirect advertising and promotion, including so-called "corporate social responsibility" initiatives, and also banned Internet and vending machine sales. As a result, Iran has effectively prohibited all direct or indirect TAPS, whether obvious or disguised. In addition, several government ministries have put mechanisms in place to ensure enforcement, and there has been overall good compliance with the ban, including at the point of sale, which had been one of the relatively less compliant areas. Iran provides a good example of how a country can effectively ban TAPS through political commitment and multisectoral coordination.

mpower

Raise taxes on tobacco

Article 6 of the **WHO Framework Convention on Tobacco Control** states: " … price and tax measures are an effective and important means of reducing tobacco consumption … [Parties should adopt] … measures which may include: … tax policies and … price policies on tobacco products so as to contribute to the health objectives aimed at reducing tobacco consumption" (*3*).

RECENT ACHIEVEMENTS AND DEVELOPMENTS

TaXSiM model developed

To assist countries with tobacco tax policy analysis, impact assessment, decision-making and policy implementation, WHO developed the Tobacco Tax Simulation (TaXSiM) model, which was launched online in December 2012 (http://www.who.int/tobacco/economics/taxsim/en/index.html). TaXSiM is an innovative tool that can be used to describe the current market and tax situation for cigarettes within a particular country or tax jurisdiction, and then to forecast the impact of tax changes on final consumer prices, cigarette consumption and government tax revenues. A particular strength of the model is that it examines outcomes on a brand-wise basis, which highlights how different tax policies can affect different segments of the tobacco market.

32 countries with 530 million people have sufficiently high tax rates.

RAISE TAXES ON TOBACCO – HIGHEST ACHIEVING COUNTRIES, 2012

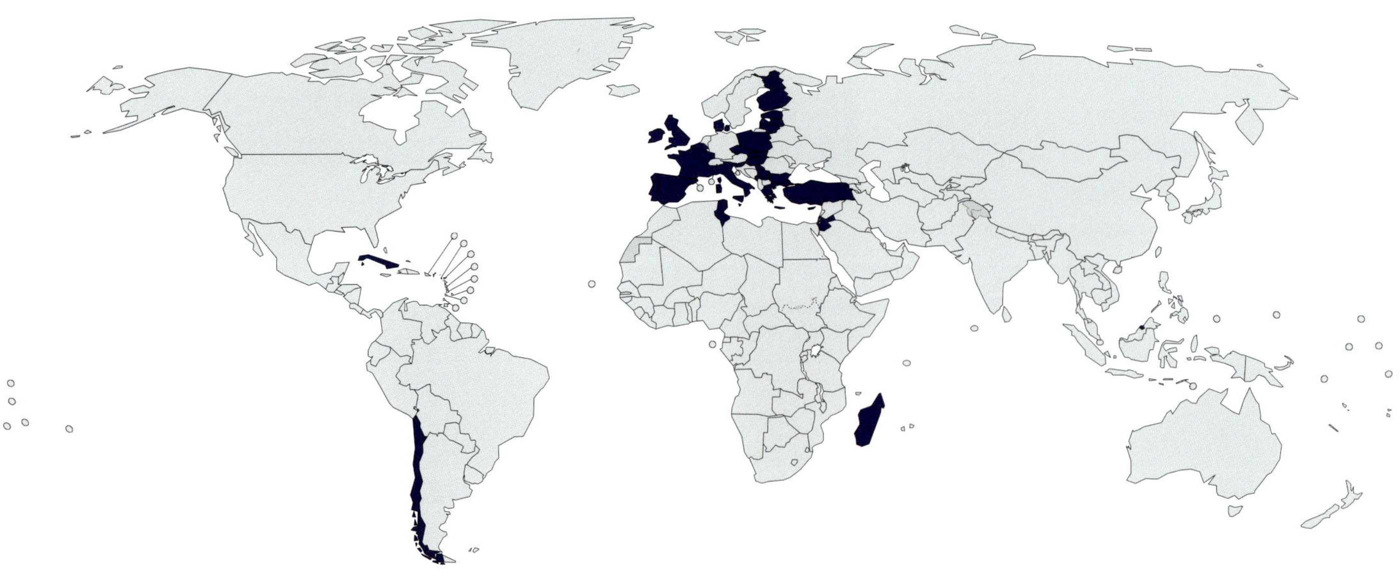

Countries and territories with the highest level of achievement: Belgium, Brunei Darussalam*, Bulgaria, Chile, Cuba*, Cyprus*, Czech Republic, Denmark*, Estonia, Finland, France, Greece, Hungary, Ireland, Israel, Italy, Jordan, Latvia, Lithuania, Madagascar, Malta, Montenegro*, Poland, Portugal, Serbia*, Slovakia, Slovenia, Spain, Tunisia, Turkey, United Kingdom of Great Britain and Northern Ireland and West Bank and Gaza Strip.

* Country newly at the highest level since 31 July 2010.

Raising taxes is the best way to reduce tobacco use

Raising taxes to increase the price of tobacco products is the most effective means to reduce tobacco use and encourage smokers to quit (*91*). Higher taxes are especially effective in reducing tobacco use among lower-income groups and preventing youth from starting to smoke (*91*). An increase in the retail price of cigarettes by 10% will reduce consumption in high-income countries by about 4% and in low- and middle-income countries by up to 8%; smoking prevalence is usually decreased by about half those rates (*92*).

Higher taxes increase government revenues

Tobacco taxes are generally well accepted by the public, including tobacco users, because most people understand at least generally that tobacco use is harmful even when they are unaware of specific health harms (*91*). Higher tax rates will increase government revenues, and this additional funding could be used for tobacco control programmes as well as other important health and social initiatives. Using tax revenues in this manner will further increase public support for higher taxes (*91*).

Strong tax administration improves compliance

Higher taxes do not necessarily lead to increases in smuggling and other tax avoidance activities; strong enforcement is more important to preventing smuggling than tax rates (*91*). Countries should strengthen their tax administration and customs enforcement capacity to prevent smuggling and/or tax evasion (*92*).

TOTAL TAX ON CIGARETTES

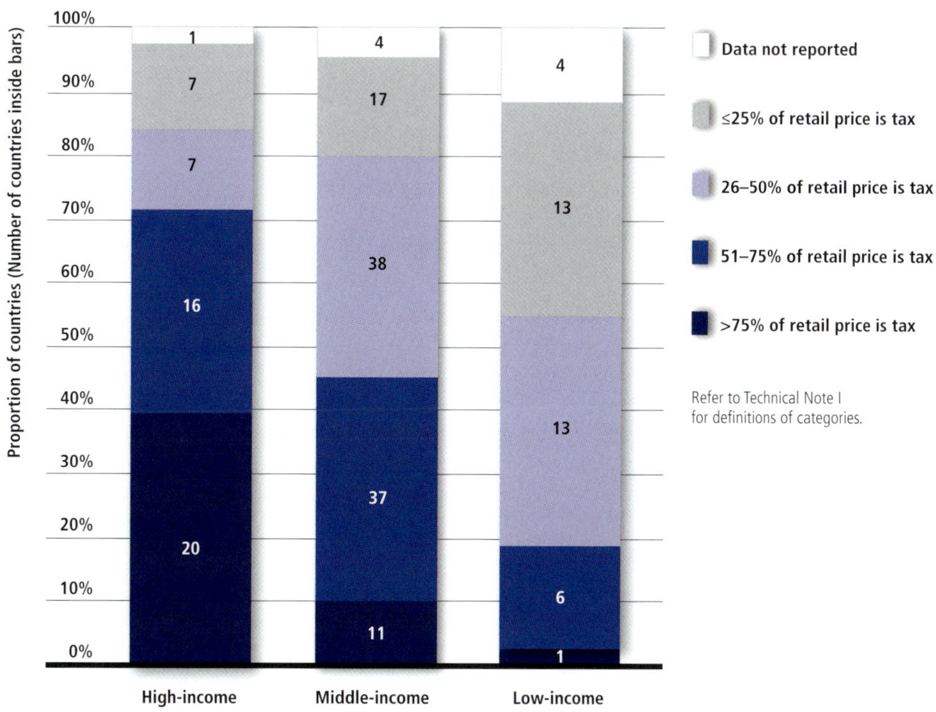

Refer to Technical Note I for definitions of categories.

Taxes must keep pace with inflation and economic growth

Taxes need to be increased periodically to offset the effects of inflation and of rising incomes and purchasing power (*93*). If the real price of tobacco after inflation does not increase faster than consumer purchasing power, consumption will increase because tobacco becomes relatively more affordable (*93*).

Raising the price of tobacco through increased taxes is the least-achieved MPOWER measure

Although raising the price of tobacco through increased tobacco taxes is the most effective way to reduce tobacco use, it is the least-achieved MPOWER measure, with only 32 countries with 530 million people (8% of the world's population) having sufficiently high tax rates. Since 2010, six countries (Brunei Darussalam, Cuba, Cyprus, Denmark, Montenegro and Serbia) increased tax rates so that at least 75% of the retail price of cigarettes is tax. One country fell from this highest achievement level. Low- and middle-income countries are least likely to impose sufficiently high tax rates.

As indicated in Technical Note III on tobacco taxes, the change in tax as a share of price is not only dependent on tax changes but also on changes in the retail price, and occasionally on other changes (e.g., countries applying a tax on declared customs value of imported tobacco products priced in other countries' currencies, which are then subject to changes in exchange rates). Therefore, despite an increase in the tax, the tax share could remain the same or go down; similarly, a tax share can increase even if there is no change or even a decrease in the tax.

Regardless of whether the tax share increased or not, it is important to highlight that a large number of countries have increased their tax rates since 2010. Of the 178 countries for which data were available in both 2010 and 2012, 97 countries increased their excise taxes. Of those 97 countries, 7 increased both specific and ad valorem excise tax components, 14 increased their ad valorem excise, 51 increased their specific excise and another 25 increased their overall excise tax by different means (e.g. introducing one type

WEIGHTED AVERAGE RETAIL PRICE AND TAXATION (EXCISE AND TOTAL) OF MOST SOLD BRANDS OF CIGARETTES, 2012

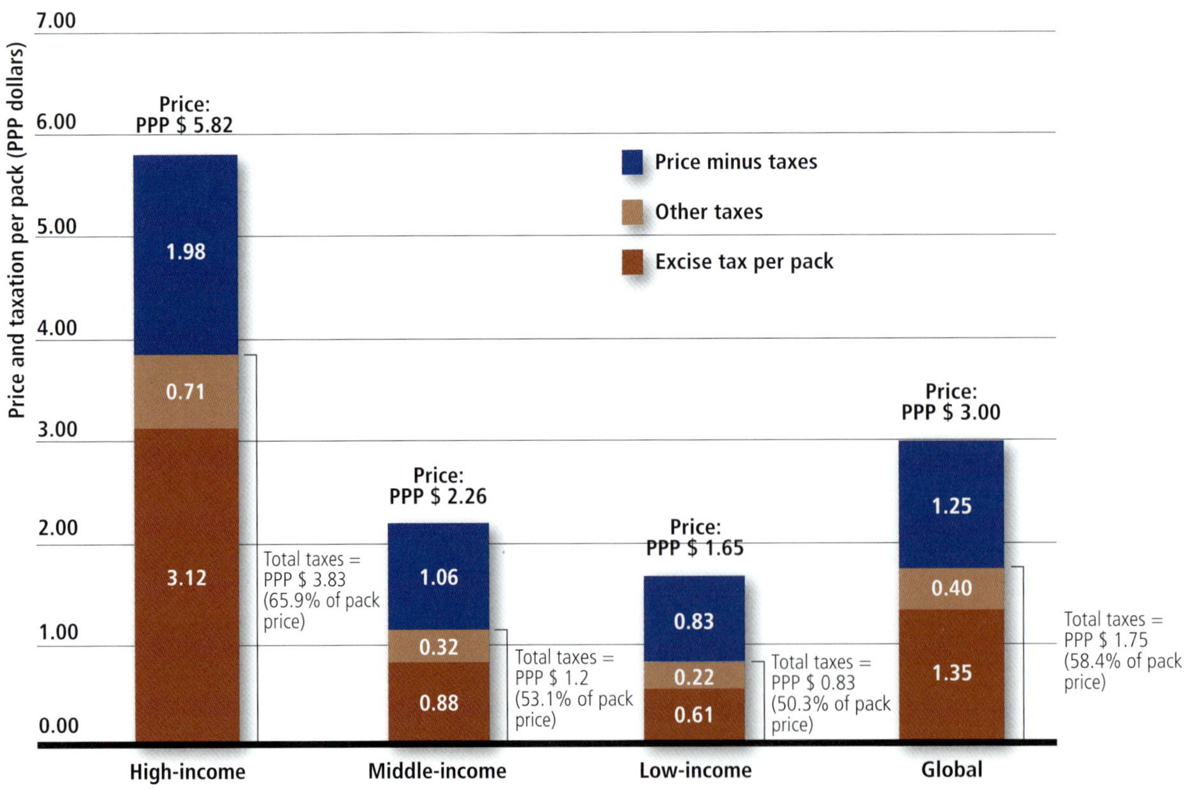

Note: Averages are weighted by WHO estimates of number of current cigarette smokers in each country.
Prices are expressed in Purchasing Power Parity (PPP) adjusted dollars or international dollars to account for differences in the purchasing power across countries. Based on 48 high-income, 95 middle-income and 30 low-income countries with data on price of most sold brand, excise and other taxes and PPP conversion factors. Numbers do not exactly add up to the total because of rounding errors.

of excise, increasing specific and at the same time reducing ad valorem, introducing specific and removing ad valorem). For some countries the tax increase was only a few per cent, but for others it was substantial, in some cases by many multiples. Table 9.1 in Appendix IX includes a note showing which countries increased their excise taxes.

Of the 445 million people (6.3% of the world's population) who live in the world's 100 largest cities, only 15 million (in five cities) are covered by sufficiently high taxes on cigarette products. In all five cities, the same high tax rates operate at a national level. No city has yet independently introduced taxes on tobacco products so that at least 75% of the retail price is tax.

Costa Rica earmarks tobacco tax revenue for tobacco control programmes

After a five-year effort, in 2012 Costa Rica passed a comprehensive tobacco control bill that incorporated several provisions of the WHO FCTC and built upon the experiences of other Latin American countries, including Uruguay, Panama, Brazil and Colombia, among others. Among the law's features was an increase in tobacco taxes by the equivalent of US$ 0.80 per pack of cigarettes, with all of the new tax revenue earmarked for government tobacco control programmes and other health initiatives. The total tax as a share of the most sold brand increased from 55.7% in 2008 to 71.5% in 2012, with the price increasing by 73% from 750 Costa Rican Colon (CRC) to 1300 CRC in the same period. In early 2013, funding from the first full year of increased tax revenue was distributed as follows: approximately US$ 81 million to the Social Security Fund for diagnosis, treatment and prevention of diseases associated with smoking and to strengthen the National Cancer Network; US$ 27 million to the Ministry of Health to monitor and enforce the nation's Health Promotion Act; US$ 13 million to the Alcoholism and Drug Dependence Institute for prevention and cessation research; and US$ 13 million to the Costa Rican Institute of Sport and Recreation to promote physical activity. This compares with the US$ 144 million spent each year on treatment of diseases associated with tobacco use, about 6% of the country's total health expenditures. Taxes will automatically increase each year, ensuring that they keep pace with inflation, and a system to track payment of tobacco taxes was implemented. There has been strong popular support for the new law, which has achieved high compliance.

PRICE AND TAX, PACK OF MOST SOLD BRAND AND REVENUES FROM TOBACCO TAXES

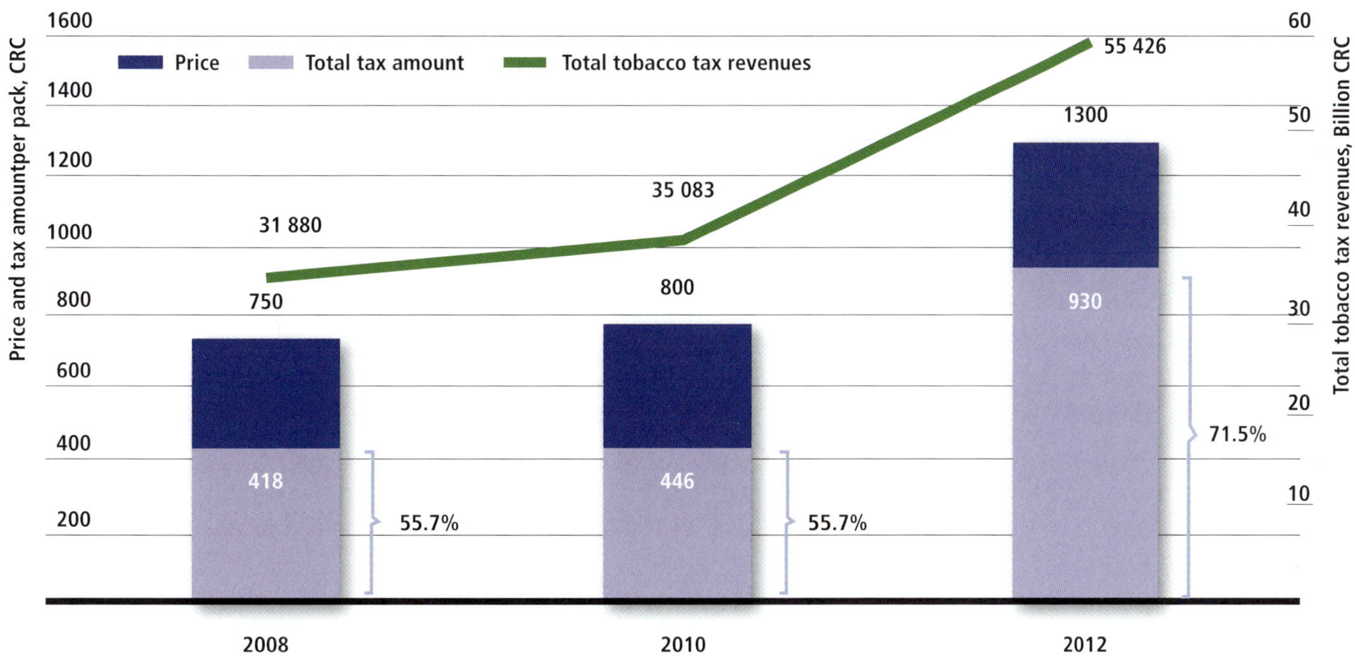

Countries must act decisively to end the epidemic of tobacco use

Article 5 of the **WHO Framework Convention on Tobacco Control** states: "Each Party shall develop, implement, periodically update and review comprehensive multisectoral national tobacco control strategies, plans and programmes ... [and] establish or reinforce and finance a national coordinating mechanism or focal points for tobacco control" (*3*). In addition, WHO FCTC Article 26.2 indicates that "Each Party shall provide financial support in respect of its national activities intended to achieve the objective of the Convention" (*3*).

A national tobacco control programme (NTCP) is needed to lead each country's tobacco control efforts

The WHO FCTC suggests that every Party establish and finance a national tobacco control coordination mechanism to build the capacity needed to implement effective and sustainable policies to reverse the tobacco epidemic (*91*). The ministry of health or equivalent government agency should take the lead on strategic planning and policy setting, with other ministries or agencies reporting to this centralized authority.

Subnational implementation is important

In larger countries, decentralizing the NTCP authority to subnational levels may allow more flexibility in programme implementation and facilitate effectively reaching all regions and populations in the country (*92*). Since many tobacco control interventions are carried out at regional, local and community levels, public health and government leaders at subnational levels need adequate resources to build implementation capacity (*92*). National tobacco control programmes must also ensure that population subgroups with disproportionately high rates of tobacco use are reached by policies and programmes to eliminate these social inequities (*93*).

RECENT ACHIEVEMENTS AND DEVELOPMENTS

Philippines develops five-year National Tobacco Control Strategy

The Philippines started tobacco control efforts in 1987. Since then, the country has made progressive achievements to strengthen tobacco control, including enacting tobacco control legislation, despite tobacco industry opposition. However, because nearly 3 in 10 Philippine adults continue to smoke, in 2011 the Philippine Department of Health in conjunction with WHO conducted an assessment of the country's capacity to implement effective tobacco control measures and reduce tobacco use. This review took place in the context of the Philippine government's universal health coverage strategy, and assessed national leadership, infrastructure, partnerships, and human and financial resources.

After a series of consultations with key government and civil society stakeholders, a new five-year National Tobacco Control Strategy for 2011-2016 was initiated to achieve and reinforce a social environment that will help build a "Tobacco-free Philippines: Healthier People, Communities, and Environments." This will be accomplished through well-planned and defined strategies to advocate, enable and mobilize multisectoral support for stronger tobacco policies and programmes that completely implement the WHO FCTC. The process in the Philippines is an excellent example of collaboration between government and civil society, as well as with WHO and other international partners.

NATIONAL TOBACCO CONTROL PROGRAMMES

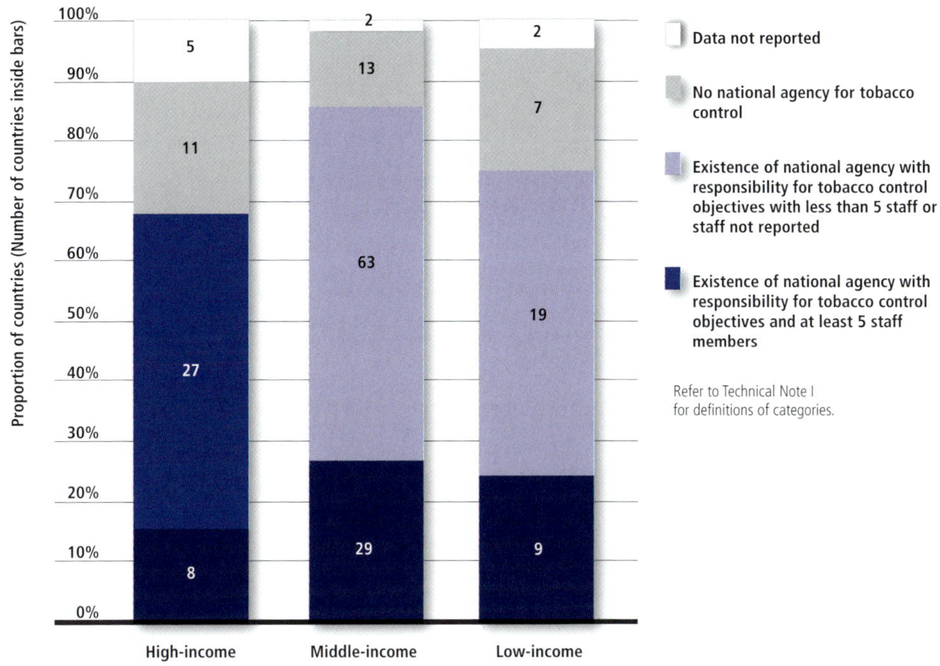

National tobacco control programmes require support from partners within government as well as all segments of civil society.

Civil society must be involved

NTCPs require support from partners within government as well as all segments of civil society (except the tobacco industry and its allies) (*92*).The continued involvement of legitimate nongovernmental organizations and other civil society groups is essential to continued progress on national and global tobacco control efforts (*91*).

More countries have an adequately staffed national tobacco control programme

Nearly two thirds of the world's population (4.5 billion people) live in one of the 46 countries that has a national agency responsible for tobacco control with at least five full-time staff (or full-time equivalents). Another 109 countries (with 32% of the world's population) would attain the highest level by increasing the number of staff available to work full-time on tobacco control. Middle-income countries are most likely to have a national agency with sufficient staffing. There are 39 countries and one territory with no national agency or national objectives on tobacco control, or for which no data are available.

Governments collect nearly US$ 145 billion in tobacco excise tax revenues each year, but spend less than US$ 1 billion combined on tobacco control – 96% of this is spent by high-income countries.

TOBACCO CONTROL IS UNDERFUNDED

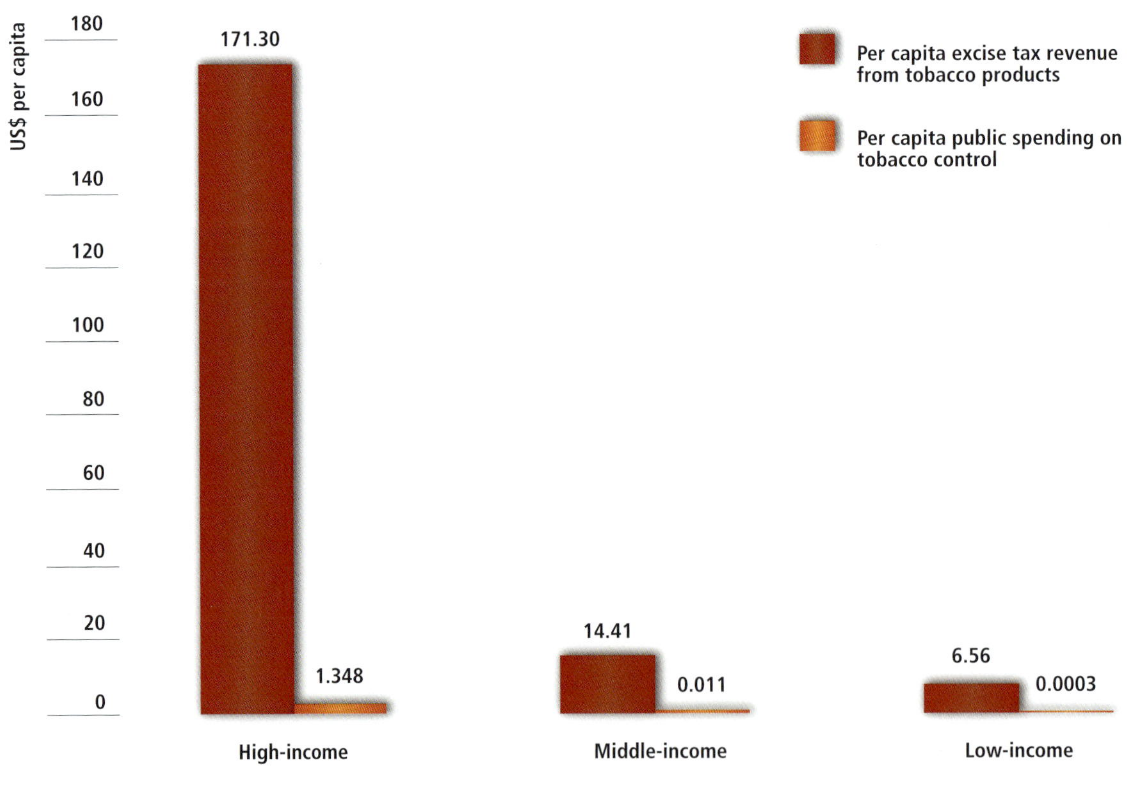

Note: Based on 62 countries with available tobacco excise revenue data for 2012; expenditure on tobacco control for several of these countries was estimated from figures between 2007 and 2012, adjusting for inflation. Tax revenues are tobacco product (or cigarette) excise revenues in 2011–2012 for included countries. The revenues here pertain to excise tax rather than all taxes on tobacco products. Per capita value is calculated by using UN forecasted number of population age 15+ for the year 2012.

Sustainable funding for tobacco control in Viet Nam

In June 2012, The Viet Nam National Assembly approved a tobacco control law that, along with measures to reduce tobacco consumption, established the Tobacco Control Fund – an effective mechanism to ensure sustainable funding for the national tobacco control programme. Under the new law, this funding is secured through a compulsory contribution from tobacco manufacturers and importers, and is calculated based on a percentage of excise tax-based prices. The contribution started at 1% on 1 May 2013 (the date the law came into force), and will rise to 1.5% in May 2016 and 2% in May 2019.

The Tobacco Control Fund will support a broad spectrum of tobacco control programmes, including communication and education, development and expansion of smoke-free regulations, cessation services, implementing alternative economic activities for tobacco industry workers and capacity building for tobacco control practitioners. Although Viet Nam will need additional time and effort to fully establish and operate its Tobacco Control Fund, this is an excellent example of what countries with strong commitment can do to ensure sustainable funding for tobacco control programmes.

Conclusion

Substantial progress has been made in global tobacco control since adoption of the WHO Framework Convention on Tobacco Control ten years ago.

Since WHO introduced the six demand reduction measures (MPOWER) in 2008 in line with the WHO FCTC, the number of countries successfully establishing one or more of the measures at the highest level of achievement and the number of people covered by those measures have more than doubled.

As a result, hundreds of millions of tobacco users are protected from the harms of tobacco by governments to improve their health and the health of others, and hundreds of millions of non-smokers are less likely to start. Despite this progress, significant gaps remain in establishing effective tobacco control measures in most countries.

Only one country, Turkey, has established all measures at the highest level, and only three additional countries have put four measures in place at the highest level. Although most countries have started taking steps to address the tobacco epidemic, more than half of all countries have yet to establish even a single measure at the highest level.

This *WHO Report on the Global Tobacco Epidemic, 2013* shows that any country can establish an effective tobacco control programme to reduce tobacco use, regardless of its political structure or income level.

- In total, more than 2.3 billion people – a third of the world's population – are now protected by at least one of the measures at the highest level of achievement. Nearly 1 billion people are protected by two or more measures at the highest level.
- Nearly 1.3 billion people are newly protected by at least one measure applied nationally at the highest level since 2007, with progress made in all areas.
- Creation of smoke-free public places and workplaces continues to be the most commonly established measure at the highest level of achievement. There are 32 countries that passed complete smoking bans covering all work places, public places and public transportation means between 2007 and 2012, protecting nearly 900 million additional people. Since 2010, 12 countries and one territory, with 350 million people, passed strong smoke-free laws at a national level.
- More than half a billion people in nine countries have gained access to appropriate cessation services in the past five years. However, there has been little progress since 2010, as only four additional countries with a combined population of 85 million were newly provided access to cost-covered services including a toll-free national quit line.

- Effective health warning labels on tobacco packaging continue to be established by more countries. In the past five years, a total of 20 countries with 657 million people put strong warning label requirements in place, with 11 countries (with 265 million people) doing so since 2010.
- National mass media campaigns, first assessed in 2010, have been conducted in the past two years by about one fifth of countries, which have more than half the world's population.
- Complete bans on all tobacco advertising, promotion and sponsorship have been put in place to protect more than half a billion people in 16 countries in the past five years. Since 2010, six countries with nearly 400 million people newly established this measure at the highest level.
- Raising taxes to increase the price of tobacco products remains the measure least likely to be established. Only 14 countries and one territory with 166 million people have increased their tax rates to sufficiently high levels since 2008, and only six countries with 29 million people have done so in the past two years.
- Adequately staffed national tobacco control government structures have been established by six countries with 413 million people since 2008. In the past two years, three countries with 150 million people newly established a structure to manage national tobacco control programmes.

Much more remains to be done to ensure that recent successes in tobacco control can be further expanded. Even as the number of countries establishing complete tobacco control measures has increased, more than half do not yet provide high-level protection for their people on any measure. And while the number of people covered by high-level measures has increased substantially, two thirds of the world's population have yet to be fully protected in any one area, let alone all of them.

The successes demonstrated by many countries in using demand reduction measures to build capacity to implement the WHO Framework Convention on Tobacco Control show that it is possible to effectively address the tobacco epidemic and save lives, regardless of size or income. However, efforts to incorporate all provisions of the WHO Framework Convention into national tobacco control programmes must be accelerated in all countries to save even more lives.

References

1. *Gender, women, and the tobacco epidemic.* Geneva, World Health Organization, 2010 (http://www.who.int/tobacco/publications/gender/women_tob_epidemic/en/index.html, accessed 15 June 2013).

2. *Forty-ninth World Health Assembly, Resolution WHA49.17.* International framework convention for tobacco control. Geneva, World Health Organization, 1996 (http://www.who.int/tobacco/framework/wha_eb/wha49_17/en/index.html, accessed 15 June 2013).

3. *WHO Framework Convention on Tobacco Control.* Geneva, World Health Organization, 2003 (updated 2004, 2005; http://whqlibdoc.who.int/publications/2003/9241591013.pdf, accessed 15 June 2013).

4. *Draft action plan for the prevention and control of noncommunicable diseases 2013-2020: Report by the Secretariat.* Geneva: World Health Organization, 2013 (http://apps.who.int/gb/ebwha/pdf_files/EB132/B132_7-en.pdf, accessed 15 June 2013).

5. *WHO Framework Convention on Tobacco Control guidelines for implementation.* Geneva, World Health Organization, 2013 (http://www.who.int/fctc/guidelines/adopted/guidel_2011/en, accessed 15 June 2013).

6. *Briefing 6: Adoption of guidelines for implementation of Article 13 (Tobacco advertising, promotion and sponsorship) and recommendations on further measures relating to cross-border tobacco advertising, promotion and sponsorship.* Geneva, World Health Organization, 2008 (http://www.fctc.org/dmdocuments/COP-3_policy_briefing_Article_13_Advertising2.pdf, accessed 15 June 2013).

7. *Cigarette report for 2003.* Washington, DC, Federal Trade Commission, 2005 (http://www.ftc.gov/reports/cigarette05/050809cigrpt.pdf, accessed 15 June 2013).

8. *Cigarette report for 2007 and 2008.* Washington, DC, Federal Trade Commission, 2011 (http://www.ftc.gov/os/2011/07/110729cigarettereport.pdf, accessed 15 June 2013).

9. *Preventing tobacco use among youth and young adults: a report of the Surgeon General.* Atlanta, US Department of Health and Human Services, Centers for Disease Control and Prevention, 2012 (http://www.surgeongeneral.gov/library/reports/preventing-youth-tobacco-use/index.html, accessed 15 June 2013).

10. *The role of the media in promoting and reducing tobacco use.* Bethesda, MD, US Department of Health and Human Services, National Institutes of Health, National Cancer Institute, 2008 (Tobacco Control Monograph No. 19, NIH Pub. No. 07-6242). (http://www.cancercontrol.cancer.gov/brp/tcrb/monographs/19/index.html, accessed 15 June 2013).

11. *Social determinants of health and well-being among young people. Health behaviour in school-aged children (HBSC) study: International report from the 2009–2010 survey.* Geneva, World Health Organization, 2012 (http://www.euro.who.int/__data/assets/pdf_file/0003/163857/Social-determinants-of-health-and-well-being-among-young-people.pdf, accessed 15 June 2013).

12. Di Franza JR et al. Tobacco acquisition and cigarette brand selection among youth, *Tobacco Control*, 1994, 3:334–338.

13. Di Franza JR et al. Tobacco promotion and the initiation of tobacco use: assessing the evidence for causality. *Pediatrics*, 2006, 117:e1237–e1248.

14. Brown A, Moodie C. The influence of tobacco marketing on adolescent smoking intentions via normative beliefs. *Health Education Research*, 2009, 24:721–733.

15. Burton D et al. Perceptions of smoking prevalence by youth in countries with and without a tobacco advertising ban. *Journal of Health Communication*, 2010, 6:656–664.

16. Hanewinkel R et al. Cigarette advertising and teen smoking initiation. *Pediatrics*, 2011, 127:e271–e278.

17. Lovato C, Watts A, Stead LF. Impact of tobacco advertising and promotion on increasing adolescent smoking behaviours. *Cochrane Database of Systematic Reviews*, 2011, (10):CD 003439.

18. Amos A et al. Women and tobacco: a call for including gender in tobacco control research, policy and practice. *Tobacco Control*, 2012, 21:236–243.

19. Lee K et al. The strategic targeting of females by transnational tobacco companies in South Korea following trade liberalization. *Global Health*, 2009, 5:2.

20. Lee S, Ling PM, Glantz SA. The vector of the tobacco epidemic: tobacco industry practices in low- and middle-income countries. *Cancer Causes and Control*, 2012, 23(Suppl. 1):117–129.

21. Boutayeb A, Boutayeb S. The burden of non communicable diseases in developing countries. *International Journal for Equity in Health*, 2005, 4:2.

22. Doku D. The tobacco industry tactics – a challenge for tobacco control in low and middle income countries. *African Health Sciences*, 2010, 10:201–203.

23. Nimpitakpong P, Pittayakulmongko C. Worldwide news and comment: Thailand: young female 'ambassadors' promote cigarettes. *Tobacco Control*, 2011, 20:393.

24. Hefler M. Worldwide news and comment: Indonesia/world: using music to target youth. *Tobacco Control*, 2012, 21:82–86.

25. Shahrir S et al. Tobacco sales and promotion in bars, cafes and nightclubs from large cities around the world. *Tobacco Control*, 2011, 20:285–290.

26. Simpson D. News analysis: Brazil: Marlboro interactive games promotion. *Tobacco Control*, 2011, 20:178–181.

27. Hafez N, Ling PM. How Philip Morris built Marlboro into a global brand for young adults: implications for international tobacco control. *Tobacco Control*, 2005, 14:262–271.

28. *Empower women: Combating industry marketing in the WHO European Region.* Geneva, World Health Organization, 2010 (http://www.euro.who.int/__data/assets/pdf_file/0014/128120/e93852.pdf, accessed 15 June 2013).

29. Pollay RW. Targeting youth and concerned smokers: Evidence from Canadian tobacco industry documents. *Tobacco Control*, 2000, 9:136–147.

30. GTSS Data website. Atlanta, Centers for Disease Control and Prevention (CDC), National Center for Chronic Disease Prevention and Health Promotion, Office on Smoking and Health, 2013. (http://www.cdc.gov/tobacco/global/gtss, accessed 15 June 2013).

31. Saffer H, Chaloupka F. The effect of tobacco advertising bans on tobacco consumption. *Journal of Health Economics*, 2000, 19:1117–1137.

32. Yang T et al. Tobacco advertising, environmental smoking bans, and smoking in Chinese urban areas. *Drug and Alcohol Dependence*, 2012, 124:121–127.

33. Arora M et al. Impact of tobacco advertisements on tobacco use among urban adolescents in India: results from a longitudinal study. *Tobacco Control*, 2012, 21:318–324.

34. Henricksen L. Comprehensive tobacco marketing restrictions: promotion, packaging, price and place. *Tobacco Control*, 2012, 21:147–153.

35. Harris F et al. Effects of the 2003 advertising/promotion ban in the United Kingdom on awareness of tobacco marketing: findings from the International Tobacco Control (ITC) Four Country Survey. *Tobacco Control*, 2006, 15(Suppl. 3):iii26–iii33.

36. Kasza KA et al. The effectiveness of tobacco marketing regulations on reducing smokers' exposure to advertising and promotion: findings from the International Tobacco Control (ITC) Four Country Survey. *International Journal of Environmental Research and Public Health*, 2011, 2:321–340.

37. Emery S, Choi WS, Pierce JP. The social costs of tobacco advertising and promotions. *Nicotine and Tobacco Research*, 1999, 1(Suppl. 2):S83–S91.

38. Pierce JP. Tobacco industry marketing, population-based tobacco control, and smoking behavior. *American Journal of Preventive Medicine*, 2007, 33(6 Suppl.):S327–S334.

39. Centers for Disease Control and Prevention (CDC). Adult awareness of tobacco advertising, promotion, and sponsorship – 14 countries. *Morbidity and Mortality Weekly Report*, 2012, 61:365–369.

40. Jha P, Chaloupka FJ, eds. *Curbing the epidemic: governments and the economics of tobacco control.* Washington, DC, The World Bank, 1999 (http://transition.usaid.gov/policy/ads/200/tobacco.pdf, accessed 15 June 2013).

41. Galduroz JC et al. Decrease in tobacco use among Brazilian students: a possible consequence of the ban on cigarette advertising? *Addictive Behaviours*, 2007, 32:1309–1313.

42. *Tobacco control at a glance.* Washington, DC, The World Bank, 2003 (http://siteresources.worldbank.org/INTPHAAG/Resources/AAGTobacControlEngv46-03.pdf, accessed 15 June 2013).

43. Warner K. *Tobacco Control Policy*, 1st ed. San Francisco, CA, Jossey-Bass, 2006.

44. Ling PM, Glantz SA. Why and how the tobacco industry sells cigarettes to young adults: Evidence from industry documents. *American Journal of Public Health*, 2002, 92:908–916.

45. Centers for Disease Control and Prevention (CDC). Decline in smoking prevalence – New York City, 2002-2006. *Morbidity and Mortality Weekly Report*, 2007, 56: 604–608.

46. Saffer H. Tobacco advertising and promotion. In: Jha P, Chaloupka FJ, eds. *Tobacco control in developing countries*. Oxford, Oxford University Press, 2000:215–236.

47. *It can be done: a smoke-free Europe*. Copenhagen, World Health Organization Regional Office for Europe, 1990.

48. Carter SM. Going below the line: creating transportable brands for Australia's dark market. *Tobacco Control*, 2003, 12(Suppl. 3):iii87–iii94.

49. Weinberger MG et al. Cigarette advertising: tactical changes in the pre and post broadcast era. In: Hunt HK, ed. *Advertising in a new age: proceedings of the annual conference of the American Academy of Advertising*. Provo, UT, American Academy of Advertising, 1981:136–141.

50. Assunta M, Chapman S. "The world's most hostile environment": how the tobacco industry circumvented Singapore's advertising ban. *Tobacco Control*, 2004, 13(Suppl. 2):ii51–ii57.

51. *Select Committee on Health*. Second report. London, Government of Great Britain, House of Commons, 2000 (http://www.parliament.the-stationery-office.co.uk/pa/cm199900/cmselect/cmhealth/27/2701.htm, accessed 15 June 2013).

52. Roemer R. *Legislative action to combat the world tobacco epidemic*, 2nd ed. Geneva, World Health Organization, 1993.

53. *A long history of empty promises: the cigarette companies' ineffective youth anti-smoking programs*. Washington, DC, Campaign for Tobacco-Free Kids, 1999 (http://tobaccofreekids.org/research/factsheets/pdf/0010.pdf, accessed 15 June 2013).

54. Madkour AS et al. Tobacco advertising/promotions and adolescents' smoking risk in Northern Africa. *Tobacco Control*, 2013 [published online 8 Jan].

55. *Building blocks for tobacco control: a handbook*. Geneva, World Health Organization, WHO Tobacco Free Initiative, 2004 (http://www.who.int/entity/tobacco/resources/publications/general/HANDBOOK%20Lowres%20with%20cover.pdf, accessed 15 June 2013).

56. Crofton J, Simpson D. *Tobacco: a global threat*. Hong Kong, Macmillan Education, 2002.

57. Rosenberg NJ, Siegel M. Use of corporate sponsorship as a tobacco marketing tool: a review of tobacco industry sponsorship in the USA, 1995–99. *Tobacco Control*, 2001, 10:239–246.

58. Hammond D et al. Impact of female-oriented cigarette packaging in the United States. *Nicotine and Tobacco Research*, 2011, 13:579–588.

59. Limb M. "Slick" cigarette packaging encourages children to smoke, UK charity says. *British Medical Journal*, 2012, 344:e3030.

60. Cohen JE et al. Changes in retail tobacco promotions in a cohort of stores before, during, and after a tobacco product display ban. *American Journal of Public Health*, 2011, 101:1879–1881.

61. Spanopoulos D et al. Tobacco display and brand communication at the point of sale: implications for adolescent smoking behaviour. *Tobacco Control*, 2013 [published online 28 Feb].

62. Thomson G et al. Evidence and arguments on tobacco retail displays: marketing an addictive drug to children? *New Zealand Medical Journal*, 2008, 121:87–98.

63. Hoek J et al. How do tobacco retail displays affect cessation attempts? Findings from a qualitative study. *Tobacco Control*, 2010, 19:334–337.

64. McNeill A et al. Evaluation of the removal of point-of-sale tobacco displays in Ireland. *Tobacco Control*, 2011, 20:137–143.

65. Scheffels J, Lavik R. Out of sight, out of mind? Removal of point-of-sale tobacco displays in Norway. *Tobacco Control*, 2013, 22(e1):e37–e42.

66. Phillips, B. Cigarette sales already down ahead of tobacco display ban. *The Grocer*, 31 March 2012:5.

67. Kim AE et al. Influence of tobacco displays and ads on youth: a virtual store experiment. *Pediatrics*, 2013, 131:e88–e95.

68. Burch T, Wander N, Collin J. Uneasy money: the Instituto Carlos Slim de la Salud, tobacco philanthropy and conflict of interest in global health. *Tobacco Control*, 2010, 19:e1–e9.

69. Fooks G. News analysis: World: Disasters are 'brand aid' opportunities for tobacco. *Tobacco Control*, 2011, 20:4.

70. Fooks G et al. The limits of Corporate Social Responsibility: techniques of neutralization, stakeholder management and political CSR. *Journal of Business Ethics*, 2013, 112:283–299.

71. Fooks GJ et al. Corporate social responsibility and access to policy élites: an analysis of tobacco industry documents. *PLoS Medicine*, 2011, 8:e1001076.

72. Morgenstern M et al. Smoking in movies and adolescent smoking initiation: longitudinal study in six European countries. *American Journal of Preventive Medicine*, 2013, 44:339–344.

73. *BAT's African Footprint*. London, Action on Smoking and Health, 2008 (http://www.ash.org.uk/files/documents/ASH_685.pdf, accessed 15 June 2013).

74. Seidenberg AB et al. Storefront cigarette advertising differs by community demographic profile. *American Journal of Health Promotion*, 2010, 24:e26–e31.

75. Shafey O et al. Cigarette advertising and female smoking prevalence in Spain, 1982–1997: case studies in international tobacco surveillance. *Cancer*, 2004, 100:1744–1749.

76. *United States v. Philip Morris USA Inc., 449 F.* Supp. 2d 1 (D.D.C. 2006), *aff'd in part & vacated in part,* 566 F.3d 1095 (D.C. Cir. 2009) (per curiam), *cert. denied,* 561 U.S. ___, 130 S. Ct. 3501 (2010).

77. Kenyon AT, Liberman J. *Controlling cross-border tobacco: advertising, promotion and sponsorship – implementing the FCTC*. University of Melbourne Legal Studies Research Paper No. 161. Melbourne, Centre for Media and Communications Law, University of Melbourne, 2006 (http://papers.ssrn.com/sol3/papers.cfm?abstract_id=927551, accessed 15 June 2013).

78. *Report on the implementation of the EU Tobacco Advertising Directive*. Brussels, European Commission Directorate-General for Health & Consumers, 2008 (http://ec.europa.eu/health/archive/ph_determinants/life_style/tobacco/documents/com_20080520_en.pdf, accessed 15 June 2013).

79. Freeman B, Chapman S. Open source marketing: Camel cigarette brand marketing in the "Web 2.0" world. *Tobacco Control*, 2009, 18:212–217.

80. Freeman B. New media and tobacco control. *Tobacco Control*, 2012, 21:139–144.

81. Freeman B, Chapman S. British American Tobacco on Facebook: undermining Article 13 of the global World Health Organization Framework Convention on Tobacco Control. *Tobacco Control*, 2010, 19:e1–e9.

82. Novello AC. Campaigns for young people. In: Slama K, ed. *Tobacco and health: proceedings of the Ninth World Conference on Tobacco and Health*. New York, Plenum Press, 1995:41–45.

83. *Income taxes: disallowance of deductions: advertising*, 2011. California Assembly Bill 1218 (died in committee pursuant to Art. IV, Sec. 10(c) of the California Constitution, 1 Feb 2012).

84. Wakefield MA et al. The cigarette pack as image: new evidence from tobacco industry documents. *Tobacco Control*, 2002, 11(Suppl. 1):i73–i80.

85. Freeman B, Chapman S, Rimmer M. The case for the plain packaging of tobacco products. *Addiction*, 2008, 4:580–590.

86. *Tobacco industry interference with tobacco control*. Geneva, World Health Organization, 2008 (http://whqlibdoc.who.int/publications/2008/9789241597340_eng.pdf, accessed 15 June 2013).

87. *Examples of implementation of Article 5.3 communicated through the reports of the Parties*. Geneva, World Health Organization, 2013 (http://www.who.int/fctc/parties_experiences/en/index.html, accessed 15 June 2013).

88. *Global Adult Tobacco Survey (GATS). Fact sheet: Turkey 2012*. Geneva, World Health Organization, 2013 (http://www.who.int/tobacco/surveillance/survey/gats/gats_turkey_2012_fact_sheet_may_2013.pdf, accessed 15 June 2013).

89. *Global Adult Tobacco Survey: 2011 GATS, Thailand*. Nonthaburi, Ministry of Public Health, Department of Disease Control, Bureau of Tobacco Control, 2012 (http://whothailand.healthrepository.org/handle/123456789/1918, accessed 15 June 2013).

90. *WHO report on the global tobacco epidemic, 2008: the MPOWER package*. Geneva, World Health Organization, 2008 (http://www.who.int/tobacco/mpower/gtcr_download/en/index.html, accessed 15 June 2013).

91. *WHO report on the global tobacco epidemic, 2009: implementing smoke-free environments*. Geneva, World Health Organization, 2009 (http://www.who.int/tobacco/mpower/2009/en/index.html, accessed 15 June 2013).

92. *MPOWER: a policy package to reverse the tobacco epidemic*. Geneva, World Health Organization, 2008 (http://www.who.int/tobacco/mpower/mpower_english.pdf, accessed 15 June 2013).

93. *WHO report on the global tobacco epidemic, 2011: warning about the dangers of tobacco*. Geneva, World Health Organization, 2011 (http://www.who.int/tobacco/global_report/2011/en/index.html, accessed 15 June 2013).

94. Wakefield M et al. Smokers' responses to television advertisements about the serious harms of tobacco use: pre-testing results from 10 low- to middle-income countries. *Tobacco Control*, 2013, 22:24–31.

95. Geist HJ. Global assessment of deforestation related to tobacco farming. *Tobacco Control*, 1999, 8:18–28.

TECHNICAL NOTES

APPENDICES

Appendices VI to XII are available online at http://www.who.int/tobacco/

TECHNICAL NOTE I

Evaluation of existing policies and compliance

This report provides summary indicators of country achievements for each of the six MPOWER measures, and the methodology used to calculate each indicator is described in this Technical Note. To ensure consistency and comparability, the data collection and analysis methodology used in this report are largely based on previous editions of the report. Some of the methodology employed in earlier reports, however, has been revised and strengthened for the present report. Where revisions have been made, data from previous reports have been re-analysed so that results are comparable across years.

Data sources

Data were collected using the following sources:

- For all areas: official reports from WHO FCTC Parties to the Conference of the Parties (COP) and their accompanying documentation.[1]
- For M: tobacco prevalence surveys not yet reported under the COP reporting mechanism were collected from the WHO Global Infobase and through an extensive literature search. Technical Note II provides the detailed methodology used for the calculation of the prevalence estimates.
- For P, W (pack warnings) and E: original tobacco control legislation, including regulations, adopted in all Member States related to smoke-free environments, packaging and labelling measures and tobacco advertising, promotion and sponsorship.
- For W (mass media): data on anti-tobacco mass media campaigns were obtained from Member States. In order to avoid unnecessary data collection, WHO conducted a screening for anti-tobacco mass media campaigns in all WHO country offices. In countries where potentially eligible mass media campaigns were identified, focal points in each country were contacted for further information on these campaigns and data on eligible campaigns were gathered and recorded systematically.
- For R: the prices of the most sold brand of cigarettes, the cheapest brand and the brand Marlboro were collected through regional data collectors. Information on the taxation of cigarettes (and, for some countries in South East Asia Region, bidis) and revenues from tobacco taxation as well as any supporting documents were collected from ministries of finance. Technical Note III provides the detailed methodology used.

Based on these sources of information, WHO made an assessment for each indicator as of 31 December 2012. Exceptions to this cut-off date were tobacco product prices and taxes (cut-off date 31 July 2012) and anti-tobacco mass media campaigns (cut-off date 30 June 2012).

Data validation

For each country, every data point for which the source was legislation was assessed independently by two different expert staff from two different WHO offices, generally one from WHO headquarters and the other from the respective regional office. Any inconsistencies found were reviewed by the two WHO expert staff involved and a third expert staff member not yet involved in the appraisal of the legislation. These were resolved by: (i) checking the original text of the legislation; (ii) trying to obtain consensus from the two expert staff involved in the data collection; and (iii) the decision of the third expert in cases where differences remained. Data were also checked for completeness and logical consistency across variables.

Data sign-off

Final, validated data for each country were sent to the respective government for review and sign-off. To facilitate review by governments, a summary sheet was generated for each country and was sent for review prior to the close of the report database. In cases where national authorities requested data changes, the requests were assessed by WHO expert staff according to both the legislation and the clarification shared by the national authorities, and data were updated or left unchanged. In cases where national authorities explicitly did not approve data, this is specifically noted in the appendix tables. Further details about the data processing procedure are available from WHO.

Data analysis

The report provides summary measures or indicators of country achievements for each of the six MPOWER measures. It is important to note that data for the report are based on existing legislation and reflect the status of adopted but not necessarily implemented legislation, as long as the law clearly indicates a date of entry into force and is not undergoing a legal challenge. The summary measures developed for the *WHO Report on the Global Tobacco Epidemic, 2013* are the same as those used for the 2011 report, except for the indicator on anti-tobacco mass media campaigns, which was slightly improved.

The report provides analysis of progress made since 2010 and since the first report (2007). For each indicator, 2010 and 2007 data were compared with 2012 data. Indicators from previous years have been recalculated, according to legislation/materials received after the assessment period of the respective report or according to changes in the methodology, so that the results are comparable across years.

When country or population totals for MPOWER measures are referred to collectively in the analysis section of this report, only the implementation of tobacco control policies (smoke-free legislation, cessation services, warning labels, advertising and promotion bans, and tobacco taxes) is included in these totals. Monitoring of tobacco use is reported separately. When changes in population coverage since 2010 or 2007 are presented, again only implementation of policies is included.

Correction to previously published data

The 2010 data published in the last report were reviewed, and about 3% of data points were corrected. In most cases, review was conducted because legislation or policies were in place at the time of the last report but details were not available to WHO in time for publication. As a result of these corrections, one country was downgraded from the highest group of smoke-free legislation, two countries for cessation services, one country for pack warnings, nine countries for bans on advertising, promotion and sponsorship, and one country for tax rates.

Monitoring

The strength of a national tobacco surveillance system is conveyed by the frequency and periodicity of nationally representative youth and adult surveys in countries. To assess each country's tobacco use surveillance system, the following information is noted:

- the year of the most recent survey;
- whether the survey was representative of the country's population;
- whether a similar survey was repeated at least every five years (periodicity); and
- whether adults, youth or both were surveyed.

Surveys were considered recent if data were collected in 2007 or later. Surveys were considered representative if the sample was selected scientifically to represent the national population. Surveys were considered periodic if the same survey or a similar survey was conducted at least once every five years. Surveys were considered "youth surveys" if these surveys provided statistically robust information on persons up to 17 years of age. Where it was not possible to obtain all the above information on a particular survey, the survey was excluded from the assessment. Where the survey was subnational or covered only a portion of the general population, it was excluded from the assessment.

The groupings for the Monitoring indicator are listed below.

(white)	No known data or no recent* data or data that are not both recent* and representative**
(light brown)	Recent* and representative** data for either adults or youth
(brown)	Recent* and representative** data for both adults and youth
(dark red)	Recent*, representative** and periodic*** data for both adults and youth

* Data from 2007 or later.
** Survey sample representative of the national population.
*** Collected at least every five years.

Smoke-free legislation

There is a wide range of places and institutions that can be made smoke-free by law. Smoke-free legislation can take place at the national or subnational level. The report includes data on national legislation as well as legislation in subnational jurisdictions. The assessment of subnational smoke-free legislation includes all first-level administrative boundaries (first administrative subdivisions of a country), as determined by the United Nations Geographical Information Working Group. In addition, smoke-free legislation status of other subnational jurisdictions is reported when data and respective legislation were provided by country focal points. Subnational data reported in Appendix VI only reflect the status of subnational legislation and do not take into account the status of legislation at the national/federal level. Legislation was assessed to determine whether smoke-free laws provided for a complete[2] indoor smoke-free environment at all times, in all the facilities of each of the following eight places:

- health-care facilities;
- educational facilities other than universities;
- universities;
- government facilities;
- indoor offices and workplaces not considered in any other category;
- restaurants or facilities that serve mostly food;
- cafés, pubs and bars or facilities that serve mostly beverages;
- public transport.

Groupings for the Smoke-free legislation indicator are based on the number of places where indoor smoking is completely prohibited. In addition, countries where at least 90% of the population was covered by complete subnational indoor smoke-free legislation are grouped in the top category.

In a few countries, in order to significantly expand the creation of smoke-free places, including restaurants and bars, it was politically necessary to include exceptions to the law that allowed for the provision of designated smoking rooms (DSRs) with requirements so technically complex and strict that, for practical purposes, few or no establishments are expected to implement them. In order to meet the criteria for "very strict technical requirements", the legislation had to include at least three out of the six following characteristics (and must include at least criteria 5 or 6).

The designated smoking room must:

1. be a closed indoor environment;
2. be furnished with automatic doors, generally kept closed;
3. be non-transit premises for non-smokers;
4. be furnished with appropriate forced-ventilation mechanical devices;
5. have appropriate installations and functional openings installed, and air must be expelled from the premises;
6. be maintained, with reference to surrounding areas, in a depression not lower than 5 Pascal.

The few countries whose laws provide for DSRs with very strict technical requirements have not been categorized in the analyses for this section because their smoke-free legislation substantially departs from the recommendations of WHO FCTC Article 8 guidelines, and it has been difficult to measure if the law resulted in the intended very low number of DSRs in all of these countries.

The groupings for the Smoke-free legislation indicator are listed below.

	Data not reported/not categorized
	Up to two public places completely smoke-free
	Three to five public places completely smoke-free
	Six to seven public places completely smoke-free
	All public places completely smoke-free (or at least 90% of the population covered by complete subnational smoke-free legislation)

In addition to the data being used for the above groupings of the Smoke-free legislation indicator, other related data such as information on fines and enforcement were collected and are reported in Appendix VI.

Tobacco dependence treatment

The indicator of achievement in treatment for tobacco dependence is based on whether the country has available:

- nicotine replacement therapy (NRT);
- cessation services;
- reimbursement for any of the above; and
- a national toll-free quit line.

Despite the low cost of quit lines, few low- or middle-income countries have implemented such programmes. Thus, national toll-free quit lines are included as a qualification only for the highest category. Reimbursement for tobacco dependence treatment is considered only for the top two categories to take restricted national budgets of many lower-income countries into consideration.

The top three categories reflect varying levels of government commitment to the availability of nicotine replacement therapy and cessation support.

The groupings for the Tobacco dependence treatment indicator are listed below.

	Data not reported
	None
	NRT* and/or some cessation services** (neither cost-covered)
	NRT* and/or some cessation services** (at least one of which is cost-covered)
	National quit line, and both NRT* and some cessation services** cost-covered

* Nicotine replacement therapy.

** Smoking cessation support available in any of the following places: health clinics or other primary care facilities, hospitals, office of a health professional, the community.

In addition to data used for the grouping of the Tobacco dependence treatment indicator, other related data such as information on countries' essential medicines lists, non-NRT tobacco dependence treatment, etc. were collected and are reported in Appendix VI.

Warning labels

The section of the report devoted to assessing each country's achievements in health warnings notes the following information about characteristics of cigarette pack warnings:

- whether specific health warnings are mandated;
- the mandated size of the warnings, as a percentage of the front and back of the cigarette pack;
- whether the warnings appear on individual packages as well as on any outside packaging and labelling used in retail sale;
- whether the warnings describe specific harmful effects of tobacco use on health;
- whether the warnings are large, clear, visible and legible (e.g. specific colours and font styles and sizes are mandated);
- whether the warnings rotate;
- whether the warnings are written in (all) the principal language(s) of the country;
- whether the warnings include pictures or pictograms.

The size of the warnings on both the front and back of the cigarette pack were averaged to calculate the percentage of the total pack surface area that is covered by the warnings. This information was combined with the warning characteristics to construct the groupings for the Health warnings indicator.

The groupings for the Health warnings indicator are listed below.

	Data not reported
	No warnings or small warnings[1]
	Medium size warnings[2] missing some[3] appropriate characteristics[4] OR large warnings[5] missing many[6] appropriate characteristics[4]
	Medium size warnings[2] with all appropriate characteristics[4] OR large warnings[5] missing some[3] appropriate characteristics[4]
	Large warnings[5] with all appropriate characteristics[4]

1 Average of front and back of package is less than 30%.

2 Average of front and back of package is between 30 and 49%.

3 One or more.

4 Appropriate characteristics:
- specific health warnings mandated;
- appearing on individual packages as well as on any outside packaging and labelling used in retail sale;
- describing specific harmful effects of tobacco use on health;
- are large, clear, visible and legible (e.g. specific colours and font style and sizes are mandated);
- rotate;
- include pictures or pictograms;
- written in (all) the principal language(s) of the country.

5 Average of front and back of the package is at least 50%.

6 Four or more.

In addition to the data used for the grouping of the Health warnings indicator, other related data such as the appearance of the quit line number, etc. were collected and are reported in Appendix VI.

Anti-tobacco mass media campaigns

Countries undertake communication activities to serve varied goals, including improving public relations, creating attention for an issue, building support for public policies, and prompting behaviour change. Anti-tobacco communication campaigns, which are a core tobacco control intervention, must have specified features in order to be minimally effective: they must be of sufficient duration and must be designed to effectively support tobacco control priorities, including increasing knowledge, changing social norms, promoting cessation, preventing tobacco uptake, and increasing support for good tobacco control policies.

With this in mind, and consistent with the definition of "anti-tobacco mass media campaigns" in the last report, only mass media campaigns of at least three weeks in duration that were designed to support tobacco control efforts and implemented between January 2011 and June 2012 were considered eligible for analysis. For the sake of logistical feasibility and cross-country comparability, only national level campaigns were considered eligible.

Eligible campaigns were assessed according to the following characteristics, which signify the use of a comprehensive communication approach:

1. The campaign was part of a comprehensive tobacco control programme.
2. Before the campaign, research was undertaken or reviewed to gain a thorough understanding of the target audience.
3. Campaign communications materials were pre-tested with the target audience and refined in line with campaign objectives.
4. Air time (radio, television) and/or placement (billboards, print advertising, etc.) was obtained by purchasing or securing it using either the organization's own internal resources or an external media planner or agency (this information indicates whether the campaign adopted a thorough media planning and buying process to effectively and efficiently reach its target audience).
5. The implementing agency worked with journalists to gain publicity or news coverage for the campaign.
6. Process evaluation was undertaken to assess how effectively the campaign had been implemented.
7. An outcome evaluation process was implemented to assess campaign impact.
8. The campaign was aired on television and/or radio.

The eighth criterion was added this year because television and radio are important mass media for tobacco control: first, they tend to have the greatest population reach in nearly all countries in the world; and second, TV and radio campaigns tend to be more impactful than static media (e.g. outdoors or print) because of their audio-visual nature. The definition and grouping of countries in the 2011 report has similarly been refined. Finally, to enable greater accuracy, an additional step was added in the submission of campaigns: materials from campaigns had to be submitted and verified based on the eligibility criteria for all countries.

The groupings for the Mass media campaigns indicator are listed below.

	Data not reported
	No national campaign conducted between January 2011 and June 2012 with a duration of at least three weeks
	National campaign conducted with one to four appropriate characteristics
	National campaign conducted with 5–6 appropriate characteristics, or with 7 characteristics excluding airing on television and/or radio
	National campaign conducted with at least seven appropriate characteristics including airing on television and/or radio

Bans on advertising, promotion and sponsorship

The report includes data on legislation in national as well subnational jurisdictions. The assessment of subnational legislation on advertising, promotion and sponsorship bans includes all first-level administrative boundaries (first administrative subdivisions of a country), as determined by the United Nations Geographical Information Working Group. In addition, status of legislation on advertising, promotion and sponsorship bans for other subnational jurisdictions is reported when data and respective legislation were provided by country focal points. Subnational data reported in Appendix VI reflect only the status of subnational legislation and do not take into account the status of legislation at the national/federal level.

Country-level achievements in banning tobacco advertising, promotion and sponsorship were assessed based on whether the bans covered the following types of advertising:

- national television and radio;
- local magazines and newspapers;
- billboards and outdoor advertising;
- point of sale;
- free distribution of tobacco products in the mail or through other means;
- promotional discounts;
- non-tobacco products identified with tobacco brand names (brand stretching);[3]
- brand names of non-tobacco products used for tobacco products (brand-sharing); [4]
- appearance of tobacco brands or products in television and/or films (product placement);
- sponsored events, including corporate social responsibility programmes.

The first four types of advertising listed are considered "direct" advertising, and the remaining six are considered "indirect" advertising. Complete bans on tobacco advertising, promotion and sponsorship usually start with bans on direct advertising in national media and progress to bans on indirect advertising as well as promotion and sponsorship.

Bans that cover national television, radio and print media were used as the basic criteria for the two lowest groups, and the remaining groups were constructed based on how comprehensively the law covers bans of other forms of direct and indirect advertising included in the questionnaire. In cases where the law did not explicitly address cross-border advertising, it was interpreted that advertising at both domestic and international levels was covered by the ban only if advertising was totally banned at national level.

The groupings for the Bans on advertising, promotion and sponsorship indicator are listed below.

	Data not reported
	Complete absence of ban, or ban that does not cover national television (TV), radio and print media
	Ban on national TV, radio and print media only
	Ban on national TV, radio and print media as well as on some (but not all) other forms of direct* and/or indirect** advertising
	Ban on all forms of direct* and indirect** advertising

* Direct advertising bans:

- national television and radio;
- local magazines and newspapers;
- billboards and outdoor advertising;
- point of sale.

** Indirect advertising bans:

- free distribution of tobacco products in the mail or through other means;
- promotional discounts;
- non-tobacco goods and services identified with tobacco brand names (brand stretching);
- brand names of non-tobacco products used for tobacco products (brand sharing);
- appearance of tobacco brands or products in television and/or films (product placement) OR appearance of tobacco products in television and/or films;
- sponsored events, including corporate social responsibility programmes.

In addition to the data being used for the grouping of the Bans on advertising, promotion and sponsorship indicator, other related data, such as information on Corporate Social Responsibility activities, were collected and are reported in Appendix VI.

Tobacco taxes

Countries are grouped according to the percentage contribution of all tobacco taxes to the retail price. Taxes assessed include excise tax, value added tax (sometimes called "VAT"), import duty (when the cigarettes were imported) and any other taxes levied. Only the price of the most popular brand of cigarettes is considered. In the case of countries where different levels of taxes are applied to cigarettes are based on either length, quantity produced or type (e.g. filter vs. non-filter), only the rate that applied to the most popular brand is used in the calculation.

Given the lack of information on country and brand-specific profit margins of retailers and wholesalers, their profits were assumed to be zero (unless provided by the national data collector).

The groupings for the Tobacco tax indicator are listed below. In the regional summary table, tax rates are rounded but more precise data with two decimals are available in Appendix IX. Please refer to Technical Note III for more details.

	Data not reported
	< 25% of retail price is tax
	26–50% of retail price is tax
	51–75% of retail price is tax
	>75% of retail price is tax

National tobacco control programmes

Classification of countries' national tobacco control programmes is based on the existence of a national agency with responsibility for tobacco control objectives. Countries with at least five full-time equivalent staff members working at the national agency with responsibility for tobacco control meet the criteria for the highest group.

The groupings for the National tobacco control programme indicator are listed below.

	Data not reported
	No national agency for tobacco control
	Existence of national agency with responsibility for tobacco control objectives with no or < 5 full-time equivalent staff members
	Existence of national agency with responsibility for tobacco control objectives and at least 5 full-time equivalent staff members

Compliance assessment

Compliance with national and comprehensive subnational smoke-free legislation as well as with advertising, promotion and sponsorship bans (covering both direct and indirect marketing) was assessed by up to five national experts, who assessed the compliance in these two areas as "minimal", "moderate" or "high". These five experts were selected according to the following criteria:

- person in charge of tobacco prevention in the country's ministry of health, or the most senior government official in charge of tobacco control or tobacco-related conditions;
- the head of a prominent nongovernmental organization dedicated to tobacco control;
- a health professional (e.g. physician, nurse, pharmacist or dentist) specializing in tobacco-related conditions;
- a staff member of a public health university department;
- the tobacco control focal point of the WHO country office.

The experts performed their assessments independently. Summary scores were calculated by WHO from the individual compliance assessments.

Two points were assigned for high compliance, one point for moderate compliance and no points for minimal compliance. The total points were divided by the maximum possible points (reflecting the number of assessors) and multiplied by 10 to yield a score between 0 and 10.

The compliance assessment was obtained for legislation adopted by 30 April 2012. For countries with more recent legislation, compliance data are reported as "not applicable". Compliance with smoke-free legislation was not assessed in cases where the law provides for DSRs with very strict technical requirements.

The country-reported answers are listed in Appendix VI. Appendix I summarizes this information. Compliance scores are represented separately from the grouping (i.e. compliance is not included in the calculation of the grouping categories).

1 Parties report on the implementation of the WHO Framework Convention on Tobacco Control according to Article 21. The objective of reporting is to enable Parties to learn from each other's experience in implementing the WHO FCTC. Parties' reports are also the basis for review by the COP of the implementation of the Convention. Parties submit their initial report two years after entry into force of the WHO FCTC for that Party, and then every subsequent three years, through the reporting instrument adopted by COP. Since 2012, all Parties report at the same time, once every two years. For more information please refer to http://www.who.int/fctc/reporting/en.

2 "Complete" is used in this report to mean that smoking is not permitted, with no exemptions allowed, except in residences and indoor places that serve as equivalents to long-term residential facilities, such as prisons and long-term health and social care facilities such as psychiatric units and nursing homes. Ventilation and any form of designated smoking rooms and/or areas do not protect from the harms of second-hand tobacco smoke, and the only laws that provide protection are those that result in the complete absence of smoking in all public places.

3 When legislation did not explicitly ban the identification of non-tobacco products with tobacco brand names (brand stretching) and did not provide a definition of tobacco advertising and promotion, it was interpreted that brand stretching was covered by the existing ban of all forms of advertising and promotion when the country was a Party to the WHO FCTC, assuming that the WHO FCTC definitions apply.

4 When legislation did not explicitly ban the use of brand names of non-tobacco products for tobacco products (brand sharing) and did not provide a definition of tobacco advertising and promotion, it was interpreted that brand sharing was covered by the existing ban of all forms of advertising and promotion when the country was a Party to the WHO FCTC, assuming that the WHO FCTC definitions apply.

TECHNICAL NOTE II

Smoking prevalence in WHO Member States

Monitoring the prevalence of tobacco use is central to any surveillance system involved with tobacco control. Reliable prevalence data provide the information needed to assess the impact of tobacco control actions adopted by a country and can be used by tobacco control workers in their efforts to counter the tobacco epidemic. This report contains country-provided data for both smoking and smokeless tobacco use among youth and adults, as well as WHO-modelled age-standardized prevalence estimates for smoking among adults (Appendix VII).

Collection of tobacco use prevalence surveys

For this report, the following sources of information were explored:

- reports submitted to the WHO FCTC Secretariat by Parties to the Conference of Parties;
- information collected through WHO tobacco focussed surveys conducted under the aegis of the Global Tobacco Surveillance System – in particular the Global Youth Tobacco Survey (GYTS) and the Global Adult Tobacco Survey (GATS);
- tobacco information collected through other WHO surveys including the WHO STEPwise Surveys, the Global School-based Student Health Surveys and the World Health Surveys;
- other systems-based surveys undertaken by other organizations, including surveys such as the (European-based) Health Behaviour in School-aged Children surveys and global Demographic Health Surveys.

In addition, an extensive search was conducted through WHO regional and WHO country offices where possible to try to identify as many country-specific surveys that are not part of an international surveillance system – such as the Survey of Lifestyles, Attitude and Nutrition in the Republic of Ireland, or the Social Weather Station Surveys in the Philippines.

Much of the information identified here is also stored on the WHO Global Infobase (a portal of information on eight risk factors for noncommunicable diseases including tobacco: http://www.who.int/infobase). Surveys that met the following criteria were collected:

- provide country survey summary data for one or more of six tobacco use definitions: daily tobacco user, current tobacco user, daily tobacco smoker, current tobacco smoker, daily cigarette smoker, or current cigarette smoker;
- include randomly selected participants who were representative of the general population;
- present prevalence values by age and sex; and
- are officially recognized by the national health authority.

Member States were contacted to obtain an official report from recently undertaken surveys.

Analysis and presentation of tobacco use prevalence indicators

Data collected from countries' prevalence surveys are presented in this report in two forms.

1. *Crude prevalence rates* (Appendix VIII): these present the actual estimate of tobacco use in a country as measured by the survey, and can be used to generate an estimate of the number of smokers for the relevant indicator (e.g. current smokers, daily smokers) in the population. Crude prevalence rates from the most recent youth and adult surveys from each country are presented in this report.
2. *Adjusted and age-standardized prevalence rates* (Appendix VII): these rates are constructed solely for the purpose of comparing adult tobacco use prevalence across multiple countries or across multiple time periods for the same country. These rates must not be used to estimate the number of smokers in the population. The methods for age-standardizing and adjusting for survey differences are described separately below. The estimates presented in Appendix VII have been both adjusted and age-standardized.

Crude prevalence. The crude prevalence, a summary measure of tobacco use in a population, reflects the actual use of tobacco in a country (e.g. prevalence of cigarette smoking by adults aged 15 years and above). The crude rate, expressed as a percentage of the total population, refers to the number of smokers per 100 population of the country. When this crude prevalence rate is multiplied by the country's population, the result is the number of smokers in the country.

Adjusted prevalence. Adjustments to data are typically done when collecting information from heterogeneous sources that originate from different surveys and do not employ standardized survey instruments. These differences render difficult the comparison of prevalence rates between surveys and between countries. The following four indicators of smoking were collated using all adult survey information identified in the search process described earlier:

- current prevalence of tobacco smoking;[1]
- daily prevalence of tobacco smoking;[1]
- current prevalence of cigarette smoking;
- daily prevalence of cigarette smoking.

These indicators provide for the most complete representation of tobacco smoking across countries and at the same time help minimize attrition of countries from further analysis because of lack of adequate data. Although differences exist in the types of tobacco products used in different countries and grown or manufactured in different regions of the world, data on cigarette smoking and tobacco smoking are the most widely reported and are common to all countries, thereby permitting statistical analyses.[2]

WHO developed a regression method that attempts to adjust the reported survey results to enable comparisons between countries. The general principle that underlies the regression method is that if data are partly missing or are incomplete for a country, then the regression technique uses data available for the United Nations subregion[3] in which the country is located to generate estimates for that country. The regression models are run separately for males and females in order to obtain age-specific prevalence rates for each region. These estimates are then substituted for the country falling within the subregion for the missing indicator. Note that the technique cannot be used where countries have no surveys at all, or insufficient data (i.e. one single survey run in 2009 or earlier, or no surveys run since 2002); these countries were excluded from the analysis.

Adjusting for differences between surveys

Differences in age groups covered by the survey. In order to estimate smoking prevalence rates for standard age ranges (by five-year groups from age 15 until age 80 and thereafter from 80 to 100 years), the association between age and daily smoking is examined for males and females separately for each country using scatter plots. For this exercise, data from the latest nationally representative survey are chosen; in some cases more than one survey is chosen if male and female prevalence rates stem from different surveys or if the additional survey supplements data for the extreme age intervals. To obtain age-specific prevalence rates for five-year age intervals, regression models using daily smoking prevalence estimates from a first order, second order and third order function of age are graphed against the scatter plot and the best fitting curve is chosen. For the remaining indicators, a combination of methods is applied: regression models are run at the subregional level to obtain age-specific rates for current and daily cigarette smoking, and an equivalence relationship is applied between smoking prevalence rates and cigarette smoking where cigarette smoking is dominant to obtain age-specific prevalence rates for current and daily cigarette smoking for the standard age intervals.

Differences in the types of indicators of tobacco use measured. If data are available for current tobacco smoking and current cigarette smoking only, then definitional adjustments are made to account for the missing daily tobacco smoking and daily cigarette smoking data. Likewise, if data are available for current and daily tobacco smoking only, then tobacco type adjustments are made across tobacco types to generate estimates for current and daily cigarette smoking.

Differences in geographical coverage of the survey within the country. If data are available for urban or rural areas only, then adjustments are made by observing the relationship between urban and rural areas in countries falling within the relevant subregion. Results from this urban-rural regression exercise are applied to countries to allow a scaling-up of prevalence to the national level. As an example, if a country has prevalence rates for daily smoking of tobacco in urban areas only, the regression results from the rural-urban smoking relationship are used to obtain rural prevalence rates for daily smoking. These are then combined with urban prevalence rates using urban-rural population ratios as weights to generate a national prevalence estimate as well as national age-specific rates.

Differences in survey year. For this report, smoking prevalence estimates are generated for the year 2011. Smoking prevalence data are sourced from surveys conducted in countries in different years. To obtain smoking prevalence estimates for 2011, trend information is used either to project into the future for countries with data older than 2011 or backtracked for countries with data later than 2011. This is achieved by incorporating trend information from all available surveys for each country. For countries without historical data, trend information from the respective subregion in which they fall is used. For countries that completed a survey in 2011, no adjustment is done.

Age-standardized prevalence. Tobacco use generally varies widely by sex and across age groups. Comparison of crude rates between two or more countries at one point in time, or of one country at different points in time, can be misleading if the two populations being compared have significantly different age distributions or differences in tobacco use by sex. The method of age-standardization is commonly used to overcome this problem and allows for meaningful comparison of prevalence between countries, once all other comparison issues described above have been addressed. The method involves applying the age-specific rates by sex in each population to one standard population. When presenting age-standardized prevalence rates, this report uses the WHO Standard Population, a fictitious population whose age distribution is largely reflective of the population age structure of low- and middle-income countries. The resulting age-standardized rates refer to the number of smokers per 100 WHO Standard Population. As a result, the rates generated using this process are only hypothetical numbers with no inherent meaning. They are only meaningful when comparing rates obtained from one country with those obtained in another country. The age-standardized rates are shown in Appendix VII.

1 Tobacco smoking includes cigarette, cigar, pipe, hookah, shisha, water-pipe and any other form of smoked tobacco.

2 For countries where prevalence of smokeless tobacco use is reported, we have published these data.

3 For a complete listing of countries by UN region, please refer to pages ix to xiii of *World Population Prospects: The 2010 Revision* published by the UN Department of Economic and Social Affairs in 2011 at http://esa.un.org/wpp/Documentation/pdf/WPP2010_Volume-I_Comprehensive-Tables.pdf. Please note that, for the purposes of this analysis, the Eastern Africa subregion was divided into two regions: Eastern Africa Islands and Remainder of Eastern Africa; and the Melanesia, Micronesia and Polynesia subregions were combined into one subregion.

TECHNICAL NOTE III

Tobacco taxes in WHO Member States

This report includes appendices containing information on the share of total and excise taxes in the price of the most widely sold brand of cigarettes, based on tax policy information collected from each country. This note contains information on the methodology used by WHO to estimate the share of total and tobacco excise taxes in the price of a pack of 20 cigarettes using country-reported data.

1. Data collection

Data were collected between July 2012 and January 2013 by WHO regional data collectors. The two main inputs into calculating the share of total and excise taxes were (1) prices and (2) tax rates and structure.

Prices were collected for the most widely sold brand of cigarettes, two other popular brands, the least-expensive brand and the brand Marlboro for July 2012.

Data on tax structure were collected through contacts with ministries of finance. The validity of this information was checked against other sources. These sources, including tax law documents, decrees and official schedules of tax rates and structures as well as trade information, when available, were either provided by data collectors or were downloaded from ministerial websites or from other United Nations databases such as Comtrade (http://comtrade.un.org/db). Other secondary data sources were also purchased for data validation.

The tax data collected focus on indirect taxes levied on tobacco products (e.g. excise taxes of various types, import duties, value added taxes), which usually have the most significant policy impact on the price of tobacco products. Within indirect taxes, excise taxes are the most important because they are applied exclusively to tobacco, and contribute the most to substantially increasing the price of tobacco products and subsequently reducing consumption. Thus, rates, amounts, and point of application of excise taxes are central components of the data collected.

Certain other taxes, in particular direct taxes such as corporate taxes, can potentially impact tobacco prices to the extent that producers pass them on to final consumers. However, because of the practical difficulty of obtaining information on these taxes and the complexity in estimating their potential impact on price in a consistent manner across countries, they are not considered.

The table below describes the types of tax information collected.

2. Data analysis

The price of the most popular brand of cigarettes was considered in the calculation of the tax as a share of the retail price reported in table 9.1 in Appendix IX. In the case of countries where different levels of taxes are applied on cigarettes

1. Amount-specific excise taxes	An amount-specific excise tax is a tax on a selected good produced for sale within a country, or imported and sold in that country. In general, the tax is collected from the manufacturer/wholesaler or at the point of entry into the country by the importer, in addition to import duties. These taxes come in the form of an amount per stick, per pack, per 1000 sticks, or per kilogram. Example: US$ 1.50 per pack of 20 cigarettes.
2. Ad valorem excise taxes	An ad valorem excise tax is a tax on a selected good produced for sale within a country, or imported and sold in that country. In general, the tax is collected from the manufacturer/wholesaler or at the point of entry into the country by the importer, in addition to import duties. These taxes come in the form of a percentage of the value of a transaction between two independent entities at some point of the production/distribution chain; ad valorem taxes are generally applied to the value of the transactions between the manufacturer and the retailer/wholesaler. Example: 27% of the retail price.
3. Import duties	An import duty is a tax *on* a selected good imported into a country to be consumed in that country (i.e. the goods are not in transit to another country). In general, import duties are collected from the importer at the point of entry into the country. These taxes can be either amount-specific or ad valorem. Amount-specific import duties are applied in the same way as amount-specific excise taxes. Ad valorem import duties are generally applied to the CIF (cost, insurance, freight) value, i.e. the value of the unloaded consignment that includes the cost of the product itself, insurance and transport and unloading. Example: 50% import duty levied on CIF.
4. Value added taxes and sales taxes	The value added tax (VAT) is a "multi-stage" tax on all consumer goods and services applied proportionally to the price the consumer pays for a product. Although manufacturers and wholesalers also participate in the administration and payment of the tax all along the manufacturing/distribution chain, they are all reimbursed through a tax credit system, so that the only entity who pays in the end is the final consumer. Most countries that impose a VAT do so on a base that includes any excise tax and customs duty. Example: VAT representing 10% of the retail price. Some countries, however, impose sales taxes instead. Unlike VAT, sales taxes are levied at the point of retail sale on the total value of goods and services purchased. For the purposes of the report, care was taken to ensure the VAT and/or sales tax shares were computed in accordance with country-specific rules.
5. Other taxes	Information was also collected on any other tax that is not called an excise tax or VAT or sales tax, but that applies to either the quantity of tobacco or to the value of a transaction of tobacco product, with as much detail as possible regarding what is taxed (the tax base) and the purpose for which the tax is collected..

based on length of cigarette, quantity produced or type (e.g. filter vs. non-filter), only the relevant rate that applied to the most sold brand was used in the calculation. In the case of Canada and the United States of America, national average estimates calculated for prices and taxes reflect the fact that different rates are applied by each state/province over and above the applicable federal tax. In the case of Brazil, which applies different VAT rates per states, an average VAT rate was applied. In India, which also has varying VAT rates per state, the VAT rate applicable in Delhi was used.

The import duty was only applied to the most popular brand of cigarettes imported into the country. Import duty is not applied on total tax calculation for countries reporting that the most popular brand, even if an international brand, was produced locally.

"Other taxes" are all other indirect taxes not reported as excise taxes or VAT. These taxes were, however, treated as excises if they had a special rate applied to tobacco products. For example, Thailand reported the tax earmarked from tobacco and alcohol for the ThaiHealth Promotion Foundation as "other tax". However, since this tax is applied only on tobacco and alcohol products, it acts like an excise tax and it was considered an excise in the calculations.

The next step of the exercise was to convert all tax rates into the same base, in our case, the tax-inclusive retail sale price (hereafter referred to as *P*). Standardizing bases is important in calculating tax share correctly, as the example in the table shows. Country B applies the same ad valorem tax rate as Country A, but ends up with higher tax rate and a higher final price because the tax is applied later in the distribution chain. Comparing reported ad valorem tax rates without taking into account the stage at which the tax is applied could therefore lead to biased results.

	TAX INCLUSIVE RETAIL SALES PRICE OF CIGARETTES	COUNTRY A (US$)	COUNTRY B (US$)
[A]	Manufacturer's price (same in both countries)	2.00	2.00
[B]	Country A: ad valorem tax on manufacturer's price (20%) = 20% x [A]	**0.40**	-
[C]	Countries A and B: specific excise	2.00	2.00
[D]	Retailer's and wholesaler's profit margin (same in both countries)	0.20	0.20
[E]	Country B: ad valorem tax on retailer's price (20%) = 20% x [F]	-	**1.05**
[F]	Final price = *P* = [A]+[B]+[C]+[D]+[E]	4.60	5.25

3. Calculation

Denote S_{ts} as the share of taxes on the price of a widely consumed brand of cigarettes (20-cigarette pack or equivalent). Then

$$S_{ts} = S_{as} + S_{av} + S_{id} + S_{VAT} \quad ①$$

Where:

S_{ts} = Total share of taxes on the price of a pack of cigarettes;

S_{as} = Share of amount-specific excise taxes (or equivalent) on the price of a pack of cigarettes;

S_{av} = Share of ad valorem excise taxes (or equivalent) on the price of a pack of cigarettes;

S_{id} = Share of import duties on the price of a pack of cigarettes (if the most popular brand is imported);

S_{VAT} = Share of the value added tax on the price of a pack of cigarettes.

Calculating S_{as} is fairly straightforward and involves dividing the specific tax amount for a 20-cigarette pack by the total price. Unlike S_{as}, the share of ad valorem taxes, S_{av} is much more difficult to calculate and involves making some assumptions described below. Import duties are sometimes amount-specific, sometimes value-based. S_{id} is therefore calculated the same way as S_{av} if it is amount-specific and the same way as S_{av} if it is value-based. VAT rates reported for countries are usually applied on the VAT-exclusive retail sale price but are also sometimes reported on VAT-inclusive prices. S_{VAT} is calculated to consistently reflect the share of the VAT in VAT-inclusive retail sale price.

The price of a pack of cigarettes can be expressed as the following:[1]

$$P = [(M + M \times ID) + (M + M \times ID) \times T_{av}\% + T_{as} + \pi] \times (1 + VAT\%)$$

$$P = [M \times (1 \times ID) \times (1 + T_{av}\%) + T_{as} + \pi] \times (1 + VAT\%) \quad ②$$

Where:

P = Price per pack of 20 cigarettes of the most popular brand consumed locally;

M = Manufacturer's/distributor's price, or import price if the brand is imported;

ID = Total import duties (where applicable) on a pack of 20 cigarettes[2];

T_{av} = Statutory rate of ad valorem tax;

T_{as} = Amount-specific excise tax on a pack of 20 cigarettes;

π = Retailer's, wholesaler's and importer's profit margins (sometimes expressed as a mark-up);

VAT = Statutory rate of value added tax.

Changes to this formula were made based on country-specific considerations such as the base for the ad valorem tax and excise tax, the existence or not of ad valorem and specific excise taxes, and whether the most popular brand was locally produced or imported. In many cases (particularly in low- and middle-income countries) the base for ad valorem excise tax was the manufacturer's/distributor's price.

Given knowledge of price (*P*) and amount-specific excise tax (T_{as}), the share S_{as} is easy to recover ($=T_{as}/P$). The case of ad valorem taxes (and, where applicable, S_{id}) is more complicated because the base (M) needs to be recovered in order to calculate the amount of ad valorem tax. In most of the cases M was not known (unless specifically reported by the country), and therefore needed to be estimated.

Using equation (2), it is possible to recover M:

$$M = \frac{\frac{P}{1 + VAT\%} - \pi - T_{as}}{(1 + T_{av}\%) \times (1 + ID)} \quad ③$$

π, or wholesalers' and retailers' profit margins are rarely publicly disclosed and will vary from country to country. For domestically produced most-popular brands, we considered π to be nil (i.e. =0) in the calculation of M because the retailer's and wholesaler's margins are assumed to be small. Setting the margin to 0, however, would result in an overestimation of M and therefore of the base for the ad valorem tax. This will in turn result in an overestimation of the amount of ad valorem tax. Since the goal of this exercise is to measure how high the share of tobacco taxes is in the price of a typical pack of cigarettes, assuming that the retailer's/wholesaler's profit (π) is nil, therefore, does not penalize countries by underestimating their ad valorem taxes. In light of this it was decided that unless and until country-specific information was made available to WHO, the retailer's wholesalers' margin would be assumed to be nil for the domestically produced brands.

For those countries where the most popular brand is imported, assuming π to be nil would grossly overestimate the base for the ad valorem tax because the importer's profit needs to be taken into account. The import duty is applied on CIF values, and the consequent excise taxes are usually applied on import duty inclusive CIF values. The importer's profit or own price is added on tax inclusive CIF value. For domestically produced cigarettes, the producer's price includes its own profit so it is automatically included in M but this is not the case for imported products where the tax is imposed on the import duty inclusive of CIF value but excluding the importer's profit. So calculating M as in equation (3) would imply assuming importer's profit to be zero.

The importer's profit is assumed to be relatively significant and ignoring it would therefore substantially overestimate M. For this reason, M had to be estimated differently for imported products: M^* (or the CIF value) was calculated either based on information reported by countries or using secondary sources (data from the United Nations Comtrade database). M^* was normally calculated as the import price of cigarettes in a country (value of imports divided by the quantity of imports for the importing country). However, in exceptional cases where no such data were available (Angola, Guyana and Niue), the export price was considered instead (in that case, the CIF value was approximated as the export price plus an additional 10 US cents).[3] The ad valorem and other taxes were then calculated in the same way as for local cigarettes, using M^* rather than M as the base, where applicable.

In the case of VAT, in most of the cases the base was P excluding the VAT (or, similarly, the manufacturer's/distributor's price plus all excise taxes). In other words:

$$S_{VAT} = VAT\% \times (P - S_{VAT}), \text{ equivalent to} \quad ④$$
$$S_{VAT} = VAT\% \div (1 + VAT\%)$$

So in sum, the tax rates are calculated this way:

$$S_{ts} = S_{id} + S_{as} + S_{av} + S_{VAT} \quad ⑤$$

$$S_{as} = T_{as} \div P$$

$$S_{av} = (T_{av}\% \times M) \div P$$
or
$$(T_{av}\% \times M^* \times (1 + S_{id})) \div P$$
if the most popular brand was imported

$$S_{id} = (T_{ID}\% \times M^*) \div P$$
(if the import duty is value-based)
or
$$ID \div P$$
(if it is specific)

$$S_{VAT} = VAT\% \div (1 + VAT\%)$$

4. Prices

Primary collection of price data in this and previous reports involved surveying retail outlets. Two aspects that emerged in the 2010 round of field data collection informed the current round of data collection:

- Different brands were sometimes reported between 2008 and 2010 making price comparability difficult across time.
- Lower prices were sometimes reported in 2010 compared to 2008 (despite no change in taxes or other major economic events). The concern in such instances was that prices in the two years were being collected from different retail shops in countries where prices vary by type of retail outlet.

To improve comparability of 2008 and 2010 data, the data cleaning process necessitated particular assumptions (further details can be found in Technical note III of the *WHO Report on the Global Tobacco Epidemic, 2011*).

For the 2012 round of data collection, a more comprehensive approach was used to actively reduce primary data collection errors and improve the ability to validate price data:

- In addition to the most sold brand reported in previous years, prices of two additional popular brands were requested.[4]
- For each brand, prices were required from three different types of retail outlets.

Questionnaires sent to data collectors were pre-populated with the names of the three highest selling brands in each country. The three popular brands were identified using data bought from Euromonitor[5] and the Tobacco Merchants Association (TMA),[6] which provide brand market shares for more than 80 countries. For 10 additional countries, information was collected by WHO through its close collaboration with ministries of finance. For the countries where such data were not available, the questionnaire was pre-filled with the brand reported in previous years as the most sold brand and data collectors were asked to provide the price of two other popular brands.

Where brand market shares were available, calculations of average prices and taxes were also done (details in Section 6 below).

The information collected from the additional prices helped address the problem of price consistency over time in two ways:

- The brand market share information collected helped confirm for at least 90 countries that the most sold brand reported actually did represent the highest share of cigarettes sold on the market. In the few cases where we discovered that the brand reported in 2008 and 2010 was not the most sold brand, the brand was changed for all years and price and corresponding tax information was corrected (e.g. for Mongolia and Nepal).
- Collection of one brand from three different types of shops helped identify countries where prices tend to vary by retail location. This helped data analysts identify from where the price was collected in previous years. Generally, prices were chosen from the type 2 retail shop as defined below.

The three types of retail shops were defined as follows:

1. Supermarket/hypermarket: chain or independent retail outlets with a selling space of over 2500 square metres and a primary focus on selling food/beverages/tobacco and other groceries. Hypermarkets also sell a range of non-grocery merchandise.
2. Kiosk/newsagent/tobacconist/independent food store: small convenience stores, retail outlets selling predominantly food, beverages and tobacco or a combination of these (e.g. kiosk, newsagent or tobacconist) or a wide range of predominantly grocery products (independent food stores or independent small grocers).
3. Street vendors: sell goods in small amounts to consumers but not from a fixed location (not applicable to all countries).

Another change made for this year's exercise was the price used for the 27 countries of the European Union (EU). In the past, price and tax information was taken entirely from the EU's Taxation and Customs Union website.[7] The price used by the EU in the past to calculate tax rates was the most popular price category (MPPC), which was assumed to be similar to the most sold brand price category collected in this report. However, since 2011, the EU calculates and reports tax rates based on the Weighted Average Price (WAP) and therefore information on the MPPC was no longer readily available for a number of EU countries. Consequently, in order to be consistent with past years' estimates and to ensure comparability with other countries, WHO decided to collect first-hand prices of the most sold brand (based on brand market shares reported from secondary sources) to calculate the 2012 rates. Excise and VAT rates are still collected from the EU published tables. This means, however, that tax shares as computed and reported here will not necessarily be similar to the rates published by the EU. This is mainly due to the calculation of the specific excise tax rates as a percentage of the retail price, which will vary depending on the price used.

See details of the difference in price and tax share for the EU countries in the table on the left.

Comparisons of prices and total tax shares are computed from WHO's most sold brand (MSB) survey and EU weighted average price (WAP).

	Total tax share (% of retail price)		Retail price (20 cigarettes)		
Country	WHO Estimates	EU Reported rates	WHO reported MSB	EU reported WAP	Currency
Austria	74.23%	76.40%	4.50	3.95	EUR
Belgium	76.08%	76.86%	5.26	4.67	EUR
Bulgaria	83.58%	86.65%	4.60	4.30	BGN
Cyprus	75.86%	75.47%	3.75	3.82	EUR
Czech Republic	78.43%	77.69%	68.00	67.84	CZK
Denmark	79.33%	80.61%	40.00	39.14	DKK
Estonia	76.88%	84.38%	3.10	2.43	EUR
Finland	79.88%	80.70%	4.90	4.50	EUR
France	79.86%	80.60%	6.20	5.70	EUR
Germany	73.03%	75.91%	5.26	4.86	EUR
Greece	82.16%	83.70%	3.70	3.25	EUR
Hungary	83.66%	85.39%	757.89	718.48	HUF
Ireland	78.97%	82.78%	9.10	8.47	EUR
Italy	75.18%	75.88%	5.00	4.28	EUR
Latvia	79.14%	81.28%	1.80	1.67	LVL
Lithuania	75.30%	78.39%	8.50	7.77	LTL
Luxembourg	70.59%	70.12%	4.60	3.84	EUR
Malta	76.92%	77.49%	4.20	4.14	EUR
Netherlands	72.18%	78.45%	5.68	5.03	EUR
Poland	79.59%	84.28%	11.60	10.01	PLN
Portugal	76.02%	80.72%	4.20	3.73	EUR
Romania	73.25%	80.24%	13.50	11.19	RON
Slovakia	83.89%	82.52%	2.63	2.72	EUR
Slovenia	80.12%	79.60%	2.80	2.86	EUR
Spain	79.30%	80.35%	4.20	3.76	EUR
Sweden	73.83%	80.83%	53.00	46.80	SEK
UK	80.12%	84.82%	6.60	6.00	GBP

Note: WHO estimates pertain to most sold brand prices collected in July 2012. EU reported rates and weighted average prices pertain to data collected by the EU, also reported for July 2012.

5. Considerations in interpreting tax share changes

It is important to note that the change in the tax as a share of the price is not only dependent on tax changes but also on changes in the price. Therefore, despite an increase in tax, the tax share could remain the same or go down; similarly, sometimes a tax share can increase even if there is no change or even an increase in the tax.

In the current database, there are cases where taxes increased between 2010 and 2012 but the share of tax as a percentage of the price went down. This is mainly due to the fact that, in absolute terms, the price increase was larger than the tax increase (particularly in the case of specific excise tax increases). For example, in Nepal, the specific excise tax increased from 445 NPR per 1000 cigarettes in 2010 to 533 NPR per 1000 cigarettes in 2012 (a 20% increase) while the price of the most sold brand increased from 35 to 45 NPR per pack (a 29% increase). In terms of tax share, however, the excise represented 25.4% of the price in 2010 while it represented 23.7% of the price in 2012. This is because prices rose more than taxes.

On the other hand, there are cases where increases (decreases) in the tax as a share of the price occurred despite no change in the tax. In the current database, this was attributable to one of the following reasons:

- In some instances, price increased independently of tax change (leading to a decrease in the tax share).
- In the case of imported products, the CIF value had to be estimated using secondary data, as explained above. The CIF values were provided in US$ and converted to local currency, an exercise which introduced other external factors that also had an impact on the calculations of taxes as a percentage of the retail price (for either of the following reasons or a combination of the two).
  - CIF value in US$ decreased (increased) between 2010 and 2012, making the base for the application of the tax lower (higher), therefore leading to a lower (higher) tax percentage despite no change in the tax rate.
  - The exchange rate decreased (increased) between 2010 and 2012, leading to a lower (higher) CIF value in the local currency, leading also to a smaller (larger) base for the application of the tax and also leading to a lower (higher) tax percentage.

Finally, when new, improved information was provided in terms of taxation and prices for some countries, corrections were made in the calculations of tax rates for 2008 and 2010 estimates, as needed.

6. New estimates: average price and tax estimates (see table 9.2 in Appendix IX)

Data on the most sold brand prices tend to be more readily available across countries; this underlies the decision to use the most sold brand in successive editions of the GTCR. However, an estimation of tax share that best reflects the tax burden within a market would ideally be based on the average price and taxes levied on all brands sold in that market.

This year, in addition to collecting and reporting most sold brand prices and tax shares, WHO attempted to get at country-level average estimates of the tax share based on an estimate of the average price of a pack of cigarettes. Average calculations were made for a total of 101 countries. This exercise was more complex due to the additional data required:

- Three popular brands were used for the average estimate of the price.
- For each of the three brands identified, a price was collected from three different types of outlet stores (see definition of the types of outlets in Section 4 above).

Data sources:

1. As stated earlier, the three popular brands were identified, and wherever possible, questionnaires were pre-populated using secondary sources. The main source was Euromonitor but this was supplemented by data from TMA and WHO's internal data.
2. The prices of the three brands from the three different types of retail outlets were collected by WHO through regional and country data collectors (nine prices in total for each country).
3. Brand market share weights used to calculate the average were taken from the same sources as noted in point 1.
4. Euromonitor provides information on the distribution of cigarettes in 26 different types of outlets. We selected 10 of these types, and consolidated them into three groups as defined in Section 4 above. In the few countries where brand market shares were available but the shares of cigarette sales by type of distribution outlet were not available, an approximation was made using the retail distribution of a country with similar attributes (e.g. region, types of products consumed, belonging to the same economic bloc, etc.).

Calculation:

1. Average price:

   First, averages were calculated for each brand weighted by the outlet distribution. In many cases, the outlet share data collected and categorized in the three broad groups did not add up to 100%, reflecting the fact that there are other retail outlet types. So, based on their proportional weight, they were first re-normalized to total 100%. When prices were the same across different stores for any brand in any particular country, equal weights (33.33%) were assigned to all three types of stores. The retail outlet distribution weights were then used to calculate the average price for each brand.

Or:

$$SSj = \frac{ss_j}{\Sigma_{j=1}^{3} ss_j} * 100\% \quad ⑥$$

$$APi = \Sigma_{j=1}^{3} Pij * SSj \quad ⑦$$

Where,

SSj = Estimated outlet share of store type (j) for brand (i) where ∀j = 1,2,3

ssj = Reported or estimated outlet share of store type (j) for brand (i) where ∀ = 1,2,3

Pij = Reported price of brand (i) in store type (j)

APi = Estimated average price of brand (i) where ∀i = 1,2,3

Once the average prices are obtained for each brand, they are multiplied by the brand-specific market share to get the overall average price of cigarettes in the country. It is understood that in most countries more than three brands are consumed, but because of difficulty in collecting prices for all brands, the three most sold brands were identified to calculate the average price. In some countries two to three brands can capture more than 90% of the market consumption, but in countries such as China, the three most popular brands represent less than 20% of the market share. However, the three brands covered more than 50% of the total market in 63 of the 101 countries covered. In all cases, the brand market shares of the three most popular brands were re-normalized to add up to 100% based on their proportional weight.

$$BSi = \frac{bs_i}{\Sigma_{j=1}^{3} bs_i} * 100\% \quad ⑧$$

$$AP = \Sigma_{i=1}^{3} APi * BSi \quad ⑨$$

Where,

BSi = Estimated market share of brand (i)

bs_i = Reported or estimated market share of brand (i) where ∀i=1,2,3

AP = Estimated average price of a cigarette pack in the country

2. Average tax share

The average tax share was calculated in two steps. First, the tax share of each brand was calculated separately. This helps account for specificities of each brand (e.g. if a different tax rate applies to different brands or if the brand is imported or not). The price used for each brand was the price weighted by the retail outlet distribution. The method used to calculate the tax share of each brand was the same as for the most sold brand. Then, the overall tax share in any country was obtained by taking the average of the three brands' tax shares. The average tax share was weighted by each brand's market share.

$$etax_{i,n} = \phi\ (tax_{i,n}, APi) \quad ⑩$$

$$ATi = \sum_{n=1}^{5} etax_{i,n} \quad ⑪$$

$$AT = \sum_{i=1}^{3} Ati * BSi \quad ⑫$$

Where,

$tax_{i,n}$ = Reported tax data by type of tax (n) for brand (i), where ∀n = 1, ..., 5 and ∀i = 1,2,3 The 5 types of tax (n=1,..., 5) are: specific excise, ad valorem excise, import duty, value added or sales tax, and other taxes.

$etax_{i,n}$ = Estimated total rate of type n for brand (i); a function of average price APi

ATi = Estimated average total share of brand (i)

AT = Overall average tax share estimated for any particular country.

APi and BSi defined in formulas (7) and (8) above.

Differences in tax share levels between average prices and most sold brand prices did not vary greatly, ranging between 0% and 10% for the vast majority of the countries covered.

1 This formula applies when the ad valorem tax is applied on the manufacturer's/distributor's price, the import duty is applied on the manufacturer's/distributor's price or the CIF value and the VAT is applied on the VAT-exclusive retail price. Other scenarios exist (e.g. ad valorem rate applies on the retail price) but they are not described here because they are usually more straightforward to calculate.

2 Import duties may vary depending on the country of origin in cases of preferential trade agreements. WHO tried to determine the origin of the pack and relevance of using such rates where possible.

3 In previous years, when CIF value was not available through secondary sources, the export price (plus 10 US cents) was used instead. This is the first year that data were collected directly from countries to estimate the CIF value. Data were reported for many countries in Africa and the values reported have shown that in many instances (particularly in West Africa) the CIF value was much lower than the export price, which in theory does not make sense (usually the CIF is equal to the export price plus insurance and transport costs). This could be due to tax evasion where importers report a lower value at port of entry to reduce their tax liability. The estimated CIF values were therefore corrected for 2010 and 2008 to concur with the lower values reported in 2012, therefore reducing the tax share for some countries in Africa, sometimes substantially.

4 The brands are used for internal purposes for data validation and are not published in the report.

5 Euromonitor International's Passport, 2012.

6 The Tobacco Merchants Association (TMA), 2012.

7 See http://ec.europa.eu/taxation_customs/taxation/excise_duties/tobacco_products/rates/index_en.htm.

APPENDIX I: **REGIONAL SUMMARY OF MPOWER MEASURES**

Appendix I provides an overview of selected tobacco control policies. For each WHO region an overview table is presented that includes information on monitoring and prevalence, smoke-free environments, treatment of tobacco dependence, health warnings and packaging, advertising, promotion and sponsorship bans, and taxation levels, based on the methodology outlined in Technical Note I.

Country-level data were often but not always provided with supporting documents such as laws, regulations, policy documents, etc. Available documents were assessed by WHO and this appendix provides summary measures or indicators of country achievements for each of the six MPOWER measures. It is important to note that data for the report are based on existing legislation and reflect the status of adopted but not necessarily implemented legislation, as long as the law clearly indicates a date of entry into force and is not undergoing a legal challenge. The summary measures developed for the *WHO Report on the Global Tobacco Epidemic, 2013* are the same as those used for the 2011 report, except for the indicator on anti-tobacco mass media campaigns, which was slightly improved. The methodology used to calculate each indicator is described in Technical Note I. This review, however, does not constitute a thorough and complete legal analysis of each country's legislation. Except for smoke-free environments and bans on tobacco advertising, promotion and sponsorship, data were collected at the national/federal level only and, therefore, provide incomplete policy coverage for Member States where subnational governments play an active role in tobacco control.

Daily smoking prevalence for the population aged 15 and over in 2011 is an indicator estimated by WHO from tobacco use surveys published by Member States. Tobacco smoking is one of the most widely reported indicators in country surveys. The calculation of WHO estimates to allow international comparison is described in Technical Note II.

Africa

Table 1.1.1
Summary of MPOWER measures

... Data not reported/not available.

– Data not required/not applicable.

2012 INDICATOR AND COMPLIANCE

<table>
<tr><th rowspan="2">COUNTRY</th><th rowspan="2">ADULT DAILY SMOKING PREVALENCE (2011)</th><th rowspan="2">M MONITORING</th><th>P SMOKE-FREE POLICIES</th><th rowspan="2">O CESSATION PROGRAMMES</th><th colspan="2">W WARNINGS</th><th>E ADVERTISING BANS</th><th rowspan="2">R TAXATION</th></tr>
<tr><th>LINES REPRESENT LEVEL OF COMPLIANCE</th><th>HEALTH WARNINGS</th><th>MASS MEDIA</th><th>LINES REPRESENT LEVEL OF COMPLIANCE</th></tr>
<tr><td>Algeria</td><td>...</td><td></td><td>|</td><td></td><td></td><td></td><td>|||||||</td><td>55%</td></tr>
<tr><td>Angola</td><td>...</td><td></td><td>–</td><td></td><td></td><td></td><td>–</td><td>16%</td></tr>
<tr><td>Benin</td><td>9%</td><td></td><td>|||</td><td></td><td></td><td></td><td>||||||</td><td>13%</td></tr>
<tr><td>Botswana</td><td>17%</td><td></td><td>–</td><td></td><td></td><td></td><td>|||||</td><td>52%</td></tr>
<tr><td>Burkina Faso</td><td>...</td><td></td><td></td><td></td><td></td><td></td><td>||||||</td><td>25%</td></tr>
<tr><td>Burundi</td><td>...</td><td></td><td>–</td><td></td><td></td><td></td><td>–</td><td>54%</td></tr>
<tr><td>Cameroon</td><td>...</td><td></td><td>|||||</td><td></td><td></td><td></td><td>|||||||</td><td>19%</td></tr>
<tr><td>Cape Verde</td><td>6%</td><td></td><td>|||</td><td></td><td></td><td></td><td>...</td><td>28%</td></tr>
<tr><td>Central African Republic</td><td>...</td><td></td><td>–</td><td></td><td></td><td></td><td>–</td><td>...</td></tr>
<tr><td>Chad</td><td>10%</td><td></td><td>...</td><td></td><td></td><td></td><td>...</td><td>25%</td></tr>
<tr><td>Comoros</td><td>10%</td><td></td><td>|||||</td><td></td><td></td><td></td><td>|||||||</td><td>30%</td></tr>
<tr><td>Congo</td><td>4%</td><td></td><td>–</td><td></td><td></td><td></td><td>|||||||||</td><td>32%</td></tr>
<tr><td>Côte d'Ivoire</td><td>...</td><td></td><td>||||||</td><td></td><td></td><td></td><td>–</td><td>44%</td></tr>
<tr><td>Democratic Republic of the Congo</td><td>8%</td><td></td><td></td><td></td><td></td><td></td><td>||||||</td><td>39%</td></tr>
<tr><td>Equatorial Guinea</td><td>...</td><td></td><td>...</td><td></td><td></td><td></td><td>–</td><td>34%</td></tr>
<tr><td>Eritrea</td><td>4%</td><td></td><td>–</td><td></td><td></td><td></td><td>||||||||</td><td>55%</td></tr>
<tr><td>Ethiopia</td><td>...</td><td></td><td>–</td><td></td><td></td><td></td><td>–</td><td>50%</td></tr>
<tr><td>Gabon</td><td>9%</td><td></td><td>–</td><td></td><td></td><td></td><td>–</td><td>35%</td></tr>
<tr><td>Gambia</td><td>15%</td><td></td><td>–</td><td></td><td></td><td></td><td>|||||||</td><td>35%</td></tr>
<tr><td>Ghana</td><td>8%</td><td></td><td>–</td><td></td><td></td><td></td><td>–</td><td>23%</td></tr>
<tr><td>Guinea</td><td>11%</td><td></td><td>||||</td><td></td><td></td><td></td><td>|||</td><td>37%</td></tr>
<tr><td>Guinea-Bissau</td><td>...</td><td></td><td>–</td><td></td><td></td><td></td><td>–</td><td>17%</td></tr>
<tr><td>Kenya</td><td>10%</td><td></td><td>–</td><td></td><td></td><td></td><td>|||||||</td><td>49%</td></tr>
<tr><td>Lesotho</td><td>...</td><td></td><td>||||||</td><td></td><td></td><td></td><td>–</td><td>45%</td></tr>
<tr><td>Liberia</td><td>9%</td><td></td><td>...</td><td></td><td></td><td></td><td>–</td><td>13%</td></tr>
<tr><td>Madagascar</td><td>...</td><td></td><td>|||</td><td></td><td></td><td></td><td>|||||||||</td><td>76%</td></tr>
<tr><td>Malawi</td><td>11%</td><td></td><td>–</td><td></td><td></td><td></td><td>–</td><td>35%</td></tr>
<tr><td>Mali</td><td>14%</td><td></td><td>–</td><td></td><td></td><td></td><td>||||||||</td><td>22%</td></tr>
<tr><td>Mauritania</td><td>15%</td><td></td><td>...</td><td></td><td></td><td></td><td>–</td><td>15%</td></tr>
<tr><td>Mauritius</td><td>18%</td><td></td><td>|||||</td><td></td><td></td><td></td><td>|||||||||</td><td>73%</td></tr>
<tr><td>Mozambique</td><td>...</td><td></td><td>|||||</td><td></td><td></td><td></td><td>|||||</td><td>24%</td></tr>
<tr><td>Namibia</td><td>15%</td><td></td><td>||</td><td></td><td></td><td></td><td>||||||||||</td><td>48%</td></tr>
<tr><td>Niger</td><td>3%</td><td></td><td>|</td><td></td><td></td><td></td><td>||||||||</td><td>31%</td></tr>
<tr><td>Nigeria</td><td>4%</td><td></td><td>|||||</td><td></td><td></td><td></td><td>–</td><td>21%</td></tr>
<tr><td>Rwanda</td><td>...</td><td></td><td>–</td><td></td><td></td><td></td><td>–</td><td>66%</td></tr>
<tr><td>Sao Tome and Principe</td><td>4%</td><td></td><td>–</td><td></td><td></td><td></td><td>–</td><td>12%</td></tr>
<tr><td>Senegal</td><td>7%</td><td></td><td>|||</td><td></td><td></td><td></td><td>|||</td><td>30%</td></tr>
<tr><td>Seychelles</td><td>17%</td><td></td><td>|||||||||</td><td></td><td></td><td></td><td>||||||||||</td><td>67%</td></tr>
<tr><td>Sierra Leone</td><td>31%</td><td></td><td>–</td><td></td><td></td><td></td><td>–</td><td>20%</td></tr>
<tr><td>South Africa</td><td>14%</td><td></td><td>–</td><td></td><td></td><td></td><td>||||||||</td><td>46%</td></tr>
<tr><td>Swaziland</td><td>6%</td><td></td><td>–</td><td></td><td></td><td></td><td>–</td><td>...</td></tr>
<tr><td>Togo</td><td>6%</td><td></td><td>|||</td><td></td><td></td><td></td><td>... ⊙</td><td>12%</td></tr>
<tr><td>Uganda</td><td>7%</td><td></td><td>|||||| ☆</td><td></td><td></td><td></td><td>–</td><td>40%</td></tr>
<tr><td>United Republic of Tanzania</td><td>...</td><td></td><td>–</td><td></td><td></td><td></td><td></td><td>28%</td></tr>
<tr><td>Zambia</td><td>11%</td><td></td><td>|||</td><td></td><td></td><td></td><td>–</td><td>28%</td></tr>
<tr><td>Zimbabwe</td><td>12%</td><td></td><td>||||||||</td><td></td><td></td><td></td><td>–</td><td>58%</td></tr>
</table>

mpower

CHANGE SINCE 2010

Row	P SMOKE-FREE POLICIES	O CESSATION PROGRAMMES	W HEALTH WARNINGS	E ADVERTISING BANS	R TAXATION
	CHANGE IN POWER INDICATOR GROUP, UP OR DOWN, SINCE 2010				
1					
2					▲
3					
4					▲
5			▲		
6					
7	▲				
8					
9					▼
10		▲			
11				▼	
12	▲		▲		
13					
14					
15					
16					
17		▲		▲	
18					▲
19					▼
20		▲	▲	▲	
21			▲	▲	
22		▲			
23		▲			▼
24					
25					
26			▲		
27					▲
28			▲	▼	
29					
30					
31					▼
32		▲			
33			▲		
34					
35					
36					
37					
38			▲		
39					
40					▼
41					▼
42				▲	
43					
44					
45					
46					

ADULT DAILY SMOKING PREVALENCE*: AGE-STANDARDIZED PREVALENCE RATES FOR ADULT DAILY SMOKERS OF TOBACCO (BOTH SEXES COMBINED), 2011

Colour	Category
. . .	Estimates not available
(grey)	30% or more
(light purple)	From 20% to 29.9%
(blue)	From 15% to 19.9%
(dark navy)	Less than 15%

* The figures should be used strictly for the purpose of drawing comparisons across countries and must not be used to estimate absolute number of daily tobacco smokers in a country.

MONITORING: PREVALENCE DATA

Colour	Category
(white)	No known data or no recent data or data that are not both recent and representative
(light brown)	Recent and representative data for either adults or youth
(brown)	Recent and representative data for both adults and youth
(dark red)	Recent, representative and periodic data for both adults and youth

SMOKE-FREE POLICIES: POLICIES ON SMOKE-FREE ENVIRONMENTS

Colour	Category
(white)	Data not reported/not categorized
(grey)	Up to two public places completely smoke-free
(light purple)	Three to five public places completely smoke-free
(blue)	Six to seven public places completely smoke-free
(dark navy)	All public places completely smoke-free (or at least 90% of the population covered by complete subnational smoke-free legislation)

CESSATION PROGRAMMES: TREATMENT OF TOBACCO DEPENDENCE

Colour	Category
(white)	Data not reported
(grey)	None
(light purple)	NRT and/or some cessation services (neither cost-covered)
(blue)	NRT and/or some cessation services (at least one of which is cost-covered)
(dark navy)	National quit line, and both NRT and some cessation services cost-covered

HEALTH WARNINGS: HEALTH WARNINGS ON CIGARETTE PACKAGES

Colour	Category
(white)	Data not reported
(grey)	No warnings or small warnings
(light purple)	Medium size warnings missing some appropriate characteristics OR large warnings missing many appropriate characteristics
(blue)	Medium size warnings with all appropriate characteristics OR large warnings missing some appropriate characteristics
(dark navy)	Large warnings with all appropriate characteristics

MASS MEDIA: ANTI-TOBACCO CAMPAIGNS

Colour	Category
(white)	Data not reported
(grey)	No national campaign conducted between January 2011 and June 2012 with duration of at least three weeks
(light purple)	National campaign conducted with 1–4 appropriate characteristics
(blue)	National campaign conducted with 5–6 appropriate characteristics, or with 7 characteristics excluding airing on television and/or radio
(dark navy)	National campaign conducted with at least seven appropriate characteristics including airing on television and/or radio

ADVERTISING BANS: BANS ON ADVERTISING, PROMOTION AND SPONSORSHIP

Colour	Category
(white)	Data not reported
(grey)	Complete absence of ban, or ban that does not cover national television, radio and print media
(light purple)	Ban on national television, radio and print media only
(blue)	Ban on national television, radio and print media as well as on some but not all other forms of direct and/or indirect advertising
(dark navy)	Ban on all forms of direct and indirect advertising

TAXATION: SHARE OF TOTAL TAXES IN THE RETAIL PRICE OF THE MOST WIDELY SOLD BRAND OF CIGARETTES

Colour	Category
(white)	Data not reported
(grey)	≤ 25% of retail price is tax
(light purple)	26–50% of retail price is tax
(blue)	51–75% of retail price is tax
(dark navy)	>75% of retail price is tax

COMPLIANCE: COMPLIANCE WITH BANS ON ADVERTISING, PROMOTION AND SPONSORSHIP, AND ADHERENCE TO SMOKE-FREE POLICY

Symbol	Category
||||||||||	Complete compliance (8/10 to 10/10)
|||||||	Moderate compliance (3/10 to 7/10)
||	Minimal compliance (0/10 to 2/10)

SYMBOLS LEGEND

☆	Separate, completely enclosed smoking rooms are allowed if they are separately ventilated to the outside and/or kept under negative air pressure in relation to the surrounding areas. Given the difficulty of meeting the very strict requirements delineated for such rooms, they appear to be a practical impossibility but no reliable empirical evidence is presently available to ascertain whether they have been constructed.
⊙	Policy adopted but not implemented by 31 December 2012.
»	Data not substantiated by a copy of the legislation.
▲▼	Change in POWER indicator group, up or down, between 2010 and 2012. Some 2010 data were revised in 2012. 2012 grouping rules were applied to both years.

Refer to Technical Note I for definitions of categories

The Americas

Table 1.1.2
Summary of MPOWER measures

. . . Data not reported/not available.
– Data not required/not applicable.

2012 INDICATOR AND COMPLIANCE

COUNTRY	ADULT DAILY SMOKING PREVALENCE (2011)	M MONITORING	P SMOKE-FREE POLICIES (LINES REPRESENT LEVEL OF COMPLIANCE)	O CESSATION PROGRAMMES	W WARNINGS: HEALTH WARNINGS	W WARNINGS: MASS MEDIA	E ADVERTISING BANS (LINES REPRESENT LEVEL OF COMPLIANCE)	R TAXATION
Antigua and Barbuda	. . .		ǀǀǀǀǀǀǀ				–	7%
Argentina	17%		ǀǀǀǀǀ				ǀǀǀǀǀǀǀ	68%
Bahamas	. . .		–				. . .	38%
Barbados	5%		. . .				–	49%
Belize	4%		–				–	21%
Bolivia (Plurinational State of)	5%						ǀǀǀǀ	42%
Brazil	15%		ǀǀǀǀǀǀǀǀ ⊙				ǀǀǀǀǀǀ	63%
Canada	13%		ǀǀǀǀǀǀǀǀǀǀ				ǀǀǀǀǀǀǀǀǀǀ	64%
Chile	27%		ǀǀǀǀǀ				ǀǀǀǀǀǀ	81%
Colombia	14%		. . .				. . .	44%
Costa Rica	6%		ǀǀǀǀǀǀǀǀ				ǀǀǀǀǀǀǀǀǀǀ	72%
Cuba	. . .		ǀǀǀǀ				–	75%
Dominica	5%		–				–	23%
Dominican Republic	14%						–	59%
Ecuador	. . .		ǀǀǀǀǀǀǀǀ				ǀǀǀǀǀǀǀǀǀ	73%
El Salvador	5%		–				. . .	52%
Grenada	. . .		–				–	. . .
Guatemala	3%		. . .				. . .	49%
Guyana	10%		ǀǀǀǀǀ				–	30%
Haiti	. . .		–				–	. . .
Honduras	. . .		ǀǀǀǀǀǀǀ				ǀǀǀǀǀǀǀǀ	34%
Jamaica	. . .		–				ǀǀǀǀǀǀǀǀǀǀ	46%
Mexico	7%		ǀǀǀǀǀ ☆				ǀǀǀǀǀ	67%
Nicaragua	. . .		. . .				. . .	29%
Panama	5%		ǀǀǀǀǀǀǀǀ				ǀǀǀǀǀǀǀǀǀ	57%
Paraguay	13%		. . .				–	17%
Peru	. . .		ǀǀǀǀǀǀǀǀ				ǀǀǀǀǀ	42%
Saint Kitts and Nevis	5%		–				–	20%
Saint Lucia	. . .		–				–	20%
Saint Vincent and the Grenadines	. . .		–				–	15%
Suriname	. . .		–				–	61%
Trinidad and Tobago	. . .		ǀǀǀǀǀǀǀǀ				ǀǀǀǀǀǀǀǀ	33%
United States of America	. . .		. . .				. . .	43%
Uruguay	20%		ǀǀǀǀǀǀǀǀǀǀ				ǀǀǀǀǀǀǀǀǀǀ	69%
Venezuela (Bolivarian Republic of)	. . .		ǀǀǀǀǀǀǀǀǀǀ				ǀǀǀǀǀǀǀǀǀǀ	71%

mpower

CHANGE SINCE 2010

P SMOKE-FREE POLICIES	O CESSATION PROGRAMMES	W HEALTH WARNINGS	E ADVERTISING BANS	R TAXATION
CHANGE IN POWER INDICATOR GROUP, UP OR DOWN, SINCE 2010				
▲		▲	▲	
	▲			
	▲			
	▲			
▲			▲	
		▲		
▲		▲	▲	
				▲
				▼
▲		▲	▲	
▼	▲	▲	▲	
				▼
				▼
	▲			
				▼
				▼
	▲			
▲				

ADULT DAILY SMOKING PREVALENCE*: AGE-STANDARDIZED PREVALENCE RATES FOR ADULT DAILY SMOKERS OF TOBACCO (BOTH SEXES COMBINED), 2011

. . .	Estimates not available
	30% or more
	From 20% to 29.9%
	From 15% to 19.9%
	Less than 15%

* The figures should be used strictly for the purpose of drawing comparisons across countries and must not be used to estimate absolute number of daily tobacco smokers in a country.

MONITORING: PREVALENCE DATA

	No known data or no recent data or data that are not both recent and representative
	Recent and representative data for either adults or youth
	Recent and representative data for both adults and youth
	Recent, representative and periodic data for both adults and youth

SMOKE-FREE POLICIES: POLICIES ON SMOKE-FREE ENVIRONMENTS

	Data not reported/not categorized
	Up to two public places completely smoke-free
	Three to five public places completely smoke-free
	Six to seven public places completely smoke-free
	All public places completely smoke-free (or at least 90% of the population covered by complete subnational smoke-free legislation)

CESSATION PROGRAMMES: TREATMENT OF TOBACCO DEPENDENCE

	Data not reported
	None
	NRT and/or some cessation services (neither cost-covered)
	NRT and/or some cessation services (at least one of which is cost-covered)
	National quit line, and both NRT and some cessation services cost-covered

HEALTH WARNINGS: HEALTH WARNINGS ON CIGARETTE PACKAGES

	Data not reported
	No warnings or small warnings
	Medium size warnings missing some appropriate characteristics OR large warnings missing many appropriate characteristics
	Medium size warnings with all appropriate characteristics OR large warnings missing some appropriate characteristics
	Large warnings with all appropriate characteristics

MASS MEDIA: ANTI-TOBACCO CAMPAIGNS

	Data not reported
	No national campaign conducted between January 2011 and June 2012 with duration of at least three weeks
	National campaign conducted with 1–4 appropriate characteristics
	National campaign conducted with 5–6 appropriate characteristics, or with 7 characteristics excluding airing on television and/or radio
	National campaign conducted with at least seven appropriate characteristics including airing on television and/or radio

ADVERTISING BANS: BANS ON ADVERTISING, PROMOTION AND SPONSORSHIP

	Data not reported
	Complete absence of ban, or ban that does not cover national television, radio and print media
	Ban on national television, radio and print media only
	Ban on national television, radio and print media as well as on some but not all other forms of direct and/or indirect advertising
	Ban on all forms of direct and indirect advertising

TAXATION: SHARE OF TOTAL TAXES IN THE RETAIL PRICE OF THE MOST WIDELY SOLD BRAND OF CIGARETTES

	Data not reported
	≤ 25% of retail price is tax
	26–50% of retail price is tax
	51–75% of retail price is tax
	>75% of retail price is tax

COMPLIANCE: COMPLIANCE WITH BANS ON ADVERTISING, PROMOTION AND SPONSORSHIP, AND ADHERENCE TO SMOKE-FREE POLICY

‖‖‖‖	Complete compliance (8/10 to 10/10)
‖‖‖	Moderate compliance (3/10 to 7/10)
‖	Minimal compliance (0/10 to 2/10)

SYMBOLS LEGEND

☆	Separate, completely enclosed smoking rooms are allowed if they are separately ventilated to the outside and/or kept under negative air pressure in relation to the surrounding areas. Given the difficulty of meeting the very strict requirements delineated for such rooms, they appear to be a practical impossibility but no reliable empirical evidence is presently available to ascertain whether they have been constructed.
⊙	Policy adopted but not implemented by 31 December 2012.
▲▼	Change in POWER indicator group, up or down, between 2010 and 2012. Some 2010 data were revised in 2012. 2012 grouping rules were applied to both years.

Refer to Technical Note I for definitions of categories

South-East Asia

Table 1.1.3
Summary of MPOWER measures

. . . Data not reported/not available.

– Data not required/not applicable.

2012 INDICATOR AND COMPLIANCE

<table>
<tr><th rowspan="2">COUNTRY</th><th rowspan="2">ADULT DAILY SMOKING PREVALENCE (2011)</th><th rowspan="2">M
MONITORING</th><th>P
SMOKE-FREE POLICIES</th><th rowspan="2">O
CESSATION PROGRAMMES</th><th colspan="2">W
WARNINGS</th><th>E
ADVERTISING BANS</th><th rowspan="2">R
TAXATION</th></tr>
<tr><th>LINES REPRESENT LEVEL OF COMPLIANCE</th><th>HEALTH WARNINGS</th><th>MASS MEDIA</th><th>LINES REPRESENT LEVEL OF COMPLIANCE</th></tr>
<tr><td>Bangladesh</td><td>23%</td><td></td><td>|||</td><td></td><td></td><td></td><td>||||||||</td><td>71%</td></tr>
<tr><td>Bhutan</td><td>11%</td><td></td><td>||||||||</td><td></td><td></td><td></td><td>||||||||</td><td>-</td></tr>
<tr><td>Democratic People's Republic of Korea</td><td>. . .</td><td></td><td>. . .</td><td></td><td></td><td></td><td>–</td><td>. . .</td></tr>
<tr><td>India</td><td>12%</td><td></td><td>||||| ☆</td><td></td><td></td><td></td><td>|||||</td><td>43%</td></tr>
<tr><td>Indonesia</td><td>29%</td><td></td><td>|||</td><td></td><td></td><td></td><td>. . .</td><td>51%</td></tr>
<tr><td>Maldives</td><td>21%</td><td></td><td>. . .</td><td></td><td></td><td></td><td>|||||</td><td>49%</td></tr>
<tr><td>Myanmar</td><td>17%</td><td></td><td>|||||</td><td></td><td></td><td></td><td>||||||</td><td>50%</td></tr>
<tr><td>Nepal</td><td>27%</td><td></td><td>||||||</td><td></td><td></td><td></td><td>||||||||</td><td>35%</td></tr>
<tr><td>Sri Lanka</td><td>12%</td><td></td><td>||||||||||</td><td></td><td></td><td></td><td>|||||||||</td><td>74%</td></tr>
<tr><td>Thailand</td><td>19%</td><td></td><td>|||||||</td><td></td><td></td><td></td><td>||||||</td><td>70%</td></tr>
<tr><td>Timor-Leste</td><td>. . .</td><td></td><td>|</td><td></td><td></td><td></td><td>–</td><td>35%</td></tr>
</table>

mpower

CHANGE SINCE 2010

P SMOKE-FREE POLICIES	O CESSATION PROGRAMMES	W HEALTH WARNINGS	E ADVERTISING BANS	R TAXATION
CHANGE IN POWER INDICATOR GROUP, UP OR DOWN, SINCE 2010				
	▲			
		▲		
				▲
▲		▲		
		▲		
	▲			
				▲

ADULT DAILY SMOKING PREVALENCE*: AGE-STANDARDIZED PREVALENCE RATES FOR ADULT DAILY SMOKERS OF TOBACCO (BOTH SEXES COMBINED), 2011

. . .	Estimates not available
	30% or more
	From 20% to 29.9%
	From 15% to 19.9%
	Less than 15%

* The figures should be used strictly for the purpose of drawing comparisons across countries and must not be used to estimate absolute number of daily tobacco smokers in a country.

MONITORING: PREVALENCE DATA

	No known data or no recent data or data that are not both recent and representative
	Recent and representative data for either adults or youth
	Recent and representative data for both adults and youth
	Recent, representative and periodic data for both adults and youth

SMOKE-FREE POLICIES: POLICIES ON SMOKE-FREE ENVIRONMENTS

	Data not reported/not categorized
	Up to two public places completely smoke-free
	Three to five public places completely smoke-free
	Six to seven public places completely smoke-free
	All public places completely smoke-free (or at least 90% of the population covered by complete subnational smoke-free legislation)

CESSATION PROGRAMMES: TREATMENT OF TOBACCO DEPENDENCE

	Data not reported
	None
	NRT and/or some cessation services (neither cost-covered)
	NRT and/or some cessation services (at least one of which is cost-covered)
	National quit line, and both NRT and some cessation services cost-covered

HEALTH WARNINGS: HEALTH WARNINGS ON CIGARETTE PACKAGES

	Data not reported
	No warnings or small warnings
	Medium size warnings missing some appropriate characteristics OR large warnings missing many appropriate characteristics
	Medium size warnings with all appropriate characteristics OR large warnings missing some appropriate characteristics
	Large warnings with all appropriate characteristics

MASS MEDIA: ANTI-TOBACCO CAMPAIGNS

	Data not reported
	No national campaign conducted between January 2011 and June 2012 with duration of at least three weeks
	National campaign conducted with 1–4 appropriate characteristics
	National campaign conducted with 5–6 appropriate characteristics, or with 7 characteristics excluding airing on television and/or radio
	National campaign conducted with at least seven appropriate characteristics including airing on television and/or radio

ADVERTISING BANS: BANS ON ADVERTISING, PROMOTION AND SPONSORSHIP

	Data not reported
	Complete absence of ban, or ban that does not cover national television, radio and print media
	Ban on national television, radio and print media only
	Ban on national television, radio and print media as well as on some but not all other forms of direct and/or indirect advertising
	Ban on all forms of direct and indirect advertising

TAXATION: SHARE OF TOTAL TAXES IN THE RETAIL PRICE OF THE MOST WIDELY SOLD BRAND OF CIGARETTES

	Data not reported
	≤ 25% of retail price is tax
	26–50% of retail price is tax
	51–75% of retail price is tax
	>75% of retail price is tax

COMPLIANCE: COMPLIANCE WITH BANS ON ADVERTISING, PROMOTION AND SPONSORSHIP, AND ADHERENCE TO SMOKE-FREE POLICY

|||||||||| ||||||||| ||||||||	Complete compliance (8/10 to 10/10)
||||||| |||||| ||||| |||| |||	Moderate compliance (3/10 to 7/10)
|| |	Minimal compliance (0/10 to 2/10)

SYMBOLS LEGEND

☆	Separate, completely enclosed smoking rooms are allowed if they are separately ventilated to the outside and/or kept under negative air pressure in relation to the surrounding areas. Given the difficulty of meeting the very strict requirements delineated for such rooms, they appear to be a practical impossibility but no reliable empirical evidence is presently available to ascertain whether they have been constructed.
⊙	Policy adopted but not implemented by 31 December 2012.
▲▼	Change in POWER indicator group, up or down, between 2010 and 2012. Some 2010 data were revised in 2012. 2012 grouping rules were applied to both years.

Refer to Technical Note I for definitions of categories

Europe

Table 1.1.4
Summary of MPOWER measures

. . . Data not reported/not available.

– Data not required/not applicable.

2012 INDICATOR AND COMPLIANCE

COUNTRY	ADULT DAILY SMOKING PREVALENCE (2011)	M MONITORING	P SMOKE-FREE POLICIES (LINES REPRESENT LEVEL OF COMPLIANCE)	O CESSATION PROGRAMMES	W WARNINGS: HEALTH WARNINGS	W WARNINGS: MASS MEDIA	E ADVERTISING BANS (LINES REPRESENT LEVEL OF COMPLIANCE)	R TAXATION
Albania	24%		|||				||||||||	61%
Andorra	. . .		. . . ☆				–	46%
Armenia	19%		|||				||||	25%
Austria	44%		|||||				||||||	74%
Azerbaijan	. . .		|||||||				||||||	19%
Belarus	24%		–				|||	42%
Belgium	21%		||||||| ☆				||||||||||	76%
Bosnia and Herzegovina	32%		–				|||||	75%
Bulgaria	33%		–				|||||	84%
Croatia	29%		|||||| ☆				||||||	71%
Cyprus	27%		||||||||				||||||||||	76%
Czech Republic	24%		||||||||				|||||||||	78%
Denmark	20%		–				. . .	79%
Estonia	25%		|||||||				|||||||||	77%
Finland	17%		||||||||||				|||||||||	80%
France	31%		. . . ☆				. . .	80%
Georgia	23%						|||||||	58%
Germany	24%		|||||||				|||||||||	73%
Greece	36%		. . .				. . .	82%
Hungary	29%		||||||||||				||||||||||	84%
Iceland	14%		||||||||||				||||||||||	57%
Ireland	. . .		. . .				. . .	79%
Israel	22%		. . .				. . .	84%
Italy	21%		– ☆				||||||||||	75%
Kazakhstan	20%		. . .				. . .	30%
Kyrgyzstan	20%		. . .				. . .	66%
Latvia	26%		. . .				. . .	79%
Lithuania	27%		||||||||				|||||||||	75%
Luxembourg	19%		. . . ☆				. . .	71%
Malta	22%		|||||||| ⊙				||||||||	77%
Monaco	. . .		. . .				–	. . .
Montenegro	. . .		|||||				||||||||||	81%
Netherlands	20%		–				|||||	72%
Norway	19%		||||||||||				||||||||||	73%
Poland	26%		|||||||				|||||	80%
Portugal	19%		||||||||				||||||	76%
Republic of Moldova	20%		||				||||	44%
Romania	25%		|||||||				|||||||||	73%
Russian Federation	34%		–				. . .	40%
San Marino	. . .		. . . ☆				. . .	74%
Serbia	29%		|||||				|||||||	76%
Slovakia	23%		|||||||				|||||||||	84%
Slovenia	21%		||||||||				|||||||	80%
Spain	26%		||||||||||				||||||||||	79%
Sweden	11%		–				|||||	74%
Switzerland	19%		–				||||||||	62%
Tajikistan	. . .		–				. . .	31%
The former Yugoslav Republic of Macedonia	. . .		. . .				. . .	71%
Turkey	24%		||||||||||				||||||||||	80%
Turkmenistan	. . .		. . .				–	30%
Ukraine	25%		. . .				. . .	67%
United Kingdom of Great Britain and Northern Ireland	14%		||||||||||				|||||||||	80%
Uzbekistan	10%		. . .				. . .	29%

CHANGE SINCE 2010

P SMOKE-FREE POLICIES	O CESSATION PROGRAMMES	W HEALTH WARNINGS	E ADVERTISING BANS	R TAXATION
CHANGE IN POWER INDICATOR GROUP, UP OR DOWN, SINCE 2010				
	▲			
▼				▼
	▲			
	▲			
▲				
				▲
	▲	▲		▲
	▲			
	▲			
▲		▲		
		▲		
		▲		
	▲			
	▲			▲
				▼
				▲
		▲	▲	
				▼
▲				
			▲	

ADULT DAILY SMOKING PREVALENCE*: AGE-STANDARDIZED PREVALENCE RATES FOR ADULT DAILY SMOKERS OF TOBACCO (BOTH SEXES COMBINED), 2011

. . .	Estimates not available
	30% or more
	From 20% to 29.9%
	From 15% to 19.9%
	Less than 15%

* The figures should be used strictly for the purpose of drawing comparisons across countries and must not be used to estimate absolute number of daily tobacco smokers in a country.

MONITORING: PREVALENCE DATA

	No known data or no recent data or data that are not both recent and representative
	Recent and representative data for either adults or youth
	Recent and representative data for both adults and youth
	Recent, representative and periodic data for both adults and youth

SMOKE-FREE POLICIES: POLICIES ON SMOKE-FREE ENVIRONMENTS

	Data not reported/not categorized
	Up to two public places completely smoke-free
	Three to five public places completely smoke-free
	Six to seven public places completely smoke-free
	All public places completely smoke-free (or at least 90% of the population covered by complete subnational smoke-free legislation)

CESSATION PROGRAMMES: TREATMENT OF TOBACCO DEPENDENCE

	Data not reported
	None
	NRT and/or some cessation services (neither cost-covered)
	NRT and/or some cessation services (at least one of which is cost-covered)
	National quit line, and both NRT and some cessation services cost-covered

HEALTH WARNINGS: HEALTH WARNINGS ON CIGARETTE PACKAGES

	Data not reported
	No warnings or small warnings
	Medium size warnings missing some appropriate characteristics OR large warnings missing many appropriate characteristics
	Medium size warnings with all appropriate characteristics OR large warnings missing some appropriate characteristics
	Large warnings with all appropriate characteristics

MASS MEDIA: ANTI-TOBACCO CAMPAIGNS

	Data not reported
	No national campaign conducted between January 2011 and June 2012 with duration of at least three weeks
	National campaign conducted with 1–4 appropriate characteristics
	National campaign conducted with 5–6 appropriate characteristics, or with 7 characteristics excluding airing on television and/or radio
	National campaign conducted with at least seven appropriate characteristics including airing on television and/or radio

ADVERTISING BANS: BANS ON ADVERTISING, PROMOTION AND SPONSORSHIP

	Data not reported
	Complete absence of ban, or ban that does not cover national television, radio and print media
	Ban on national television, radio and print media only
	Ban on national television, radio and print media as well as on some but not all other forms of direct and/or indirect advertising
	Ban on all forms of direct and indirect advertising

TAXATION: SHARE OF TOTAL TAXES IN THE RETAIL PRICE OF THE MOST WIDELY SOLD BRAND OF CIGARETTES

	Data not reported
	≤ 25% of retail price is tax
	26–50% of retail price is tax
	51–75% of retail price is tax
	>75% of retail price is tax

COMPLIANCE: COMPLIANCE WITH BANS ON ADVERTISING, PROMOTION AND SPONSORSHIP, AND ADHERENCE TO SMOKE-FREE POLICY

||||||||||	Complete compliance (8/10 to 10/10)
||||||||	Moderate compliance (3/10 to 7/10)
||	Minimal compliance (0/10 to 2/10)

SYMBOLS LEGEND

☆	Separate, completely enclosed smoking rooms are allowed if they are separately ventilated to the outside and/or kept under negative air pressure in relation to the surrounding areas. Given the difficulty of meeting the very strict requirements delineated for such rooms, they appear to be a practical impossibility but no reliable empirical evidence is presently available to ascertain whether they have been constructed.
⊙	Policy adopted but not implemented by 31 December 2012.
▲▼	Change in POWER indicator group, up or down, between 2010 and 2012. Some 2010 data were revised in 2012. 2012 grouping rules were applied to both years.

Refer to Technical Note I for definitions of categories

Eastern Mediterranean

Table 1.1.5
Summary of MPOWER measures

. . . Data not reported/not available.

< Refers to a territory.

– Data not required/not applicable.

2012 INDICATOR AND COMPLIANCE

COUNTRY	ADULT DAILY SMOKING PREVALENCE (2011)	M MONITORING	P SMOKE-FREE POLICIES (LINES REPRESENT LEVEL OF COMPLIANCE)	O CESSATION PROGRAMMES	W WARNINGS: HEALTH WARNINGS	W WARNINGS: MASS MEDIA	E ADVERTISING BANS (LINES REPRESENT LEVEL OF COMPLIANCE)	R TAXATION
Afghanistan	. . .		III				IIIIII	2%
Bahrain	22%		–				IIIIIIIII	20%
Djibouti	. . .		IIIII				IIIIIIII	29%
Egypt	25%		III				IIIIII	73%
Iran (Islamic Republic of)	11%		IIIIIIIII				IIIIIIIIII	17%
Iraq	15%		IIII				IIIIII	4%
Jordan	26%		III				IIIIIIII	77%
Kuwait	17%		IIII				IIIIIIII	25%
Lebanon	31%		IIIIIIII				IIIIIIIII	43%
Libya	21%						IIIIIII	15%
Morocco	15%		IIIII				IIIIIIIIII	68%
Oman	5%		IIIIIIIII				IIIIIIII	22%
Pakistan	19%		IIIII				III	60%
Qatar	. . .		–				IIIIIIIII	22%
Saudi Arabia	17%		IIIIIIII				IIIIIIII	22%
Somalia	. . .		. . .»				–	7%
South Sudan	. . .		–				–	. . .
Sudan	. . .		–				IIIII	72%
Syrian Arab Republic	. . .		. . .				. . .	58%
Tunisia	30%		–				IIIIIIII	78%
United Arab Emirates	. . .		. . .				. . .	25%
West Bank and Gaza Strip <	21%		IIIIIIII				IIIIIIII	83%
Yemen	21%		–				IIIIII	53%

mpower

CHANGE SINCE 2010

P SMOKE-FREE POLICIES	O CESSATION PROGRAMMES	W HEALTH WARNINGS	E ADVERTISING BANS	R TAXATION
CHANGE IN POWER INDICATOR GROUP, UP OR DOWN, SINCE 2010				
	▼	▲	▲	▼
▲	▲	▲		▼
▲		▲	▲	
	▲			
		▲		▼
		▲		▼
▲		▲		▼
				▲
	▲			
		▲		▼
▲				

ADULT DAILY SMOKING PREVALENCE*: AGE-STANDARDIZED PREVALENCE RATES FOR ADULT DAILY SMOKERS OF TOBACCO (BOTH SEXES COMBINED), 2011

. . .	Estimates not available
	30% or more
	From 20% to 29.9%
	From 15% to 19.9%
	Less than 15%

* The figures should be used strictly for the purpose of drawing comparisons across countries and must not be used to estimate absolute number of daily tobacco smokers in a country.

MONITORING: PREVALENCE DATA

	No known data or no recent data or data that are not both recent and representative
	Recent and representative data for either adults or youth
	Recent and representative data for both adults and youth
	Recent, representative and periodic data for both adults and youth

SMOKE-FREE POLICIES: POLICIES ON SMOKE-FREE ENVIRONMENTS

	Data not reported/not categorized
	Up to two public places completely smoke-free
	Three to five public places completely smoke-free
	Six to seven public places completely smoke-free
	All public places completely smoke-free (or at least 90% of the population covered by complete subnational smoke-free legislation)

CESSATION PROGRAMMES: TREATMENT OF TOBACCO DEPENDENCE

	Data not reported
	None
	NRT and/or some cessation services (neither cost-covered)
	NRT and/or some cessation services (at least one of which is cost-covered)
	National quit line, and both NRT and some cessation services cost-covered

HEALTH WARNINGS: HEALTH WARNINGS ON CIGARETTE PACKAGES

	Data not reported
	No warnings or small warnings
	Medium size warnings missing some appropriate characteristics OR large warnings missing many appropriate characteristics
	Medium size warnings with all appropriate characteristics OR large warnings missing some appropriate characteristics
	Large warnings with all appropriate characteristics

MASS MEDIA: ANTI-TOBACCO CAMPAIGNS

	Data not reported
	No national campaign conducted between January 2011 and June 2012 with duration of at least three weeks
	National campaign conducted with 1–4 appropriate characteristics
	National campaign conducted with 5–6 appropriate characteristics, or with 7 characteristics excluding airing on television and/or radio
	National campaign conducted with at least seven appropriate characteristics including airing on television and/or radio

ADVERTISING BANS: BANS ON ADVERTISING, PROMOTION AND SPONSORSHIP

	Data not reported
	Complete absence of ban, or ban that does not cover national television, radio and print media
	Ban on national television, radio and print media only
	Ban on national television, radio and print media as well as on some but not all other forms of direct and/or indirect advertising
	Ban on all forms of direct and indirect advertising

TAXATION: SHARE OF TOTAL TAXES IN THE RETAIL PRICE OF THE MOST WIDELY SOLD BRAND OF CIGARETTES

	Data not reported
	≤ 25% of retail price is tax
	26–50% of retail price is tax
	51–75% of retail price is tax
	>75% of retail price is tax

COMPLIANCE: COMPLIANCE WITH BANS ON ADVERTISING, PROMOTION AND SPONSORSHIP, AND ADHERENCE TO SMOKE-FREE POLICY

||||||||||	Complete compliance (8/10 to 10/10)
|||||||	Moderate compliance (3/10 to 7/10)
||	Minimal compliance (0/10 to 2/10)

SYMBOLS LEGEND

»	Data not substantiated by a copy of the legislation.
▲▼	Change in POWER indicator group, up or down, between 2010 and 2012. Some 2010 data were revised in 2012. 2012 grouping rules were applied to both years.

Refer to Technical Note I for definitions of categories

Western Pacific

Table 1.1.6
Summary of MPOWER measures

. . . Data not reported/not available.

– Data not required/not applicable.

2012 INDICATOR AND COMPLIANCE

<table>
<tr><th rowspan="2">COUNTRY</th><th rowspan="2">ADULT DAILY SMOKING PREVALENCE (2011)</th><th rowspan="2">M
MONITORING</th><th>P
SMOKE-FREE POLICIES</th><th rowspan="2">O
CESSATION PROGRAMMES</th><th colspan="2">W
WARNINGS</th><th>E
ADVERTISING BANS</th><th rowspan="2">R
TAXATION</th></tr>
<tr><th>LINES REPRESENT LEVEL OF COMPLIANCE</th><th>HEALTH WARNINGS</th><th>MASS MEDIA</th><th>LINES REPRESENT LEVEL OF COMPLIANCE</th></tr>
<tr><td>Australia</td><td>16%</td><td></td><td>–</td><td></td><td></td><td></td><td>. . .</td><td>60%</td></tr>
<tr><td>Brunei Darussalam</td><td>13%</td><td></td><td>|||||||</td><td></td><td></td><td></td><td>||||||||||</td><td>81%</td></tr>
<tr><td>Cambodia</td><td>21%</td><td></td><td>–</td><td></td><td></td><td></td><td>|||||||||</td><td>17%</td></tr>
<tr><td>China</td><td>23%</td><td></td><td>|||</td><td></td><td></td><td></td><td>|||||</td><td>41%</td></tr>
<tr><td>Cook Islands</td><td>27%</td><td></td><td>|||||||</td><td></td><td></td><td></td><td>||||||||||</td><td>38%</td></tr>
<tr><td>Fiji</td><td>. . .</td><td></td><td>||||||||</td><td></td><td></td><td></td><td>|||||||||</td><td>41%</td></tr>
<tr><td>Japan</td><td>20%</td><td></td><td>–</td><td></td><td></td><td></td><td>–</td><td>64%</td></tr>
<tr><td>Kiribati</td><td>50%</td><td></td><td>–</td><td></td><td></td><td></td><td>–</td><td>42%</td></tr>
<tr><td>Lao People's Democratic Republic</td><td>21%</td><td></td><td>. . .</td><td></td><td></td><td></td><td>. . .</td><td>43%</td></tr>
<tr><td>Malaysia</td><td>20%</td><td></td><td>–</td><td></td><td></td><td></td><td>||||||||</td><td>57%</td></tr>
<tr><td>Marshall Islands</td><td>17%</td><td></td><td>. . .</td><td></td><td></td><td></td><td>. . .</td><td>29%</td></tr>
<tr><td>Micronesia (Federated States of)</td><td>. . .</td><td></td><td>–</td><td></td><td></td><td></td><td>–</td><td>65%</td></tr>
<tr><td>Mongolia</td><td>24%</td><td></td><td>– ⊙</td><td></td><td></td><td></td><td>||||||</td><td>49%</td></tr>
<tr><td>Nauru</td><td>47%</td><td></td><td>. . . ⊙</td><td></td><td></td><td></td><td>. . .</td><td>. . .</td></tr>
<tr><td>New Zealand</td><td>18%</td><td></td><td>||||||||||</td><td></td><td></td><td></td><td>||||||||||</td><td>74%</td></tr>
<tr><td>Niue</td><td>12%</td><td></td><td>–</td><td></td><td></td><td></td><td>–</td><td>67%</td></tr>
<tr><td>Palau</td><td>19%</td><td></td><td>|||||||||</td><td></td><td></td><td></td><td>||||||||||</td><td>57%</td></tr>
<tr><td>Papua New Guinea</td><td>36%</td><td></td><td>. . .</td><td></td><td></td><td></td><td>. . .</td><td>37%</td></tr>
<tr><td>Philippines</td><td>21%</td><td></td><td>|||||||</td><td></td><td></td><td></td><td>|||||||</td><td>29%</td></tr>
<tr><td>Republic of Korea</td><td>25%</td><td></td><td>|||||</td><td></td><td></td><td></td><td>. . .</td><td>62%</td></tr>
<tr><td>Samoa</td><td>. . .</td><td></td><td>. . .</td><td></td><td></td><td></td><td>. . .</td><td>60%</td></tr>
<tr><td>Singapore</td><td>14%</td><td></td><td>. . . ☆</td><td></td><td></td><td></td><td>. . .</td><td>66%</td></tr>
<tr><td>Solomon Islands</td><td>25%</td><td></td><td></td><td></td><td></td><td></td><td>|||||</td><td>30%</td></tr>
<tr><td>Tonga</td><td>19%</td><td></td><td>. . .</td><td></td><td></td><td></td><td>. . .</td><td>63%</td></tr>
<tr><td>Tuvalu</td><td>. . .</td><td></td><td>|||||||</td><td></td><td></td><td></td><td>|||||||||</td><td>15%</td></tr>
<tr><td>Vanuatu</td><td>11%</td><td></td><td>–</td><td></td><td></td><td></td><td>|||||||</td><td>58%</td></tr>
<tr><td>Viet Nam</td><td>19%</td><td></td><td>|||| ⊙</td><td></td><td></td><td></td><td>|||||||| ⊙</td><td>42%</td></tr>
</table>

CHANGE SINCE 2010

P SMOKE-FREE POLICIES	O CESSATION PROGRAMMES	W HEALTH WARNINGS	E ADVERTISING BANS	R TAXATION
CHANGE IN POWER INDICATOR GROUP, UP OR DOWN, SINCE 2010				
▲				▲
			▲	
				▼
	▲			▲
	▲			
▲		▲		
				▼
▲			▲	
▲				▲
				▲
	▲			
				▲
		▲	▲	

ADULT DAILY SMOKING PREVALENCE*: AGE-STANDARDIZED PREVALENCE RATES FOR ADULT DAILY SMOKERS OF TOBACCO (BOTH SEXES COMBINED), 2011

. . .	Estimates not available
	30% or more
	From 20% to 29.9%
	From 15% to 19.9%
	Less than 15%

* The figures should be used strictly for the purpose of drawing comparisons across countries and must not be used to estimate absolute number of daily tobacco smokers in a country.

MONITORING: PREVALENCE DATA

	No known data or no recent data or data that are not both recent and representative
	Recent and representative data for either adults or youth
	Recent and representative data for both adults and youth
	Recent, representative and periodic data for both adults and youth

SMOKE-FREE POLICIES: POLICIES ON SMOKE-FREE ENVIRONMENTS

	Data not reported/not categorized
	Up to two public places completely smoke-free
	Three to five public places completely smoke-free
	Six to seven public places completely smoke-free
	All public places completely smoke-free (or at least 90% of the population covered by complete subnational smoke-free legislation)

CESSATION PROGRAMMES: TREATMENT OF TOBACCO DEPENDENCE

	Data not reported
	None
	NRT and/or some cessation services (neither cost-covered)
	NRT and/or some cessation services (at least one of which is cost-covered)
	National quit line, and both NRT and some cessation services cost-covered

HEALTH WARNINGS: HEALTH WARNINGS ON CIGARETTE PACKAGES

	Data not reported
	No warnings or small warnings
	Medium size warnings missing some appropriate characteristics OR large warnings missing many appropriate characteristics
	Medium size warnings with all appropriate characteristics OR large warnings missing some appropriate characteristics
	Large warnings with all appropriate characteristics

MASS MEDIA: ANTI-TOBACCO CAMPAIGNS

	Data not reported
	No national campaign conducted between January 2011 and June 2012 with duration of at least three weeks
	National campaign conducted with 1–4 appropriate characteristics
	National campaign conducted with 5–6 appropriate characteristics, or with 7 characteristics excluding airing on television and/or radio
	National campaign conducted with at least seven appropriate characteristics including airing on television and/or radio

ADVERTISING BANS: BANS ON ADVERTISING, PROMOTION AND SPONSORSHIP

	Data not reported
	Complete absence of ban, or ban that does not cover national television, radio and print media
	Ban on national television, radio and print media only
	Ban on national television, radio and print media as well as on some but not all other forms of direct and/or indirect advertising
	Ban on all forms of direct and indirect advertising

TAXATION: SHARE OF TOTAL TAXES IN THE RETAIL PRICE OF THE MOST WIDELY SOLD BRAND OF CIGARETTES

	Data not reported
	≤ 25% of retail price is tax
	26–50% of retail price is tax
	51–75% of retail price is tax
	>75% of retail price is tax

COMPLIANCE: COMPLIANCE WITH BANS ON ADVERTISING, PROMOTION AND SPONSORSHIP, AND ADHERENCE TO SMOKE-FREE POLICY

||||||||||	Complete compliance (8/10 to 10/10)
|||||||	Moderate compliance (3/10 to 7/10)
||	Minimal compliance (0/10 to 2/10)

SYMBOLS LEGEND

☆	Separate, completely enclosed smoking rooms are allowed if they are separately ventilated to the outside and/or kept under negative air pressure in relation to the surrounding areas. Given the difficulty of meeting the very strict requirements delineated for such rooms, they appear to be a practical impossibility but no reliable empirical evidence is presently available to ascertain whether they have been constructed.
⊙	Policy adopted but not implemented by 31 December 2012.
▲▼	Change in POWER indicator group, up or down, between 2010 and 2012. Some 2010 data were revised in 2012. 2012 grouping rules were applied to both years.

Refer to Technical Note I for definitions of categories

พ่อ

APPENDIX II: **BANS ON TOBACCO ADVERTISING, PROMOTION AND SPONSORSHIP**

Appendix II provides detailed information on legislation banning tobacco advertising, promotion and sponsorship in Member States. Data are provided for each WHO region.

Data on bans on tobacco advertising, promotion and sponsorship were primarily drawn from supporting legal documents such as adopted legislation and regulations. Available documents were reviewed by WHO and discussed with countries as necessary to ensure the correct interpretation.

Africa

Table 2.1.1
Bans on tobacco advertising in Africa

* Score of 0 to 10, where 0 is low compliance. Refer to Technical Note I for more information.

⊙ Policy adopted but not implemented by 31 December 2012.

. . . Data not reported/not available.

— Data not required/not applicable.

COUNTRY		
	NATIONAL TV AND RADIO	INTERNATIONAL TV AND RADIO
Algeria	Yes	Yes[1]
Angola	No	No
Benin	Yes	Yes[1]
Botswana	Yes	No
Burkina Faso	Yes	Yes
Burundi	No	No
Cameroon	Yes	Yes[1]
Cape Verde	Yes	No
Central African Republic	No	No
Chad	Yes	Yes[1]
Comoros	Yes	Yes[1]
Congo	Yes	Yes[1]
Côte d'Ivoire	No	No
Democratic Republic of the Congo	Yes	Yes[1]
Equatorial Guinea	No	No
Eritrea	Yes	Yes[1]
Ethiopia	Yes	Yes
Gabon	No	No
Gambia	Yes	Yes[1]
Ghana	Yes	Yes[1]
Guinea	Yes	Yes[1]
Guinea-Bissau	No	No
Kenya	Yes	Yes
Lesotho	No	No
Liberia	No	No
Madagascar	Yes	Yes
Malawi	No	No
Mali	Yes	Yes[1]
Mauritania	No	No
Mauritius	Yes	Yes[1]
Mozambique	Yes	Yes[1]
Namibia	Yes	Yes[1]
Niger	Yes	Yes[1]
Nigeria	No	No
Rwanda	No	No
Sao Tome and Principe	No	No
Senegal	No	No
Seychelles	Yes	Yes
Sierra Leone	No	No
South Africa	Yes	No
Swaziland	No	No
Togo	Yes ⊙	Yes ⊙
Uganda	No	No
United Republic of Tanzania	Yes	Yes
Zambia	No	No
Zimbabwe	No	No

NOTES

1 The law does not explicitly address cross-border advertising. However, given that advertising is banned on TV and radio, it is interpreted that both domestic and international levels are covered by the ban.

2 The law does not explicitly address cross-border advertising. However, given that advertising is banned in all magazines and newspapers, it is interpreted that both domestic and international levels are covered by the ban.

BAN ON TOBACCO ADVERTISING					
LOCAL MAGAZINES AND NEWSPAPERS	INTERNATIONAL MAGAZINES AND NEWSPAPERS	BILLBOARD AND OUTDOOR ADVERTISING	POINT OF SALE	INTERNET	OVERALL COMPLIANCE OF BAN ON DIRECT ADVERTISING *
Yes	Yes[2]	Yes	No	No	7
No	No	No	No	No	—
Yes	No	Yes	No	No	6
Yes	No	Yes	Yes	No	4
Yes	Yes	Yes	No	Yes	9
No	No	No	No	No	—
Yes	Yes[2]	Yes	No	No	9
No	No	No	No	No	. . .
No	No	No	No	No	—
Yes	Yes[2]	Yes	Yes	No	. . .
No	No	Yes	No	No	6
Yes	Yes[2]	Yes	No	No	10
No	No	No	No	No	—
Yes	Yes[2]	No	No	No	6
No	No	No	No	No	—
Yes	Yes[2]	Yes	Yes	Yes	9
Yes	Yes	Yes	Yes	Yes	—
No	No	No	No	No	—
Yes	Yes[2]	Yes	Yes	No	7
Yes	Yes[2]	Yes	Yes	Yes	5
Yes	Yes[2]	Yes	Yes	Yes	—
No	No	No	No	No	—
Yes	Yes	Yes	Yes	Yes	7
No	No	No	No	No	—
No	No	No	No	No	—
Yes	Yes	Yes	Yes	Yes	8
No	No	No	No	No	—
Yes	Yes[2]	Yes	No	Yes	8
No	No	No	No	No	—
Yes	Yes[2]	Yes	Yes	Yes	9
Yes	Yes[2]	Yes	No	No	4
Yes	Yes[2]	Yes	No	No	10
Yes	Yes[2]	Yes	Yes	Yes	9
No	No	No	No	No	—
No	No	No	No	No	—
No	No	No	No	No	—
No	No	No	No	No	—
Yes	Yes	Yes	Yes	Yes	10
No	No	No	No	No	—
Yes	No	Yes	No	Yes	9
No	No	No	No	No	—
Yes ⊙	Yes ⊙	Yes ⊙	Yes ⊙	Yes ⊙	—
No	No	No	No	No	—
Yes	Yes	Yes	No	Yes	0
No	No	No	No	No	—
No	No	No	No	No	—

The Americas

Table 2.1.2
Bans on tobacco advertising in the Americas

* Score of 0 to 10, where 0 is low compliance. Refer to Technical Note I for more information.

⊙ Policy adopted but not implemented by 31 December 2012.

. . . Data not reported/not available.

— Data not required/not applicable.

COUNTRY	NATIONAL TV AND RADIO	INTERNATIONAL TV AND RADIO
Antigua and Barbuda	No	No
Argentina	Yes	Yes[1]
Bahamas	Yes	Yes[1]
Barbados	No	No
Belize	No	No
Bolivia (Plurinational State of)	Yes	Yes[1]
Brazil	Yes	Yes[1] ⊙
Canada	Yes	No
Chile[3]	Yes	Yes[1]
Colombia	Yes	Yes
Costa Rica	Yes	Yes[1]
Cuba	No	No
Dominica	No	No
Dominican Republic	No	No
Ecuador	Yes	Yes[1]
El Salvador	Yes	Yes
Grenada	No	No
Guatemala	No	No
Guyana	No	No
Haiti	No	No
Honduras	Yes	Yes[1]
Jamaica	Yes	No
Mexico	Yes	Yes
Nicaragua	Yes	Yes
Panama	Yes	Yes
Paraguay	No	No
Peru	Yes	Yes[1]
Saint Kitts and Nevis	No	No
Saint Lucia	No	No
Saint Vincent and the Grenadines	No	No
Suriname[4]	No	No
Trinidad and Tobago	Yes	Yes[1]
United States of America	Yes	No
Uruguay	Yes	Yes[1]
Venezuela (Bolivarian Republic of)	Yes	Yes[1]

NOTES

1. The law does not explicitly address cross-border advertising. However, given that advertising is banned on TV and radio, it is interpreted that both domestic and international levels are covered by the ban.
2. The law does not explicitly address cross-border advertising. However, given that advertising is banned in all magazines and newspapers, it is interpreted that both domestic and international levels are covered by the ban.
3. A new law that entered into force on 1 March 2013 establishes a ban on all forms on tobacco advertising, promotion and sponsorship.
4. A new law was approved in early 2013 which establishes a ban on all forms of tobacco advertising, promotion and sponsorship.

BAN ON TOBACCO ADVERTISING					
LOCAL MAGAZINES AND NEWSPAPERS	INTERNATIONAL MAGAZINES AND NEWSPAPERS	BILLBOARD AND OUTDOOR ADVERTISING	POINT OF SALE	INTERNET	OVERALL COMPLIANCE OF BAN ON DIRECT ADVERTISING *
No	No	No	No	No	—
Yes	Yes[2]	Yes	No	Yes	8
No	No	No	No	No	. . .
No	No	No	No	No	—
No	No	No	No	No	—
Yes	Yes[2]	Yes	No	No	7
Yes	Yes[2] ⊙	Yes	Yes ⊙	Yes	. . .
Yes	No	Yes	No	Yes	10
Yes	Yes	Yes	No	Yes	8
Yes	Yes[2]	Yes	Yes	Yes	. . .
Yes	Yes[2]	Yes	Yes	Yes	10
No	No	No	No	No	—
No	No	No	No	No	—
No	No	No	No	No	—
Yes	Yes[2]	Yes	No	Yes	10
Yes	Yes	Yes	No	Yes	. . .
No	No	No	No	No	—
No	No	No	No	No	—
No	No	No	No	No	—
No	No	No	No	No	—
Yes	Yes[2]	Yes	No	No	8
No	No	No	No	No	10
No	No	Yes	No	No	5
No	No	Yes	No	No	. . .
Yes	Yes	Yes	Yes	Yes	10
No	No	No	No	No	—
No	No	No	No	Yes	5
No	No	No	No	No	—
No	No	No	No	No	—
No	No	No	No	No	—
No	No	No	No	No	—
No	No	Yes	No	No	7
No	No	No	No	No	. . .
Yes	Yes[2]	Yes	No	Yes	10
No	No	Yes	No	No	10

South-East Asia

Table 2.1.3
Bans on tobacco advertising in South-East Asia

* Score of 0 to 10, where 0 is low compliance. Refer to Technical Note I for more information.

— Data not required/not applicable.

COUNTRY		
	NATIONAL TV AND RADIO	INTERNATIONAL TV AND RADIO
Bangladesh	Yes	Yes[1]
Bhutan	Yes	Yes[1]
Democratic People's Republic of Korea	No	No
India	Yes	Yes[1]
Indonesia	No	No
Maldives	Yes	Yes[1]
Myanmar	Yes	Yes[1]
Nepal	Yes	Yes[1]
Sri Lanka	Yes	Yes[1]
Thailand	Yes	No
Timor-Leste	No	No

NOTES

1 The law does not explicitly address cross-border advertising. However, given that advertising is banned on TV and radio, it is interpreted that both domestic and international levels are covered by the ban.

2 The law does not explicitly address cross-border advertising. However, given that advertising is banned in all magazines and newspapers, it is interpreted that both domestic and international levels are covered by the ban.

BAN ON TOBACCO ADVERTISING					
LOCAL MAGAZINES AND NEWSPAPERS	INTERNATIONAL MAGAZINES AND NEWSPAPERS	BILLBOARD AND OUTDOOR ADVERTISING	POINT OF SALE	INTERNET	OVERALL COMPLIANCE OF BAN ON DIRECT ADVERTISING *
Yes	No	No	No	No	10
Yes	Yes[2]	Yes	Yes	Yes	10
No	No	No	No	No	—
Yes	Yes[2]	Yes	No	Yes	5
No	No	No	No	No	—
Yes	Yes[2]	Yes	Yes	Yes	7
Yes	Yes[2]	Yes	No	Yes	7
Yes	Yes[2]	Yes	Yes	Yes	8
Yes	Yes[2]	Yes	Yes	Yes	9
Yes	No	Yes	Yes	Yes	8
No	No	No	No	No	—

Europe

Table 2.1.4
Bans on tobacco advertising in Europe

* Score of 0 to 10, where 0 is low compliance.
Refer to Technical Note I for more information.

. . . Data not reported/not available.

— Data not required/not applicable.

COUNTRY		
	NATIONAL TV AND RADIO	INTERNATIONAL TV AND RADIO
Albania	Yes	Yes[1]
Andorra	No	No
Armenia	Yes	Yes[1]
Austria	Yes	Yes[1]
Azerbaijan	Yes	Yes[1]
Belarus	Yes	Yes[1]
Belgium	Yes	Yes[1]
Bosnia and Herzegovina	Yes	Yes[1]
Bulgaria	Yes	Yes[1]
Croatia	Yes	Yes[1]
Cyprus	Yes	Yes[1]
Czech Republic	Yes	Yes[1]
Denmark	Yes	Yes[1]
Estonia	Yes	Yes[1]
Finland	Yes	Yes[1]
France	Yes	No
Georgia	Yes	No
Germany	Yes	Yes[1]
Greece	Yes	Yes[1]
Hungary	Yes	Yes[1]
Iceland	Yes	Yes[1]
Ireland	Yes	Yes[1]
Israel	Yes	No
Italy	Yes	Yes[1]
Kazakhstan	Yes	Yes[1]
Kyrgyzstan	Yes	Yes[1]
Latvia	Yes	Yes[1]
Lithuania	Yes	Yes[1]
Luxembourg	Yes	Yes[1]
Malta	Yes	Yes[1]
Monaco	No	No
Montenegro	Yes	Yes[1]
Netherlands	Yes	No
Norway	Yes	No
Poland	Yes	Yes[1]
Portugal	Yes	No
Republic of Moldova	Yes	Yes[1]
Romania	Yes	Yes[1]
Russian Federation	Yes	Yes
San Marino	Yes	Yes[1]
Serbia	Yes	Yes[1]
Slovakia	Yes	Yes[1]
Slovenia	Yes	Yes[1]
Spain	Yes	Yes[1]
Sweden	Yes	Yes[1]
Switzerland	Yes	Yes[1]
Tajikistan	Yes	Yes[1]
The former Yugoslav Republic of Macedonia	Yes	Yes
Turkey	Yes	Yes[1]
Turkmenistan	No	No
Ukraine	Yes	Yes
United Kingdom of Great Britain and Northern Ireland	Yes	Yes
Uzbekistan	Yes	No

NOTES

1 The law does not explicitly address cross-border advertising. However, given that advertising is banned on TV and radio, it is interpreted that both domestic and international levels are covered by the ban.

2 The law does not explicitly address cross-border advertising. However, given that advertising is banned in all magazines and newspapers, it is interpreted that both domestic and international levels are covered by the ban.

3 Tobacco advertising is prohibited on domestic internet and only restricted on global internet.

BAN ON TOBACCO ADVERTISING					
LOCAL MAGAZINES AND NEWSPAPERS	INTERNATIONAL MAGAZINES AND NEWSPAPERS	BILLBOARD AND OUTDOOR ADVERTISING	POINT OF SALE	INTERNET	OVERALL COMPLIANCE OF BAN ON DIRECT ADVERTISING *
Yes	Yes[2]	Yes	Yes	No	8
No	No	No	No	No	—
No	No	Yes	No	Yes	5
Yes	Yes[2]	Yes	Yes	No	10
Yes	Yes[2]	Yes	Yes	Yes	3
Yes	Yes[2]	Yes	No	Yes	3
Yes	No	Yes	No	Yes	10
Yes	Yes[2]	Yes	No	No	5
Yes	No	No	No	Yes	7
Yes	Yes[2]	Yes	Yes	No	7
Yes	No	Yes	Yes	Yes	10
Yes	No	Yes	No	Yes	10
Yes	Yes[2]	Yes	No	No	...
Yes	No	Yes	No	No	8
Yes	No	Yes	Yes	Yes	10
Yes	No	Yes	No	Yes	...
No	No	No	No	No	8
Yes	No	No	No	Yes	10
Yes	No	Yes	No	Yes	...
Yes	No	Yes	No	Yes	10
Yes	No	Yes	No	Yes	10
Yes	No	Yes	Yes	No	...
No	No	No	No	No	...
Yes	No	Yes	Yes	Yes	10
Yes	Yes[2]	Yes	Yes	Yes	...
Yes	Yes[2]	Yes	No	Yes	...
Yes	No	Yes	Yes	Yes	...
Yes	No	Yes	No	Yes	10
Yes	No	No	No	Yes	...
Yes	No	Yes	Yes	Yes	8
No	No	No	No	No	—
Yes	Yes[2]	Yes	No	Yes	10
Yes	No	Yes	No	Yes	7
Yes	No	Yes	Yes	Yes[3]	10
Yes	Yes[2]	Yes	Yes	Yes	5
Yes	No	Yes	Yes	Yes	7
Yes	Yes[2]	Yes	No	No	5
Yes	No	Yes	No	Yes	10
No	No	No	No	No	...
Yes	Yes[2]	Yes	No	No	...
Yes	Yes[2]	Yes	No	Yes	8
Yes	Yes[2]	Yes	No	Yes	10
Yes	Yes[2]	Yes	No	Yes	8
Yes	No	Yes	Yes	Yes	10
Yes	Yes[2]	Yes	No	Yes	5
No	No	No	No	No	8
Yes	Yes[2]	Yes	No	No	...
Yes	Yes	Yes	Yes	Yes	...
Yes	Yes[2]	Yes	Yes	Yes	10
No	No	No	No	No	—
Yes	Yes[2]	Yes	Yes	No	...
Yes	No	Yes	No	Yes	9
Yes	No	Yes	Yes	No	...

Eastern Mediterranean

Table 2.1.5
Bans on tobacco advertising in the Eastern Mediterranean

* Score of 0 to 10, where 0 is low compliance. Refer to Technical Note I for more information.

. . . Data not reported/not available.

— Data not required/not applicable.

< Refers to a territory.

COUNTRY		
	NATIONAL TV AND RADIO	INTERNATIONAL TV AND RADIO
Afghanistan	Yes	No
Bahrain	Yes	Yes[1]
Djibouti	Yes	Yes[1]
Egypt	Yes	Yes[1]
Iran (Islamic Republic of)	Yes	Yes[1]
Iraq	Yes	Yes[1]
Jordan	Yes	Yes[1]
Kuwait	Yes	Yes[1]
Lebanon	Yes	Yes[1]
Libya	Yes	Yes[1]
Morocco	Yes	Yes[1]
Oman	No	No
Pakistan	No	No
Qatar	Yes	Yes[1]
Saudi Arabia	No[3]	No[3]
Somalia	No	No
South Sudan[4]	No	No
Sudan	Yes	Yes[1]
Syrian Arab Republic	Yes	Yes[1]
Tunisia	Yes	Yes[1]
United Arab Emirates	Yes	Yes[1]
West Bank and Gaza Strip <	Yes	Yes[1]
Yemen	Yes	Yes[1]

NOTES

[1] The law does not explicitly address cross-border advertising. However, given that advertising is banned on TV and radio, it is interpreted that both domestic and international levels are covered by the ban.

[2] The law does not explicitly address cross-border advertising. However, given that advertising is banned in all magazines and newspapers, it is interpreted that both domestic and international levels are covered by the ban.

[3] Data not approved by national authorities.

[4] South Sudan has been independent since 2011. This new country has not yet adopted legislation on tobacco advertising, promotion and sponsorship.

[5] The reported compliance is a calculated average of the assessment from experts from the West Bank.

BAN ON TOBACCO ADVERTISING					
LOCAL MAGAZINES AND NEWSPAPERS	INTERNATIONAL MAGAZINES AND NEWSPAPERS	BILLBOARD AND OUTDOOR ADVERTISING	POINT OF SALE	INTERNET	OVERALL COMPLIANCE OF BAN ON DIRECT ADVERTISING *
Yes	No	No	No	No	7
Yes	Yes[2]	Yes	Yes	Yes	9
Yes	Yes[2]	Yes	Yes	Yes	8
Yes	Yes[2]	Yes	Yes	Yes	7
Yes	Yes[2]	Yes	Yes	Yes	10
Yes	Yes[2]	Yes	No	No	7
Yes	Yes[2]	Yes	Yes	Yes	10
Yes	Yes[2]	Yes	Yes	Yes	8
Yes	Yes[2]	Yes	Yes	Yes	10
Yes	Yes[2]	Yes	Yes	Yes	8
Yes	No	No	No	No	10
No	No	Yes	No	No	9
No	No	No	No	No	—
Yes	Yes[2]	Yes	Yes	Yes	9
Yes	Yes	No[3]	Yes	No[3]	8
No	No	No	No	No	—
No	No	No	No	No	—
Yes	Yes[2]	Yes	Yes	Yes	7
Yes	Yes[2]	Yes	Yes	Yes	...
Yes	Yes[2]	Yes	No	No	9
Yes	Yes[2]	Yes	Yes	No	...
Yes	Yes[2]	Yes	Yes	Yes	8[5]
Yes	Yes[2]	Yes	Yes	Yes	8

Western Pacific

Table 2.1.6
Bans on tobacco advertising in the Western Pacific

* Score of 0 to 10, where 0 is low compliance. Refer to Technical Note I for more information.

⊙ Policy adopted but not implemented by 31 December 2012.

. . . Data not reported/not available.

— Data not required/not applicable.

COUNTRY		
	NATIONAL TV AND RADIO	INTERNATIONAL TV AND RADIO
Australia	Yes	Yes
Brunei Darussalam	Yes	Yes
Cambodia	Yes	Yes[1]
China	Yes	Yes[1]
Cook Islands	Yes	No
Fiji	Yes	No
Japan	No[3]	No[3]
Kiribati	No	No
Lao People's Democratic Republic	Yes	Yes[1]
Malaysia	Yes	Yes[1]
Marshall Islands	No	No
Micronesia (Federated States of)	No	No
Mongolia	Yes	Yes
Nauru	Yes	No
New Zealand	Yes	No
Niue	No	No
Palau	Yes	No
Papua New Guinea	Yes	Yes[1]
Philippines	Yes	Yes[1]
Republic of Korea	Yes	No
Samoa	Yes	No
Singapore	Yes	Yes[1]
Solomon Islands	Yes	No
Tonga	Yes	No
Tuvalu	Yes	No
Vanuatu	Yes	No
Viet Nam	Yes	Yes[1] ⊙

NOTES

1 The law does not explicitly address cross-border advertising. However, given that advertising is banned on TV and radio, it is interpreted that both domestic and international levels are covered by the ban.

2 The law does not explicitly address cross-border advertising. However, given that advertising is banned in all magazines and newspapers, it is interpreted that both domestic and international levels are covered by the ban.

3 In practice, tobacco brand advertisements have not been broadcast on television and radio since April 1998.

BAN ON TOBACCO ADVERTISING					
LOCAL MAGAZINES AND NEWSPAPERS	INTERNATIONAL MAGAZINES AND NEWSPAPERS	BILLBOARD AND OUTDOOR ADVERTISING	POINT OF SALE	INTERNET	OVERALL COMPLIANCE OF BAN ON DIRECT ADVERTISING *
Yes	No	Yes	No	Yes	...
Yes	No	Yes	Yes	No	10
Yes	Yes[2]	Yes	No	Yes	9
Yes	Yes[2]	No	No	No	6
Yes	No	Yes	No	Yes	10
Yes	No	Yes	No	No	10
No	No	No	No	No	—
No	No	No	No	No	—
Yes	Yes[2]	Yes	No	Yes	...
Yes	Yes[2]	Yes	Yes	Yes	9
No	No	Yes	No	No	...
No	No	No	No	No	—
Yes	Yes	Yes	Yes	Yes	6
Yes	No	Yes	No	Yes	...
Yes	No	Yes	Yes	Yes	10
No	No	No	No	No	—
Yes	Yes[2]	Yes	Yes	Yes	9
Yes	Yes[2]	Yes	No	No	...
Yes	Yes[2]	Yes	No	Yes	7
No	No	Yes	No	Yes	...
Yes	No	Yes	Yes	Yes	...
Yes	Yes	Yes	Yes	Yes	...
Yes	No	Yes	No	Yes	7
Yes	No	Yes	Yes	No	...
Yes	No	Yes	Yes	Yes	10
Yes	No	Yes	Yes	Yes	7
Yes	Yes[2] ⊙	Yes	Yes	Yes	10

Africa

Table 2.2.1
Bans on tobacco promotion and sponsorship in Africa

* Score of 0 to 10, where 0 is low compliance. Refer to Technical Note I for more information.

⊙ Policy adopted but not implemented by 31 December 2012.

. . . Data not reported/not available.

— Data not required/not applicable.

COUNTRY	FREE DISTRIBUTION IN MAIL OR THROUGH OTHER MEANS	PROMOTIONAL DISCOUNTS
Algeria	No	No
Angola	No	No
Benin	No	No
Botswana	No	No
Burkina Faso[1]	No	No
Burundi	No	No
Cameroon	No	No
Cape Verde	No	No
Central African Republic	No	No
Chad	Yes	Yes
Comoros	Yes	No
Congo	Yes	No
Côte d'Ivoire	No	No
Democratic Republic of the Congo	No	No
Equatorial Guinea	No	No
Eritrea	Yes	Yes
Ethiopia	No	No
Gabon	No	No
Gambia	No	Yes
Ghana	Yes	Yes
Guinea	Yes	Yes
Guinea-Bissau	No	No
Kenya	Yes	Yes
Lesotho	No	No
Liberia	No	No
Madagascar	Yes	Yes
Malawi	No	No
Mali	Yes	Yes
Mauritania	No	No
Mauritius	Yes	Yes
Mozambique	Yes	No
Namibia	Yes	Yes
Niger	Yes	Yes
Nigeria	No	No
Rwanda	No	No
Sao Tome and Principe	No	No
Senegal	Yes	No
Seychelles	Yes	No
Sierra Leone	No	No
South Africa	Yes	Yes
Swaziland	No	No
Togo	Yes ⊙	Yes
Uganda	No	No
United Republic of Tanzania	No	Yes
Zambia	No	No
Zimbabwe	No	No

NOTES

1 Although the law does not explicitly ban the identification of non-tobacco products with tobacco brand names (brand stretching) and does not provide a definition of tobacco advertising and promotion, we interpret that brand stretching is covered by the existing ban of all forms of advertising and promotion because this country is a Party to the WHO FCTC and we assume that the WHO FCTC definition applies.

2 Although the law does not explicitly ban the usage of brand names of non-tobacco products for tobacco products (brand sharing) and does not provide a definition of tobacco advertising and promotion, we interpret that brand sharing is covered by the existing ban on all forms of advertising and promotion because this country is a Party to the WHO FCTC and we assume that the WHO FCTC definition applies.

BAN ON TOBACCO PROMOTION AND SPONSORSHIP					
NON-TOBACCO PRODUCTS IDENTIFIED WITH TOBACCO BRAND NAMES	BRAND NAME OF NON-TOBACCO PRODUCTS USED FOR TOBACCO PRODUCTS	APPEARANCE OF TOBACCO BRANDS IN TV AND/OR FILMS (PRODUCT PLACEMENT)	APPEARANCE OF TOBACCO PRODUCTS IN TV AND/OR FILMS	SPONSORED EVENTS	OVERALL COMPLIANCE OF BAN ON PROMOTION *
No	No	No	No	No	—
No	No	No	No	No	—
No	No	No	No	No	—
No	No	Yes	No	No	5
Yes	Yes	Yes	No	Yes	3
No	No	No	No	No	—
No	No	No	No	Yes	6
No	No	No	No	No	—
No	No	No	No	No	—
Yes	Yes	Yes	No	Yes	...
Yes	No	No	No	No	7
No	No	No	No	Yes	...
No	No	No	No	No	—
No	No	No	No	No	—
No	No	No	No	No	—
Yes	Yes	Yes	No	Yes	8
No	No	No	No	No	—
No	No	No	No	No	—
Yes	No	Yes	No	Yes	7
Yes	Yes	Yes	No	Yes	...
Yes[1]	Yes[2]	Yes	No	Yes	—
No	No	No	No	No	—
Yes	Yes	Yes	Yes	Yes	6
No	No	No	No	No	—
No	No	No	No	No	—
Yes	Yes	Yes	No	Yes	9
No	No	No	No	No	—
Yes	Yes	Yes	No	Yes	7
No	No	No	No	No	—
Yes	Yes	Yes	No	Yes	8
No	No	No	No	No	6
Yes	No	Yes	No	Yes	10
Yes	Yes	Yes	No	Yes	6
No	No	No	No	No	—
No	No	No	No	No	—
No	No	No	No	No	—
No	No	No	No	No	3
Yes	Yes	Yes	No	Yes	10
No	No	No	No	No	—
Yes	Yes	Yes	No	Yes	7
No	No	No	No	No	—
Yes ⊙	Yes ⊙	Yes ⊙	Yes ⊙	Yes	—
No	No	No	No	No	—
No	No	Yes	No	No	0
No	No	No	No	No	—
No	No	No	No	No	—

The Americas

Table 2.2.2

Bans on tobacco promotion and sponsorship in the Americas

* Score of 0 to 10, where 0 is low compliance. Refer to Technical Note I for more information.

⊙ Policy adopted but not implemented by 31 December 2012.

. . . Data not reported/not available.

— Data not required/not applicable.

COUNTRY		
	FREE DISTRIBUTION IN MAIL OR THROUGH OTHER MEANS	PROMOTIONAL DISCOUNTS
Antigua and Barbuda	No	No
Argentina	No	No
Bahamas	No	No
Barbados	No	No
Belize	No	No
Bolivia (Plurinational State of)	Yes	No
Brazil	Yes	Yes ⊙
Canada	Yes	Yes
Chile[1]	Yes	Yes
Colombia	Yes	Yes
Costa Rica	No	No
Cuba	No	No
Dominica	No	No
Dominican Republic	No	No
Ecuador	Yes	No
El Salvador	No	No
Grenada	No	No
Guatemala	Yes	No
Guyana	No	No
Haiti	No	No
Honduras	No	No
Jamaica	No	No
Mexico	Yes	Yes
Nicaragua	No	No
Panama	Yes	Yes
Paraguay	No	No
Peru	No	No
Saint Kitts and Nevis	No	No
Saint Lucia	No	No
Saint Vincent and the Grenadines	No	No
Suriname[3]	No	No
Trinidad and Tobago	No	No
United States of America	No	No
Uruguay	Yes	Yes
Venezuela (Bolivarian Republic of)	Yes	Yes

NOTES

1 A new law that entered into force on 1 March 2013 establishes a ban of all forms of tobacco advertising, promotion and sponsorship.

2 Although the law does not explicitly ban the usage of brand names of non-tobacco products for tobacco products (brand sharing) and does not provide a definition of tobacco advertising and promotion, we interpret that brand sharing is covered by the existing ban on all forms of advertising and promotion because this country is a Party to the WHO FCTC and we assume that the WHO FCTC definition applies.

3 A new law was approved in early 2013 which establishes a ban on all forms of tobacco advertising, promotion and sponsorship.

BAN ON TOBACCO PROMOTION AND SPONSORSHIP					
NON-TOBACCO PRODUCTS IDENTIFIED WITH TOBACCO BRAND NAMES	BRAND NAME OF NON-TOBACCO PRODUCTS USED FOR TOBACCO PRODUCTS	APPEARANCE OF TOBACCO BRANDS IN TV AND/OR FILMS (PRODUCT PLACEMENT)	APPEARANCE OF TOBACCO PRODUCTS IN TV AND/OR FILMS	SPONSORED EVENTS	OVERALL COMPLIANCE OF BAN ON PROMOTION *
No	No	No	No	No	—
Yes	Yes	Yes	Yes	Yes	5
No	No	No	No	No	—
No	No	No	No	No	—
No	No	No	No	No	—
No	No	No	No	Yes	1
Yes	Yes	Yes	Yes	Yes	5
No	No	Yes	No	Yes	10
Yes	No	Yes	No	No	4
Yes	Yes[2]	Yes	Yes	Yes	...
Yes	Yes	Yes	Yes	Yes	10
No	No	No	No	No	—
No	No	No	No	No	—
No	No	No	No	No	—
Yes	No	Yes	Yes	Yes	8
Yes	Yes	Yes	Yes	Yes	...
No	No	No	No	No	—
No	No	No	No	No	...
No	No	No	No	No	—
No	No	No	No	No	—
No	No	No	No	No	—
No	No	No	No	No	—
Yes	No	No	No	Yes	5
No	No	No	No	No	—
Yes	Yes	Yes	Yes	Yes	8
No	No	No	No	No	—
No	No	No	No	No	—
No	No	No	No	No	—
No	No	No	No	No	—
No	No	No	No	No	—
No	No	No	No	No	—
No	No	Yes	No	Yes	8
No	No	No	No	No	—
Yes	Yes	Yes	Yes	Yes	10
No	No	No	No	No	10

South-East Asia

Table 2.2.3
Bans on tobacco promotion and sponsorship in South-East Asia

* Score of 0 to 10, where 0 is low compliance. Refer to Technical Note I for more information.

. . . Data not reported/not available.

— Data not required/not applicable.

COUNTRY		
	FREE DISTRIBUTION IN MAIL OR THROUGH OTHER MEANS	PROMOTIONAL DISCOUNTS
Bangladesh	Yes	No
Bhutan	Yes	Yes
Democratic People's Republic of Korea	No	No
India	Yes	Yes
Indonesia	Yes	Yes
Maldives	Yes	Yes
Myanmar	Yes	No
Nepal	Yes	No
Sri Lanka	Yes	Yes
Thailand	Yes	Yes
Timor-Leste	No	No

NOTES

[1] Although the law does not explicitly ban the identification of non-tobacco products with tobacco brand names (brand stretching) and does not provide a definition of tobacco advertising and promotion, we interpret that brand stretching is covered by the existing ban of all forms of advertising and promotion because this country is a Party to the WHO FCTC and we assume that the WHO FCTC definition applies.

BAN ON TOBACCO PROMOTION AND SPONSORSHIP					
NON-TOBACCO PRODUCTS IDENTIFIED WITH TOBACCO BRAND NAMES	BRAND NAME OF NON-TOBACCO PRODUCTS USED FOR TOBACCO PRODUCTS	APPEARANCE OF TOBACCO BRANDS IN TV AND/OR FILMS (PRODUCT PLACEMENT)	APPEARANCE OF TOBACCO PRODUCTS IN TV AND/OR FILMS	SPONSORED EVENTS	OVERALL COMPLIANCE OF BAN ON PROMOTION *
No	No	No	No	No	5
Yes	No	No	Yes	Yes	6
No	No	No	No	No	—
Yes	Yes	Yes	Yes	Yes	5
Yes	No	No	Yes	No	. . .
Yes	Yes	Yes	Yes	Yes	3
Yes	No	No	No	Yes	5
Yes[1]	Yes	Yes	No	No	8
Yes	No	Yes	Yes	Yes	8
Yes	No	Yes	No	No	4
No	No	No	No	No	—

Europe

Table 2.2.4

Bans on tobacco promotion and sponsorship in Europe

* Score of 0 to 10, where 0 is low compliance. Refer to Technical Note I more information.

. . . Data not reported/not available.

— Data not required/not applicable.

COUNTRY	FREE DISTRIBUTION IN MAIL OR THROUGH OTHER MEANS	PROMOTIONAL DISCOUNTS
Albania	Yes	Yes
Andorra	No	No
Armenia	Yes	No
Austria	No	Yes
Azerbaijan	Yes	No
Belarus	Yes	Yes
Belgium	Yes	Yes
Bosnia and Herzegovina	No	No
Bulgaria	No	No
Croatia	Yes	Yes
Cyprus	Yes	No
Czech Republic	Yes	Yes
Denmark	Yes	No
Estonia	Yes	Yes
Finland	Yes	Yes
France	Yes	Yes
Georgia	Yes	No
Germany	No	Yes
Greece	Yes	No
Hungary	Yes	No
Iceland	Yes	Yes
Ireland	Yes	Yes
Israel	Yes	No
Italy	No	No
Kazakhstan	Yes	No
Kyrgyzstan	Yes	Yes
Latvia	No	No
Lithuania	Yes	Yes
Luxembourg	Yes	Yes
Malta	No	Yes
Monaco	No	No
Montenegro	Yes	Yes
Netherlands	Yes	Yes
Norway	Yes	Yes
Poland	Yes	Yes
Portugal	Yes	Yes
Republic of Moldova	No	No
Romania	No	No
Russian Federation	No	No
San Marino	No	No
Serbia	Yes	Yes
Slovakia	Yes	No
Slovenia	No	Yes
Spain	Yes	Yes
Sweden	Yes	Yes
Switzerland	No	No
Tajikistan	No	No
The former Yugoslav Republic of Macedonia	No	Yes
Turkey	Yes	Yes
Turkmenistan	No	No
Ukraine	Yes	Yes
United Kingdom of Great Britain and Northern Ireland	Yes	Yes
Uzbekistan	Yes	No

NOTES

1 Although the law does not explicitly ban the identification of non-tobacco products with tobacco brand names (brand stretching) and does not provide a definition of tobacco advertising and promotion, we interpret that brand stretching is covered by the existing ban of all forms of advertising and promotion because this country is a Party to the WHO FCTC and we assume that the WHO FCTC definition applies.

2 Although the law does not explicitly ban the usage of brand names of non-tobacco products for tobacco products (brand sharing) and does not provide a definition of tobacco advertising and promotion, we interpret that brand sharing is covered by the existing ban on all forms of advertising and promotion because this country is a Party to the WHO FCTC and we assume that the WHO FCTC definition applies.

3 Data not approved by national authorities.

4 The law expressly prohibits the use of tobacco products related logos on non-tobacco products or services in periodical publications, on TV and the radio and in other recordings but provides for some exceptions.

BAN ON TOBACCO PROMOTION AND SPONSORSHIP					
NON-TOBACCO PRODUCTS IDENTIFIED WITH TOBACCO BRAND NAMES	BRAND NAME OF NON-TOBACCO PRODUCTS USED FOR TOBACCO PRODUCTS	APPEARANCE OF TOBACCO BRANDS IN TV AND/OR FILMS (PRODUCT PLACEMENT)	APPEARANCE OF TOBACCO PRODUCTS IN TV AND/OR FILMS	SPONSORED EVENTS	OVERALL COMPLIANCE OF BAN ON PROMOTION *
Yes	Yes	Yes	Yes	Yes	8
No	No	No	No	No	—
No	No	No	No	No	2
No	No	Yes	No	Yes	2
No	No	Yes	No	No	8
No	No	No	No	No	3
No	No	Yes	No	Yes	9
No	No	Yes	No	Yes	5
No	No	Yes	No	No	3
Yes	No	Yes	Yes	Yes	5
Yes[1]	Yes[2]	Yes	No	Yes	10
No	No	Yes	Yes	No	7
No	Yes	No	No	Yes	. . .
No	No	No	No	No	10
Yes	No	Yes	No	Yes	8
Yes	No	Yes	Yes	Yes	. . .
No	No	Yes	Yes	Yes	6
No	No	Yes	No	No	8
No	No	Yes	No	No	. . .
Yes	Yes	Yes	No	Yes	10
Yes	Yes	Yes	Yes	Yes	10
No	No	No	No	Yes	. . .
No	No	Yes	Yes	No	. . .
No	No	Yes	No	No	10
No	No	Yes	No	No	. . .
Yes	Yes	Yes	Yes	Yes	. . .
No	No	Yes	No	No	. . .
Yes	No	Yes	No	No	7
No	No	Yes	No	Yes	. . .
Yes	Yes	Yes	No	No	8
No	No	No	No	No	—
Yes	Yes[2]	Yes	Yes	Yes	10
No	No	Yes	No	Yes	3[3]
No	Yes	Yes	No	No	10
No	No	Yes	No	No	5
No	No	Yes	Yes	Yes	5
Yes	No	Yes	No	Yes	3
Yes	No	Yes	No	No	7
No	No	Yes	Yes	No	. . .
No	No	No	No	No	—
No	No	Yes	No	No	5
No	No	No	No	Yes	7
No	Yes	Yes	No	Yes	5
Yes	Yes	Yes	No	Yes	10
No[4]	No	Yes	No	Yes	5
No	No	No	No	No	—
No	No	No	No	Yes	. . .
Yes	No	Yes	No	Yes	. . .
Yes	Yes	Yes	Yes	Yes	10
No	No	No	No	No	—
No	No	No	No	Yes	. . .
Yes	Yes	Yes	No	Yes	9
No	No	No	No	Yes	. . .

Eastern Mediterranean

Table 2.2.5
Bans on tobacco promotion and sponsorship in the Eastern Mediterranean

* Score of 0 to 10, where 0 is low compliance. Refer to Technical Note I for more information.

. . . Data not reported/not available.

— Data not required/not applicable.

< Refers to a territory.

COUNTRY		
	FREE DISTRIBUTION IN MAIL OR THROUGH OTHER MEANS	PROMOTIONAL DISCOUNTS
Afghanistan	No	No
Bahrain	Yes	Yes
Djibouti	Yes	Yes
Egypt	Yes	Yes
Iran (Islamic Republic of)	Yes	Yes
Iraq	No	No
Jordan	Yes	No
Kuwait	Yes	Yes
Lebanon	Yes	No
Libya	Yes	Yes
Morocco	Yes	Yes
Oman	No	No
Pakistan	Yes	Yes
Qatar	Yes	Yes
Saudi Arabia[4]	No	No
Somalia	No	No
South Sudan[5]	No	No
Sudan	Yes	Yes
Syrian Arab Republic	Yes	Yes
Tunisia	Yes	Yes
United Arab Emirates	No	No
West Bank and Gaza Strip <	No	Yes
Yemen	Yes	Yes

NOTES

1 Although the law does not explicitly ban the identification of non-tobacco products with tobacco brand names (brand stretching) and does not provide a definition of tobacco advertising and promotion, we interpret that brand stretching is covered by the existing ban of all forms of advertising and promotion because this country is a Party to the WHO FCTC and we assume that the WHO FCTC definition applies.

2 Although the law does not explicitly ban the usage of brand names of non-tobacco products for tobacco products (brand sharing) and does not provide a definition of tobacco advertising and promotion, we interpret that brand sharing is covered by the existing ban of all forms of advertising and promotion because this country is a Party to the WHO FCTC and we assume that the WHO FCTC definition applies.

3 Regulations pending.

4 Data not approved by national authorities.

5 South Sudan has been independent since 2011. This new country has not yet adopted legislation on tobacco advertising, promotion and sponsorship.

6 The reported compliance is a calculated average of the assessment from experts from the West Bank.

BAN ON TOBACCO PROMOTION AND SPONSORSHIP					
NON-TOBACCO PRODUCTS IDENTIFIED WITH TOBACCO BRAND NAMES	BRAND NAME OF NON-TOBACCO PRODUCTS USED FOR TOBACCO PRODUCTS	APPEARANCE OF TOBACCO BRANDS IN TV AND/OR FILMS (PRODUCT PLACEMENT)	APPEARANCE OF TOBACCO PRODUCTS IN TV AND/OR FILMS	SPONSORED EVENTS	OVERALL COMPLIANCE OF BAN ON PROMOTION *
No	No	Yes	No	No	5
Yes[1]	Yes[2]	Yes	Yes	Yes	9
Yes	Yes	Yes	Yes	Yes	7
Yes[1]	Yes[2]	Yes	Yes	No	5
Yes	Yes[2]	Yes	Yes	Yes	10
Yes	No[3]	Yes	Yes	No[3]	5
No	No	No	No	No	6
Yes[1]	Yes[2]	Yes	Yes	Yes	8
Yes	Yes[2]	Yes	Yes	Yes	8
Yes[1]	Yes[2]	Yes	Yes	Yes	5
No	No	Yes	No	No	10
No	No	No	No	Yes	7
No	No	Yes	Yes	Yes	3
Yes[1]	Yes[2]	Yes	Yes	No	9
No	No	No	No	No	—
No	No	No	No	No	—
No	No	No	No	No	—
Yes[1]	Yes[2]	Yes	Yes	No	3
Yes[1]	Yes[2]	Yes	Yes	No	. . .
Yes[1]	Yes[2]	Yes	Yes	No	7
Yes	No	Yes	Yes	Yes	. . .
Yes	Yes[2]	Yes	Yes	Yes	7[6]
Yes[1]	Yes[2]	Yes	Yes	No	3

Western Pacific

Table 2.2.6
Bans on tobacco promotion and sponsorship in the Western Pacific

* Score of 0 to 10, where 0 is low compliance. Refer to Technical Note I for more information.

⦿ Policy adopted but not implemented by 31 December 2012.

. . . Data not reported/not available.

— Data not required/not applicable.

COUNTRY		
	FREE DISTRIBUTION IN MAIL OR THROUGH OTHER MEANS	PROMOTIONAL DISCOUNTS
Australia	No	No
Brunei Darussalam	Yes	No
Cambodia	No	No
China	No	No
Cook Islands	Yes	Yes
Fiji	Yes	Yes
Japan	No	No[1]
Kiribati	No	No
Lao People's Democratic Republic	No	No
Malaysia	Yes	Yes
Marshall Islands	Yes	Yes
Micronesia (Federated States of)	No	No
Mongolia	No	Yes
Nauru	Yes	No
New Zealand	Yes	Yes
Niue	No	No
Palau	Yes	Yes
Papua New Guinea	No	No
Philippines	No	No
Republic of Korea	No	No
Samoa	Yes	No
Singapore	Yes	Yes
Solomon Islands	Yes	Yes
Tonga	Yes	Yes
Tuvalu	Yes	Yes
Vanuatu	Yes	Yes
Viet Nam	Yes	Yes

NOTES

1 No discounted prices are allowed, however promotional gifts or offers are allowed for adults.

2 Although the law does not explicitly ban the usage of brand names of non-tobacco products for tobacco products (brand sharing) and does not provide a definition of tobacco advertising and promotion, we interpret that brand sharing is covered by the existing ban of all forms of advertising and promotion because this country is a Party to the WHO FCTC and we assume that the WHO FCTC definition applies.

3 Although the law does not explicitly ban the identification of non-tobacco products with tobacco brand names (brand stretching) and does not provide a definition of tobacco advertising and promotion, we interpret that brand stretching is covered by the existing ban of all forms of advertising and promotion because this country is a Party to the WHO FCTC and we assume that the WHO FCTC definition applies.

BAN ON TOBACCO PROMOTION AND SPONSORSHIP					
NON-TOBACCO PRODUCTS IDENTIFIED WITH TOBACCO BRAND NAMES	BRAND NAME OF NON-TOBACCO PRODUCTS USED FOR TOBACCO PRODUCTS	APPEARANCE OF TOBACCO BRANDS IN TV AND/OR FILMS (PRODUCT PLACEMENT)	APPEARANCE OF TOBACCO PRODUCTS IN TV AND/OR FILMS	SPONSORED EVENTS	OVERALL COMPLIANCE OF BAN ON PROMOTION *
Yes	No	Yes	No	Yes	...
No	No	Yes	No	Yes	10
No	No	No	No	Yes	9
No	No	Yes	No	No	3
Yes	Yes	Yes	Yes	Yes	10
Yes	Yes	Yes	No	Yes	8
No	No	No	No	No	—
No	No	No	No	No	—
No	No	No	No	Yes	...
Yes	No	Yes	No	Yes	6
Yes	No	No	No	No	...
No	No	No	No	No	—
Yes	Yes	Yes	No	Yes	6
No	No	Yes	No	Yes	...
Yes	Yes[2]	Yes	No	No	10
No	No	No	No	No	—
Yes	No	No	No	Yes	10
No	No	No	No	No	—
No	No	Yes	No	Yes	7
No	No	No	No	No	—
Yes	No	No	No	Yes	...
No	No	No	No	No	...
Yes	No	Yes	No	No	3
Yes	Yes	No	No	Yes	...
Yes	Yes	Yes	Yes	Yes	8
Yes	Yes	Yes	No	Yes	6
Yes[3]	Yes[2] ⊙	Yes	No	Yes	5

Africa

Table 2.3.1
Additional bans on tobacco advertising, promotion and sponsorship in Africa

⊙ Policy adopted but not implemented by 31 December 2012.

COUNTRY	BAN ON PUBLICITY OF CORPORATE SOCIAL RESPONSIBILITY ACTIVITIES	
	BY TOBACCO COMPANIES	BY OTHER ENTITIES
Algeria	No	No
Angola	No	No
Benin	No	No
Botswana	No	No
Burkina Faso	No	No
Burundi	No	No
Cameroon	No	No
Cape Verde	No	No
Central African Republic	No	No
Chad	No	No
Comoros	No	No
Congo	No	No
Côte d'Ivoire	No	No
Democratic Republic of the Congo	No	No
Equatorial Guinea	No	No
Eritrea	No	No
Ethiopia	No	No
Gabon	No	No
Gambia	No	No
Ghana	Yes	Yes
Guinea	No	No
Guinea-Bissau	No	No
Kenya	Yes	Yes
Lesotho	No	No
Liberia	No	No
Madagascar	No	No
Malawi	No	No
Mali	No	No
Mauritania	No	No
Mauritius	Yes	Yes
Mozambique	No	No
Namibia	No	No
Niger	No	No
Nigeria	No	No
Rwanda	No	No
Sao Tome and Principe	No	No
Senegal	No	No
Seychelles	No	No
Sierra Leone	No	No
South Africa	Yes	Yes
Swaziland	No	No
Togo	Yes ⊙	Yes ⊙
Uganda	No	No
United Republic of Tanzania	Yes	Yes
Zambia	No	No
Zimbabwe	No	No

BAN ON TOBACCO COMPANIES FUNDING OR MAKING IN-KIND CONTRIBUTIONS TO SMOKING PREVENTION MEDIA CAMPAIGNS	REQUIRED ANTI-TOBACCO ADS FOR ANY VISUAL ENTERTAINMENT MEDIA PRODUCT THAT DEPICTS TOBACCO PRODUCTS, USE OR IMAGES	BAN ON TOBACCO VENDING MACHINES	SUBNATIONAL BANS ON ADVERTISING, PROMOTION AND SPONSORSHIP EXIST
No	No	No	No
No	No	No	No
No	No	No	No
No	No	No	No
No	No	Yes	No
No	No	No	No
No	No	No	No
No	No	No	No
No	No	No	No
No	No	No	No
No	No	No	No
No	No	No	No
No	No	No	No
No	No	No	No
No	No	No	No
No	No	Yes	No
No	No	No	No
No	No	No	No
No	No	No	No
Yes	No	Yes	No
No	No	No	No
No	No	No	No
No	No	Yes	No
No	No	No	No
No	No	No	No
No	No	Yes	No
No	No	No	No
No	No	Yes	No
No	No	No	No
No	No	Yes	No
Yes	Yes	No	No
Yes	No	Yes	No
No	No	Yes	No
No	Yes	No	Yes
No	No	No	No
No	No	No	No
No	No	No	No
No	No	Yes	No
No	No	No	No
No	No	No	No
No	No	No	No
Yes ⊙	No	Yes ⊙	No
No	No	No	No
No	No	No	No
No	Yes	Yes	No
No	Yes	No	No

The Americas

Table 2.3.2
Additional bans on tobacco advertising, promotion and sponsorship in the Americas

COUNTRY	BAN ON PUBLICITY OF CORPORATE SOCIAL RESPONSIBILITY ACTIVITIES	
	BY TOBACCO COMPANIES	BY OTHER ENTITIES
Antigua and Barbuda	No	No
Argentina	No	No
Bahamas	No	No
Barbados	No	No
Belize	No	No
Bolivia (Plurinational State of)	No	No
Brazil	No	No
Canada	No	No
Chile[1]	No	No
Colombia	Yes	Yes
Costa Rica	Yes	Yes
Cuba	No	No
Dominica	No	No
Dominican Republic	No	No
Ecuador	Yes	Yes
El Salvador	Yes	Yes
Grenada	No	No
Guatemala	No	No
Guyana	No	No
Haiti	No	No
Honduras	No	No
Jamaica	No	No
Mexico	No	No
Nicaragua	No	No
Panama	No	No
Paraguay	No	No
Peru	No	No
Saint Kitts and Nevis	No	No
Saint Lucia	No	No
Saint Vincent and the Grenadines	No	No
Suriname[2]	No	No
Trinidad and Tobago	No	No
United States of America	No	No
Uruguay	Yes	Yes
Venezuela (Bolivarian Republic of)	No[3]	No[3]

NOTES

1 A new law that entered into force on 1 March 2013 establishes a ban of all forms of tobacco advertising, promotion and sponsorship.

2 A new law was approved in early 2013 that establishes a ban on all forms of tobacco advertising, promotion and sponsorship.

3 Data not approved by national authorities.

BAN ON TOBACCO COMPANIES FUNDING OR MAKING IN-KIND CONTRIBUTIONS TO SMOKING PREVENTION MEDIA CAMPAIGNS	REQUIRED ANTI-TOBACCO ADS FOR ANY VISUAL ENTERTAINMENT MEDIA PRODUCT THAT DEPICTS TOBACCO PRODUCTS, USE OR IMAGES	BAN ON TOBACCO VENDING MACHINES	SUBNATIONAL BANS ON ADVERTISING, PROMOTION AND SPONSORSHIP EXIST
No	No	No	No
No	No	Yes	Yes
No	No	No	No
No	No	No	No
No	No	No	No
No	No	No	No
No	No	No	No
No	No	No	Yes
No	No	No	No
Yes	No	Yes	No
Yes	No	Yes	No
No	No	No	No
No	No	No	No
No	No	No	No
No	No	Yes	No
Yes	No	Yes	No
No	No	No	No
No	Yes	No	No
No	No	No	No
No	No	No	No
No	No	Yes	No
No	No	No	No
No	No	Yes	Yes
No	No	Yes	No
No	No	Yes	No
No	No	No	No
No	No	No	No
No	No	No	No
No	No	No	No
No	No	No	No
No	No	No	No
No	No	Yes	No
No	No	No	Yes
Yes	No	Yes	No
No[3]	No	Yes	No

South-East Asia

Table 2.3.3
Additional bans on tobacco advertising, promotion and sponsorship in South-East Asia

COUNTRY	BAN ON PUBLICITY OF CORPORATE SOCIAL RESPONSIBILITY ACTIVITIES	
	BY TOBACCO COMPANIES	BY OTHER ENTITIES
Bangladesh	No	No
Bhutan	No	No
Democratic People's Republic of Korea	No	No
India	No	No
Indonesia	No	No
Maldives	Yes	Yes
Myanmar	No	No
Nepal	No	No
Sri Lanka	No	No
Thailand	No	No
Timor-Leste	No	No

BAN ON TOBACCO COMPANIES FUNDING OR MAKING IN-KIND CONTRIBUTIONS TO SMOKING PREVENTION MEDIA CAMPAIGNS	REQUIRED ANTI-TOBACCO ADS FOR ANY VISUAL ENTERTAINMENT MEDIA PRODUCT THAT DEPICTS TOBACCO PRODUCTS, USE OR IMAGES	BAN ON TOBACCO VENDING MACHINES	SUBNATIONAL BANS ON ADVERTISING, PROMOTION AND SPONSORSHIP EXIST
No	No	No	No
No	No	Yes	No
No	No	Yes	No
No	Yes	Yes	Yes
No	No	Yes	Yes
No	Yes	Yes	No
No	No	Yes	No
No	No	No	No
No	Yes	Yes	No
No	No	Yes	No
No	No	No	No

Europe

Table 2.3.4
Additional bans on tobacco advertising, promotion and sponsorship in Europe

COUNTRY	BAN ON PUBLICITY OF CORPORATE SOCIAL RESPONSIBILITY ACTIVITIES	
	BY TOBACCO COMPANIES	BY OTHER ENTITIES
Albania	No	No
Andorra	No	No
Armenia	No	No
Austria	No	No
Azerbaijan	No	No
Belarus	No	No
Belgium	Yes	Yes
Bosnia and Herzegovina	No	No
Bulgaria	No	No
Croatia	No	No
Cyprus	No	No
Czech Republic	No	No
Denmark	No	No
Estonia	No	No
Finland	No	No
France	No	No
Georgia	Yes	Yes
Germany	No	No
Greece	No	No
Hungary	No	No
Iceland	No	No
Ireland	No	No
Israel	No	No
Italy	No	No
Kazakhstan	No	No
Kyrgyzstan	No	No
Latvia	No	No
Lithuania	No	No
Luxembourg	No	No
Malta	No	No
Monaco	No	No
Montenegro	No	No
Netherlands	No	No
Norway	No	No
Poland	No	No
Portugal	No	No
Republic of Moldova	No	No
Romania	No	No
Russian Federation	No	No
San Marino	No	No
Serbia	No	No
Slovakia	No	No
Slovenia	No	No
Spain	No	No
Sweden	No	No
Switzerland	No	No
Tajikistan	No	No
The former Yugoslav Republic of Macedonia	No	No
Turkey	Yes	Yes
Turkmenistan	No	No
Ukraine	No	No
United Kingdom of Great Britain and Northern Ireland	No	No
Uzbekistan	No	No

BAN ON TOBACCO COMPANIES FUNDING OR MAKING IN-KIND CONTRIBUTIONS TO SMOKING PREVENTION MEDIA CAMPAIGNS	REQUIRED ANTI-TOBACCO ADS FOR ANY VISUAL ENTERTAINMENT MEDIA PRODUCT THAT DEPICTS TOBACCO PRODUCTS, USE OR IMAGES	BAN ON TOBACCO VENDING MACHINES	SUBNATIONAL BANS ON ADVERTISING, PROMOTION AND SPONSORSHIP EXIST
No	No	Yes	No
No	No	No	No
No	No	No	No
No	No	No	No
No	No	Yes	No
No	No	Yes	No
Yes	No	No	Yes
No	No	Yes	Yes
No	No	Yes	No
No	No	No	No
No	No	Yes	No
No	No	No	No
No	No	No	No
No	No	Yes	No
No	No	Yes	No
No	No	Yes	No
No	No	Yes	No
No	No	No	No
No	No	Yes	No
No	No	Yes	No
No	No	Yes	No
No	No	No	No
No	No	No	No
No	No	No	No
No	No	Yes	No
No	No	Yes	No
No	No	Yes	No
No	No	Yes	No
No	No	No	No
No	No	No	No
No	No	No	No
No	No	Yes	No
No	No	No	No
No	No	No	No
No	No	No	No
Yes	No	No	No
No	No	Yes	No
No	No	Yes	No
No	No	Yes	No
No	No	No	No
No	No	Yes	No
No	No	Yes	No
No	No	Yes	No
No	No	No	No
No	No	No	No
No	No	No	Yes
No	No	Yes	No
No	No	Yes	No
No	No	Yes	No
No	No	No	No
Yes	No	Yes	No
No	No	Yes	Yes
No	Yes	Yes	No

Eastern Mediterranean

Table 2.3.5
Additional bans on tobacco advertising, promotion and sponsorship in the Eastern Mediterranean

< Refers to a territory.

COUNTRY	BAN ON PUBLICITY OF CORPORATE SOCIAL RESPONSIBILITY ACTIVITIES	
	BY TOBACCO COMPANIES	BY OTHER ENTITIES
Afghanistan	No	No
Bahrain	Yes	No
Djibouti	Yes	Yes
Egypt	No	No
Iran (Islamic Republic of)	Yes	Yes
Iraq	No[1]	No[1]
Jordan	No	No
Kuwait	No	No
Lebanon	Yes	Yes
Libya	Yes	Yes
Morocco	No	No
Oman	No	No
Pakistan	No	No
Qatar	No	No
Saudi Arabia	No[2]	No[2]
Somalia	No	No
South Sudan[3]	No	No
Sudan	No	No
Syrian Arab Republic	No	No
Tunisia	No	No
United Arab Emirates	Yes	Yes
West Bank and Gaza Strip <	Yes	Yes
Yemen	No	No

NOTES

1 Regulations pending.

2 Data not approved by national authorities.

3 South Sudan has been independent since 2011. This new country has not yet adopted legislation on tobacco advertising, promotion and sponsorship.

BAN ON TOBACCO COMPANIES FUNDING OR MAKING IN-KIND CONTRIBUTIONS TO SMOKING PREVENTION MEDIA CAMPAIGNS	REQUIRED ANTI-TOBACCO ADS FOR ANY VISUAL ENTERTAINMENT MEDIA PRODUCT THAT DEPICTS TOBACCO PRODUCTS, USE OR IMAGES	BAN ON TOBACCO VENDING MACHINES	SUBNATIONAL BANS ON ADVERTISING, PROMOTION AND SPONSORSHIP EXIST
No	No	No	No
No	No	Yes	No
Yes	No	Yes	No
No	No	No	Yes
Yes	No	Yes	No
No	No	No	Yes
No	No	Yes	No
No	No	No	No
No	No	Yes	No
Yes	No	Yes	No
No	No	Yes	No
No	No	No	Yes
No	Yes	No	No
No	No	Yes	No
No[2]	No	No	No
No	No	No	No
No	No	No	No
No	No	Yes	No
No	No	No	No
No	No	Yes	No
Yes	No	Yes	No
Yes	No	Yes	No
No	No	No	No

Western Pacific

Table 2.3.6

Additional bans on tobacco advertising, promotion and sponsorship in the Western Pacific

⊙ Policy adopted but not implemented by 31 December 2012.

COUNTRY	BAN ON PUBLICITY OF CORPORATE SOCIAL RESPONSIBILITY ACTIVITIES	
	BY TOBACCO COMPANIES	BY OTHER ENTITIES
Australia	No	No
Brunei Darussalam	No	No
Cambodia	Yes	Yes
China	No	No
Cook Islands	Yes	Yes
Fiji	No	No
Japan	No	No
Kiribati	No	No
Lao People's Democratic Republic	No	No
Malaysia	No	No
Marshall Islands	No	No
Micronesia (Federated States of)	No	No
Mongolia	Yes	Yes
Nauru	No	No
New Zealand	Yes	Yes
Niue	No	No
Palau	No	No
Papua New Guinea	No	No
Philippines	No	No
Republic of Korea	No	No
Samoa	No	No
Singapore	Yes	Yes
Solomon Islands	No	No
Tonga	No	No
Tuvalu	No	No
Vanuatu	Yes	Yes
Viet Nam	Yes ⊙	Yes ⊙

BAN ON TOBACCO COMPANIES FUNDING OR MAKING IN-KIND CONTRIBUTIONS TO SMOKING PREVENTION MEDIA CAMPAIGNS	REQUIRED ANTI-TOBACCO ADS FOR ANY VISUAL ENTERTAINMENT MEDIA PRODUCT THAT DEPICTS TOBACCO PRODUCTS, USE OR IMAGES	BAN ON TOBACCO VENDING MACHINES	SUBNATIONAL BANS ON ADVERTISING, PROMOTION AND SPONSORSHIP EXIST
No	No	No	Yes
No	No	Yes	No
No	No	No	No
No	No	Yes	Yes
No	No	Yes	No
No	No	Yes	No
No	No	No	No
No	No	No	No
No	No	Yes	Yes
No	No	Yes	No
No	Yes	Yes	No
No	No	No	Yes
Yes	No	Yes	No
No	No	Yes	No
No	No	No	No
No	No	No	No
No	No	Yes	No
No	No	No	No
No	No	No	No
No	No	No	No
No	No	Yes	No
No	No	Yes	No
No	No	Yes	No
No	No	No	No
No	No	Yes	No
No	No	Yes	No
Yes ⊙	No	Yes	No

Table 2.4.1
Subnational bans⁺ on tobacco advertising

⁺ Only subnational jurisdictions for which legislation was available are reported here.

* A ban is in effect at national level.

COUNTRY	JURISDICTION
Argentina	Buenos Aires
	Catamarca
	Chaco
	Chubut
	Ciudad Autonoma de Buenos Aires
	Cordoba
	Corrientes
	Formosa
	La Pampa
	La Rioja
	Mendoza
	Neuquen
	Rio Negro
	San Luis
	Santa Cruz
	Santa Fe
	Santiago del Estero
Australia	Australian Capital Territory
	New South Wales
	Northern Territory
	Queensland
	South Australia
	Tasmania
	Victoria
	Western Australia
Belgium	Flanders
Bosnia and Herzegovina	Federacija Bosne i Hercegovine
	Republika Srpska
Canada	Alberta
	British Columbia
	Manitoba
	New Brunswick
	Newfoundland and Labrador
	Northwest Territories
	Nova Scotia
	Nunavut
	Ontario
	Prince Edward Island
	Quebec
	Saskatchewan
	Yukon
China	Hong Kong Special Administrative Region
	Macao Special Administrative Region
Egypt	Alexandria
India	Goa
	Tamil Nadu
Indonesia	Padang Panjang
Iraq	Arbïl
	As Sulaymanayah
	Duhok

BAN ON TOBACCO ADVERTISING						
NATIONAL TV AND RADIO	INTERNATIONAL TV AND RADIO	LOCAL MAGAZINES AND NEWSPAPERS	INTERNATIONAL MAGAZINES AND NEWSPAPERS	BILLBOARD AND OUTDOOR ADVERTISING	POINT OF SALE	INTERNET
Yes	No*	Yes	No*	Yes	No	No*
No*	No*	No*	No*	No*	No	No*
Yes	Yes	Yes	Yes	Yes	No	Yes
Yes	Yes	Yes	Yes	Yes	No	Yes
Yes	No*	Yes	No*	Yes	No	No*
Yes	Yes	Yes	Yes	Yes	No	Yes
No*	No*	No*	No*	No*	No	No*
Yes	Yes	Yes	Yes	Yes	No	Yes
No*	No*	No*	No*	No*	No	No*
No*	No*	No*	No*	No*	No	No*
Yes	Yes	Yes	Yes	Yes	No	Yes
Yes	Yes	Yes	Yes	Yes	Yes	Yes
No*	No*	No*	No*	Yes	No	No*
No*	No*	No*	No*	No*	No	No*
No*	No*	No*	No*	No*	No	No*
No*	No*	No*	No*	No*	No	No*
No*	No*	No*	No*	No*	No	No*
Yes	No*	Yes	No	Yes	Yes	No*
No*	No*	Yes	No	Yes	Yes	No*
Yes	No*	Yes	No	Yes	Yes	No*
No*	No*	No*	No	No*	Yes	No*
Yes	Yes	Yes	Yes	Yes	Yes	Yes
Yes	No*	No*	No	Yes	Yes	No*
No*	No*	No*	No	Yes	No	No*
No*	No*	Yes	No	Yes	Yes	No*
Yes	No*	No*	No	No*	No	No*
Yes	Yes	Yes	Yes	Yes	No	No
Yes	Yes	Yes	Yes	Yes	No	No
No*	No	No*	No	Yes	Yes	No*
No*	No	No*	No	No*	Yes	No*
No*	No	No*	No	Yes	Yes	No*
No*	No	No*	No	No*	Yes	No*
No*	No	No*	No	No*	Yes	No*
No*	No	No*	No	No*	Yes	No*
No*	No	No*	No	No*	Yes	No*
No*	No	No*	No	No*	No	No*
No*	No	No*	No	No*	Yes	No*
No*	No	No*	No	No*	Yes	No*
No*	No	No*	No	No*	Yes	No*
No*	No	No*	No	Yes	Yes	No*
No*	No	No*	No	No*	Yes	No*
Yes	Yes	Yes	Yes	Yes	Yes	Yes
Yes	Yes	Yes	Yes	Yes	Yes	Yes
Yes	Yes	Yes	Yes	Yes	Yes	Yes
Yes	Yes	Yes	Yes	Yes	Yes	Yes
No*	No*	No*	No*	Yes	No	No*
No	No	No	No	Yes	No	No
Yes	Yes	Yes	Yes	Yes	Yes	Yes
Yes	Yes	Yes	Yes	Yes	Yes	Yes
Yes	Yes	Yes	Yes	Yes	Yes	Yes

Table 2.4.1
Subnational bans⁺ on tobacco advertising (continued)

⁺ Only subnational jurisdictions for which legislation was available are reported here.

* A ban is in effect at national level.

COUNTRY	JURISDICTION
Lao People's Democratic Republic	Vientiane Capital
Mexico	Aguascalientes
	Baja California
	Baja California Sur
	Campeche
	Chiapas
	Chihuahua
	Coahuila de Zaragoza
	Colima
	Durango
	Federal District (Mexico City)
	Guanajuato
	Guerrero
	Hidalgo
	Jalisco
	Mexico
	Michoacan de Ocampo
	Morelos
	Nayarit
	Nuevo Leon
	Oaxaca
	Puebla
	Queretaro Arteaga
	Quintana Roo
	San Luis Potosi
	Sinaloa
	Sonora
	Tabasco
	Tamaulipas
	Tlaxcala
	Veracruz de Ignacio de la Llave
	Yucatan
	Zacatecas
Micronesia (Federated States of)	Chuuk
	Pohnpei
	Yap
Nigeria	Cross River
Oman	Dhofar
	Sahar
Switzerland	Appenzell Ausserrhoden
	Basel-Landschaft
	Basel-Stadt
	Bern
	Genève
	Graubünden
	Sankt Gallen
	Solothurn
	Thurgau
	Ticino
	Uri

BAN ON TOBACCO ADVERTISING						
NATIONAL TV AND RADIO	INTERNATIONAL TV AND RADIO	LOCAL MAGAZINES AND NEWSPAPERS	INTERNATIONAL MAGAZINES AND NEWSPAPERS	BILLBOARD AND OUTDOOR ADVERTISING	POINT OF SALE	INTERNET
Yes	No*	Yes	No*	No*	No	Yes
No*	No*	No	No	No*	No	No
No*	No*	No	No	No*	No	No
No*	No*	No	No	No*	No	No
No*	No*	No	No	No*	No	No
No*	No*	No	No	No*	No	No
No*	No*	No	No	No*	No	No
No*	No*	No	No	No*	No	No
No*	No*	No	No	No*	No	No
No*	No*	No	No	No*	No	No
No*	No*	No	No	No*	No	No
No*	No*	No	No	No*	No	No
No*	No*	No	No	No*	No	No
No*	No*	No	No	No*	No	No
No*	No*	No	No	No*	No	No
No*	No*	No	No	No*	No	No
No*	No*	No	No	No*	No	No
No*	No*	No	No	No*	No	No
No*	No*	No	No	No*	No	No
No*	No*	No	No	No*	No	No
No*	No*	No	No	No*	No	No
No*	No*	No	No	No*	No	No
No*	No*	No	No	No*	No	No
No*	No*	No	No	No*	No	No
No*	No*	No	No	No*	No	No
No*	No*	No	No	No*	No	No
No*	No*	No	No	No*	No	No
No*	No*	No	No	No*	No	No
No*	No*	No	No	No*	No	No
No*	No*	No	No	No*	No	No
No*	No*	No	No	No*	No	No
No*	No*	No	No	No*	No	No
No*	No*	No	No	No*	No	No
Yes	No	Yes	No	Yes	Yes	Yes
Yes	No	Yes	No	Yes	Yes	Yes
Yes	No	Yes	No	Yes	Yes	No
Yes	No	Yes	No	Yes	No	No
No	No	No	No	No*	No	No
No	No	No	No	No*	No	No
No*	No*	No	No	Yes	No	No
No*	No*	No	No	Yes	No	No
No*	No*	No	No	Yes	No	No
No*	No*	No	No	Yes	No	No
No*	No*	No	No	Yes	No	No
No*	No*	No	No	Yes	No	No
No*	No*	No	No	Yes	No	No
No*	No*	No	No	Yes	No	No
No*	No*	No	No	Yes	No	No
No*	No*	No	No	Yes	No	No
No*	No*	No	No	Yes	No	No

Table 2.4.1
Subnational bans+ on tobacco advertising (continued)

+ Only subnational jurisdictions for which legislation was available are reported here.

* A ban is in effect at national level.

COUNTRY	JURISDICTION
Switzerland (continued)	Valais
	Vaud
	Zug
	Zürich
United Kingdom of Great Britain and Northern Ireland	England
	Northern Ireland
	Scotland
	Wales
United States of America	Alabama
	Alaska
	Arizona
	Arkansas
	California
	Colorado
	Connecticut
	Delaware
	District of Columbia
	Florida
	Georgia
	Hawaii
	Idaho
	Illinois
	Indiana
	Iowa
	Kansas
	Kentucky
	Louisiana
	Maine
	Maryland
	Massachusetts
	Michigan
	Minnesota
	Mississippi
	Missouri
	Montana
	Nebraska
	Nevada
	New Hampshire
	New Jersey
	New Mexico
	New York
	North Carolina
	North Dakota
	Ohio
	Oklahoma
	Oregon
	Pennsylvania
	Puerto Rico
	Rhode Island

BAN ON TOBACCO ADVERTISING						
NATIONAL TV AND RADIO	INTERNATIONAL TV AND RADIO	LOCAL MAGAZINES AND NEWSPAPERS	INTERNATIONAL MAGAZINES AND NEWSPAPERS	BILLBOARD AND OUTDOOR ADVERTISING	POINT OF SALE	INTERNET
No*	No*	No	No	Yes	No	No
No*	No*	No	No	Yes	No	No
No*	No*	No	No	Yes	No	No
No*	No*	No	No	Yes	No	No
Yes	Yes	Yes	No	Yes	No	Yes
Yes	Yes	Yes	No	Yes	No	Yes
Yes	Yes	Yes	No	Yes	No	Yes
Yes	Yes	Yes	No	Yes	No	Yes
No*	No	No	No	Yes	No	No
No*	No	No	No	Yes	No	No
No*	No	No	No	Yes	No	No
No*	No	No	No	Yes	No	No
No*	No	No	No	Yes	No	No
No*	No	No	No	Yes	No	No
No*	No	No	No	Yes	No	No
No*	No	No	No	Yes	No	No
No*	No	No	No	Yes	No	No
No*	No	No	No	Yes	No	No
No*	No	No	No	Yes	No	No
No*	No	No	No	Yes	No	No
No*	No	No	No	Yes	No	No
No*	No	No	No	Yes	No	No
No*	No	No	No	Yes	No	No
No*	No	No	No	Yes	No	No
No*	No	No	No	Yes	No	No
No*	No	No	No	Yes	No	No
No*	No	No	No	Yes	No	No
No*	No	No	No	Yes	No	No
No*	No	No	No	Yes	No	No
No*	No	No	No	Yes	No	No
No*	No	No	No	Yes	No	No
No*	No	No	No	Yes	No	No
No*	No	No	No	Yes	No	No
No*	No	No	No	Yes	No	No
No*	No	No	No	Yes	No	No
No*	No	No	No	Yes	No	No
No*	No	No	No	Yes	No	No
No*	No	No	No	Yes	No	No
No*	No	No	No	Yes	No	No
No*	No	No	No	Yes	No	No
No*	No	No	No	Yes	No	No
No*	No	No	No	Yes	No	No
No*	No	No	No	Yes	No	No
No*	No	No	No	Yes	No	No
No*	No	No	No	Yes	No	No
No*	No	No	No	Yes	No	No
No*	No	No	No	Yes	No	No
No*	No	No	No	Yes	No	No
No*	No	No	No	Yes	No	No

Table 2.4.1
Subnational bans+ on tobacco advertising (continued)

+ Only subnational jurisdictions for which legislation was available are reported here.

* A ban is in effect at national level.

COUNTRY	JURISDICTION
United States of America (continued)	South Carolina
	South Dakota
	Tennessee
	Texas
	Utah
	Vermont
	Virginia
	Washington
	West Virginia
	Wisconsin
	Wyoming

BAN ON TOBACCO ADVERTISING						
NATIONAL TV AND RADIO	INTERNATIONAL TV AND RADIO	LOCAL MAGAZINES AND NEWSPAPERS	INTERNATIONAL MAGAZINES AND NEWSPAPERS	BILLBOARD AND OUTDOOR ADVERTISING	POINT OF SALE	INTERNET
No*	No	No	No	Yes	No	No
No*	No	No	No	Yes	No	No
No*	No	No	No	Yes	No	No
No*	No	No	No	Yes	No	No
No*	No	No	No	Yes	No	No
No*	No	No	No	Yes	No	No
No*	No	No	No	Yes	No	No
No*	No	No	No	Yes	No	No
No*	No	No	No	Yes	No	No
No*	No	No	No	Yes	No	No
No*	No	No	No	Yes	No	No

Table 2.4.2

Subnational bans+ on tobacco promotion and sponsorship

+ Only subnational jurisdictions for which legislation was available are reported here.

* A ban is in effect at national level.

COUNTRY	JURISDICTION
Argentina	Buenos Aires
	Catamarca
	Chaco
	Chubut
	Ciudad Autonoma de Buenos Aires
	Cordoba
	Corrientes
	Formosa
	La Pampa
	La Rioja
	Mendoza
	Neuquen
	Rio Negro
	San Luis
	Santa Cruz
	Santa Fe
	Santiago del Estero
Australia	Australian Capital Territory
	New South Wales
	Northern Territory
	Queensland
	South Australia
	Tasmania
	Victoria
	Western Australia
Belgium	Flanders
Bosnia and Herzegovina	Federacija Bosne i Hercegovine
	Republika Srpska
Canada	Alberta
	British Columbia
	Manitoba
	New Brunswick
	Newfoundland and Labrador
	Northwest Territories
	Nova Scotia
	Nunavut
	Ontario
	Prince Edward Island
	Quebec
	Saskatchewan
	Yukon
China	Hong Kong Special Administrative Region
	Macao Special Administrative Region
Egypt	Alexandria
India	Goa
	Tamil Nadu
Indonesia	Padang Panjang
Iraq	Arbïl
	As Sulaymanayah
	Duhok

BAN ON TOBACCO PROMOTION AND SPONSORSHIP						
FREE DISTRIBUTION BY MAIL OR THROUGH OTHER MEANS	PROMOTIONAL DISCOUNTS	NON-TOBACCO GOODS AND SERVICES IDENTIFIED WITH TOBACCO BRAND NAMES	BRAND NAME OF NON-TOBACCO PRODUCTS USED FOR TOBACCO PRODUCTS	APPEARANCE OF TOBACCO BRANDS IN TV AND/OR FILMS (PRODUCT PLACEMENT)	APPEARANCE OF TOBACCO PRODUCTS IN TV AND/OR FILMS	SPONSORED EVENTS
No	No	No*	No*	No*	No*	Yes
No	No	No*	No*	No*	No*	No*
No	No	Yes	Yes	Yes	Yes	Yes
No	No	Yes	Yes	Yes	Yes	Yes
Yes	No	No*	No*	No*	No*	Yes
No	No	Yes	Yes	Yes	Yes	Yes
No	No	No*	No*	No*	No*	No*
No	No	Yes	Yes	Yes	Yes	Yes
No	No	No*	No*	No*	No*	No*
No	No	No*	No*	No*	No*	No*
No	No	Yes	Yes	Yes	Yes	Yes
Yes	Yes	Yes	Yes	Yes	Yes	Yes
No	No	No*	No*	No*	No*	Yes
No	No	No*	No*	No*	No*	Yes
No	No	No*	No*	No*	No*	Yes
No	No	No*	No*	No*	No*	Yes
No	No	No*	No*	No*	No*	No*
Yes	Yes	No*	No	No*	No	Yes
Yes	Yes	Yes	No	No*	No	Yes
No	No	No*	No	No*	No	Yes
Yes	Yes	No*	No	No*	No	No*
Yes	Yes	No*	No	Yes	No	Yes
Yes	No	Yes	No	No*	No	No*
Yes	Yes	No*	No	Yes	No	No*
Yes	No	Yes	No	No*	No	Yes
No*	No*	No	No	Yes	No	No*
No	No	No	No	Yes	No	Yes
Yes	Yes	No	No	Yes	Yes	Yes
No*	No*	No	No	No*	No	No*
No*	No*	No	No	No*	No	No*
No*	No*	No	No	No*	No	No*
No*	No*	No	No	No*	No	No*
No*	No*	No	No	No*	No	No*
No*	No*	No	No	No*	No	No*
No*	No*	No	No	No*	No	No*
No*	No*	No	No	No*	No	No*
No*	No*	No	No	No*	No	No*
No*	No*	No	No	No*	No	No*
Yes	Yes	No	No	No*	No	Yes
No*	No*	No	No	No*	No	No*
No*	No*	No	No	No*	No	No*
Yes	Yes	Yes	No	Yes	Yes	No
Yes	Yes	No	No	Yes	No	Yes
Yes	Yes	Yes	Yes	Yes	Yes	No
No*	No*	No*	No*	No*	No*	No*
No*	No*	No*	No*	No*	No*	No*
No*	No*	No*	No	No	No*	No
No	No	No*	No	No*	No*	No
No	No	No*	No	No*	No*	No
No	No	No*	No	No*	No*	No

Table 2.4.2
Subnational bans+ on tobacco promotion and sponsorship (continued)

+ Only subnational jurisdictions for which legislation was available are reported here.

* A ban is in effect at national level.

COUNTRY	JURISDICTION
Lao People's Democratic Republic	Vientiane Capital
Mexico	Aguascalientes
	Baja California
	Baja California Sur
	Campeche
	Chiapas
	Chihuahua
	Coahuila de Zaragoza
	Colima
	Durango
	Federal District (Mexico City)
	Guanajuato
	Guerrero
	Hidalgo
	Jalisco
	Mexico
	Michoacan de Ocampo
	Morelos
	Nayarit
	Nuevo Leon
	Oaxaca
	Puebla
	Queretaro Arteaga
	Quintana Roo
	San Luis Potosi
	Sinaloa
	Sonora
	Tabasco
	Tamaulipas
	Tlaxcala
	Veracruz de Ignacio de la Llave
	Yucatan
	Zacatecas
Micronesia (Federated States of)	Chuuk
	Pohnpei
	Yap
Nigeria	Cross River
Oman	Dhofar
	Sahar
Switzerland	Appenzell Ausserrhoden
	Basel-Landschaft
	Basel-Stadt
	Bern
	Genève
	Graubünden
	Sankt Gallen
	Solothurn
	Thurgau
	Ticino
	Uri

BAN ON TOBACCO PROMOTION AND SPONSORSHIP						
FREE DISTRIBUTION BY MAIL OR THROUGH OTHER MEANS	PROMOTIONAL DISCOUNTS	NON-TOBACCO GOODS AND SERVICES IDENTIFIED WITH TOBACCO BRAND NAMES	BRAND NAME OF NON-TOBACCO PRODUCTS USED FOR TOBACCO PRODUCTS	APPEARANCE OF TOBACCO BRANDS IN TV AND/OR FILMS (PRODUCT PLACEMENT)	APPEARANCE OF TOBACCO PRODUCTS IN TV AND/OR FILMS	SPONSORED EVENTS
No	No	No	No	No	No	No*
No*	No*	No*	No	No	No	No*
No*	No*	No*	No	No	No	No*
No*	No*	No*	No	No	No	No*
No*	No*	No*	No	No	No	No*
No*	No*	No*	No	No	No	No*
Yes	No*	Yes	No	No	No	No*
No*	No*	No*	No	No	No	No*
No*	No*	No*	No	No	No	No*
No*	No*	No*	No	No	No	No*
No*	No*	No*	No	No	No	No*
No*	No*	No*	No	No	No	No*
No*	No*	No*	No	No	No	No*
No*	No*	No*	No	No	No	No*
No*	No*	No*	No	No	No	No*
No*	No*	No*	No	No	No	No*
No*	No*	No*	No	No	No	No*
No*	No*	No*	No	No	No	No*
No*	No*	No*	No	No	No	No*
No*	No*	No*	No	No	No	No*
No*	No*	No*	No	No	No	No*
No*	No*	No*	No	No	No	No*
No*	No*	No*	No	No	No	No*
No*	No*	No*	No	No	No	No*
No*	No*	No*	No	No	No	No*
No*	No*	No*	No	No	No	No*
No*	No*	No*	No	No	No	No*
No*	No*	No*	No	No	No	No*
No*	No*	No*	No	No	No	No*
No*	No*	No*	No	No	No	No*
Yes	No*	No*	No	No	No	No*
No*	No*	No*	No	No	No	No*
Yes	No*	No*	No	No	No	No*
No	No	No	No	No	No	No
No	No	Yes	No	Yes	No	Yes
No	No	No	No	No	No	No
No	No	No	No	No	No	Yes
No	No	No	No	No	No	Yes
No	No	No	No	No	No	No*
No	No	No	No	No	No	No
No	No	No	No	No	No	No
No	No	No	No	No	No	No
No	No	No	No	No	No	No
No	No	No	No	No	No	No
No	No	No	No	No	No	No
No	No	No	No	No	No	No
No	No	No	No	No	No	No
No	No	No	No	No	No	No
No	No	No	No	No	No	No
No	No	No	No	No	No	No

Table 2.4.2
Subnational bans+ on tobacco promotion and sponsorship (continued)

+ Only subnational jurisdictions for which legislation was available are reported here.

COUNTRY	JURISDICTION
Switzerland (continued)	Valais
	Vaud
	Zug
	Zürich
United Kingdom of Great Britain and Northern Ireland	England
	Northern Ireland
	Scotland
	Wales
United States of America	Alabama
	Alaska
	Arizona
	Arkansas
	California
	Colorado
	Connecticut
	Delaware
	District of Columbia
	Florida
	Georgia
	Hawaii
	Idaho
	Illinois
	Indiana
	Iowa
	Kansas
	Kentucky
	Louisiana
	Maine
	Maryland
	Massachusetts
	Michigan
	Minnesota
	Mississippi
	Missouri
	Montana
	Nebraska
	Nevada
	New Hampshire
	New Jersey
	New Mexico
	New York
	North Carolina
	North Dakota
	Ohio
	Oklahoma
	Oregon
	Pennsylvania
	Puerto Rico
	Rhode Island

BAN ON TOBACCO PROMOTION AND SPONSORSHIP						
FREE DISTRIBUTION BY MAIL OR THROUGH OTHER MEANS	PROMOTIONAL DISCOUNTS	NON-TOBACCO GOODS AND SERVICES IDENTIFIED WITH TOBACCO BRAND NAMES	BRAND NAME OF NON-TOBACCO PRODUCTS USED FOR TOBACCO PRODUCTS	APPEARANCE OF TOBACCO BRANDS IN TV AND/OR FILMS (PRODUCT PLACEMENT)	APPEARANCE OF TOBACCO PRODUCTS IN TV AND/OR FILMS	SPONSORED EVENTS
No	No	No	No	No	No	No
No	No	No	No	No	No	No
No	No	No	No	No	No	No
No	No	No	No	No	No	No
Yes	Yes	Yes	Yes	Yes	No	Yes
Yes	Yes	Yes	Yes	Yes	No	Yes
Yes	Yes	Yes	Yes	Yes	No	Yes
Yes	Yes	Yes	Yes	Yes	No	Yes
No	No	No	No	No	No	No
No	No	No	No	No	No	No
No	No	No	No	No	No	No
No	No	No	No	No	No	No
No	No	No	No	No	No	No
No	No	No	No	No	No	No
No	No	No	No	No	No	No
No	No	No	No	No	No	No
No	No	No	No	No	No	No
No	No	No	No	No	No	No
No	No	No	No	No	No	No
No	No	No	No	No	No	No
No	No	No	No	No	No	No
No	No	No	No	No	No	No
No	No	No	No	No	No	No
No	No	No	No	No	No	No
No	No	No	No	No	No	No
No	No	No	No	No	No	No
No	No	No	No	No	No	No
No	No	No	No	No	No	No
No	No	No	No	No	No	No
No	No	No	No	No	No	No
No	No	No	No	No	No	No
No	No	No	No	No	No	No
No	No	No	No	No	No	No
No	No	No	No	No	No	No
No	No	No	No	No	No	No
No	No	No	No	No	No	No
No	No	No	No	No	No	No
No	No	No	No	No	No	No
No	No	No	No	No	No	No
No	No	No	No	No	No	No
No	No	No	No	No	No	No
No	No	No	No	No	No	No
No	No	No	No	No	No	No
No	No	No	No	No	No	No
No	No	No	No	No	No	No
No	No	No	No	No	No	No
No	No	No	No	No	No	No
No	No	No	No	No	No	No
No	No	No	No	No	No	No

Table 2.4.2
Subnational bans+ on tobacco promotion and sponsorship (continued)

+ Only subnational jurisdictions for which legislation was available are reported here.

COUNTRY	JURISDICTION
United States of America (continued)	South Carolina
	South Dakota
	Tennessee
	Texas
	Utah
	Vermont
	Virginia
	Washington
	West Virginia
	Wisconsin
	Wyoming

BAN ON TOBACCO PROMOTION AND SPONSORSHIP						
FREE DISTRIBUTION BY MAIL OR THROUGH OTHER MEANS	PROMOTIONAL DISCOUNTS	NON-TOBACCO GOODS AND SERVICES IDENTIFIED WITH TOBACCO BRAND NAMES	BRAND NAME OF NON-TOBACCO PRODUCTS USED FOR TOBACCO PRODUCTS	APPEARANCE OF TOBACCO BRANDS IN TV AND/OR FILMS (PRODUCT PLACEMENT)	APPEARANCE OF TOBACCO PRODUCTS IN TV AND/OR FILMS	SPONSORED EVENTS
No	No	No	No	No	No	No
No	No	No	No	No	No	No
No	No	No	No	No	No	No
No	No	No	No	No	No	No
No	No	No	No	No	No	No
No	No	No	No	No	No	No
No	No	No	No	No	No	No
No	No	No	No	No	No	No
No	No	No	No	No	No	No
No	No	No	No	No	No	No
No	No	No	No	No	No	No

APPENDIX III: **YEAR OF HIGHEST LEVEL OF ACHIEVEMENT IN SELECTED TOBACCO CONTROL MEASURES**

Appendix III provides information on the year in which respective countries attained the highest level of achievement for five of the MPOWER measures. Data are shown for each WHO region separately.

For *Monitoring tobacco use* the earliest year assessed is 2007. However, it is possible that while 2007 is reported as the year of highest achievement for some countries, they actually may have reached this level earlier.

Years of highest level achievement of the MPOWER measure *Raise taxes on tobacco* are not included in this appendix. The share of taxes in product price depends both on tax policy and on demand and supply factors that affect manufacturing and retail prices. Countries with tax increases might have seen the share of tax remain unchanged or even decline if the non-tax share of price rose at the same, or a higher rate, complicating the interpretation of the year of highest level of achievement. See Technical Note III for details on the construction of tax shares.

Africa

Table 3.1.1
Year of highest level of achievement in selected tobacco control measures in Africa

Note: Refer to Technical Note I for definitions of highest level of achievement. An empty cell indicates that the population is not covered by the measure at the highest level of achievement.

* Or earlier year.

⊙ Policy adopted but not implemented by 31 December 2012.

COUNTRY
Algeria
Angola
Benin
Botswana
Burkina Faso
Burundi
Cameroon
Cape Verde
Central African Republic
Chad
Comoros
Congo
Côte d'Ivoire
Democratic Republic of the Congo
Equatorial Guinea
Eritrea
Ethiopia
Gabon
Gambia
Ghana
Guinea
Guinea-Bissau
Kenya
Lesotho
Liberia
Madagascar
Malawi
Mali
Mauritania
Mauritius
Mozambique
Namibia
Niger
Nigeria
Rwanda
Sao Tome and Principe
Senegal
Seychelles
Sierra Leone
South Africa
Swaziland
Togo
Uganda
United Republic of Tanzania
Zambia
Zimbabwe

YEAR THE HIGHEST LEVEL OF ACHIEVEMENT WAS ATTAINED				
MONITOR TOBACCO USE	PROTECT PEOPLE FROM TOBACCO SMOKE	OFFER HELP TO QUIT TOBACCO USE	WARN ABOUT THE DANGERS OF TOBACCO	ENFORCE BANS ON TOBACCO ADVERTISING, PROMOTION AND SPONSORSHIP
	2010			
	2010			2010
	2012			
				2004
				2012
				2012
				2007
			2012	2003
2007*			2008	2008
	2010			
			2012	2006
	2009		2012	
2007*				
2012				2012 ⊙

The Americas

Table 3.1.2
Year of highest level of achievement in selected tobacco control measures in the Americas

Note: Refer to Technical Note I for definitions of highest level of achievement. An empty cell indicates that the population is not covered by the measure at the highest level of achievement.

* Or earlier year.

. . . Data not available.

COUNTRY
Antigua and Barbuda
Argentina
Bahamas
Barbados
Belize
Bolivia (Plurinational State of)
Brazil
Canada
Chile
Colombia
Costa Rica
Cuba
Dominica
Dominican Republic
Ecuador
El Salvador
Grenada
Guatemala
Guyana
Haiti
Honduras
Jamaica
Mexico
Nicaragua
Panama
Paraguay
Peru
Saint Kitts and Nevis
Saint Lucia
Saint Vincent and the Grenadines
Suriname
Trinidad and Tobago
United States of America
Uruguay
Venezuela (Bolivarian Republic of)

YEAR THE HIGHEST LEVEL OF ACHIEVEMENT WAS ATTAINED				
MONITOR TOBACCO USE	PROTECT PEOPLE FROM TOBACCO SMOKE	OFFER HELP TO QUIT TOBACCO USE	WARN ABOUT THE DANGERS OF TOBACCO	ENFORCE BANS ON TOBACCO ADVERTISING, PROMOTION AND SPONSORSHIP
2010	2011		2011	
2007*	2010			
			2009	
	2011	2002	2003	2012
2007*	2007	2002	2011	
2007*			2006	
	2008			2009
2010	2012			
	2011		2012	
		...	2011	
	2008			
	2010			
			2009	
	2008	2009	2005	2008
	2010		2010	
	2009			
2007*		2006		
2007*	2005	2012	2005	
	2011		2004	

South-East Asia

Table 3.1.3
Year of highest level of achievement in selected tobacco control measures in South-East Asia

Note: Refer to Technical Note I for definitions of highest level of achievement. An empty cell indicates that the population is not covered by the measure at the highest level of achievement.

* Or earlier year.

COUNTRY
Bangladesh
Bhutan
Democratic People's Republic of Korea
India
Indonesia
Maldives
Myanmar
Nepal
Sri Lanka
Thailand
Timor-Leste

YEAR THE HIGHEST LEVEL OF ACHIEVEMENT WAS ATTAINED				
MONITOR TOBACCO USE	PROTECT PEOPLE FROM TOBACCO SMOKE	OFFER HELP TO QUIT TOBACCO USE	WARN ABOUT THE DANGERS OF TOBACCO	ENFORCE BANS ON TOBACCO ADVERTISING, PROMOTION AND SPONSORSHIP
	2005			
2007*				
				2010
	2011		2011	
			2012	
2008	2010	2012	2006	

Europe

Table 3.1.4
Year of highest level of achievement in selected tobacco control measures in Europe

Note: Refer to Technical Note I for definitions of highest level of achievement. An empty cell indicates that the population is not covered by the measure at the highest level of achievement.

* Or earlier year.

. . . Data not available.

COUNTRY
Albania
Andorra
Armenia
Austria
Azerbaijan
Belarus
Belgium
Bosnia and Herzegovina
Bulgaria
Croatia
Cyprus
Czech Republic
Denmark
Estonia
Finland
France
Georgia
Germany
Greece
Hungary
Iceland
Ireland
Israel
Italy
Kazakhstan
Kyrgyzstan
Latvia
Lithuania
Luxembourg
Malta
Monaco
Montenegro
Netherlands
Norway
Poland
Portugal
Republic of Moldova
Romania
Russian Federation
San Marino
Serbia
Slovakia
Slovenia
Spain
Sweden
Switzerland
Tajikistan
The former Yugoslav Republic of Macedonia
Turkey
Turkmenistan
Ukraine
United Kingdom of Great Britain and Northern Ireland
Uzbekistan

YEAR THE HIGHEST LEVEL OF ACHIEVEMENT WAS ATTAINED				
MONITOR TOBACCO USE	PROTECT PEOPLE FROM TOBACCO SMOKE	OFFER HELP TO QUIT TOBACCO USE	WARN ABOUT THE DANGERS OF TOBACCO	ENFORCE BANS ON TOBACCO ADVERTISING, PROMOTION AND SPONSORSHIP
	2006			2006
2010				
2010				
2007*				
2008	2012			
2007*				
2010		...		
2007*				
2007*				
2010		2007		
2007*				
2010	2010			
2012				
2010				
2007*	2004	2003		
2010		...		
2007*				
2010				
2007*				
2007*				
2010				
	2010			
2007*				
2007*				
2010				
2007*		2007		
2007*				
2007*	2010			2010
2007*				
2010				
2007*	2008	2010	2012	2012
	2000			
2007*			2009	
2007*	2006	2001		

Eastern Mediterranean

Table 3.1.5

Year of highest level of achievement in selected tobacco control measures in the Eastern Mediterranean

Note: Refer to Technical Note I for definitions of highest level of achievement. An empty cell indicates that the population is not covered by the measure at the highest level of achievement.

* Or earlier year.

... Data not available.

< Refers to a territory.

COUNTRY
Afghanistan
Bahrain
Djibouti
Egypt
Iran (Islamic Republic of)
Iraq
Jordan
Kuwait
Lebanon
Libya
Morocco
Oman
Pakistan
Qatar
Saudi Arabia
Somalia
South Sudan
Sudan
Syrian Arab Republic
Tunisia
United Arab Emirates
West Bank and Gaza Strip <
Yemen

YEAR THE HIGHEST LEVEL OF ACHIEVEMENT WAS ATTAINED				
MONITOR TOBACCO USE	PROTECT PEOPLE FROM TOBACCO SMOKE	OFFER HELP TO QUIT TOBACCO USE	WARN ABOUT THE DANGERS OF TOBACCO	ENFORCE BANS ON TOBACCO ADVERTISING, PROMOTION AND SPONSORSHIP
				2011
			2008	2007
2007*			2008	
2010	2007	2008	2008	2007
2007*				
		...		1995
	2011			
	2009			2009
2007*				
	2009			
		2010		
	2011			

Western Pacific

Table 3.1.6
Year of highest level of achievement in selected tobacco control measures in the Western Pacific

Note: Refer to Technical Note I for definitions of highest level of achievement. An empty cell indicates that the population is not covered by the measure at the highest level of achievement.

* Or earlier year.

⊙ Policy adopted but not implemented by 31 December 2012.

COUNTRY
Australia
Brunei Darussalam
Cambodia
China
Cook Islands
Fiji
Japan
Kiribati
Lao People's Democratic Republic
Malaysia
Marshall Islands
Micronesia (Federated States of)
Mongolia
Nauru
New Zealand
Niue
Palau
Papua New Guinea
Philippines
Republic of Korea
Samoa
Singapore
Solomon Islands
Tonga
Tuvalu
Vanuatu
Viet Nam

YEAR THE HIGHEST LEVEL OF ACHIEVEMENT WAS ATTAINED				
MONITOR TOBACCO USE	PROTECT PEOPLE FROM TOBACCO SMOKE	OFFER HELP TO QUIT TOBACCO USE	WARN ABOUT THE DANGERS OF TOBACCO	ENFORCE BANS ON TOBACCO ADVERTISING, PROMOTION AND SPONSORSHIP
2007*	2005	2011	2004	
	2012		2007	
2007*				
2012			2008	
	2006			
2010	2012		2012	
	2009			
2008	2003	2000	2007	
2010				
	2012			
2007*		2006		
		1999	2003	
				2008
				2008
				2012 ⊙

APPENDIX IV: HIGHEST LEVEL OF ACHIEVEMENT IN SELECTED TOBACCO CONTROL MEASURES IN THE 100 BIGGEST CITIES IN THE WORLD

Appendix IV provides information on whether the populations of the 100 biggest cities in the world are covered by selected tobacco control measures at the highest level of achievement.

Cities are listed by population size in descending order. There are many ways to define geographically and measure the size of "a city". For the purposes of this report, we focused on the jurisdictional boundaries of cities, since subnational laws will apply to populations within jurisdictions. Where a large "city" includes several jurisdictions or parts of jurisdictions, it is possible that not everyone in the entire "city" is covered by the same laws. We therefore use the list of cities and their populations published in the UNSD Demographic Yearbook, since these are defined jurisdictionally. Please refer to Tables 8 and 8a at http://unstats.un.org/unsd/demographic/products/dyb/dyb2009-2010.htm to access the source data.

Refer to Technical Note I for definitions of highest level of achievement.

Table 4.1.0

Highest level of achievement in selected tobacco control measures in the 100 biggest cities in the world

N	City's population covered by national legislation or policy at the highest level of achievement
S	City's population covered by state-level legislation or policy at the highest level of achievement
C	City's population covered by city-level legislation or policy at the highest level of achievement

Notes: An empty cell indicates that the population in the respective city is not covered by the measure at the highest level of achievement. Refer to Technical Note I for definitions of highest level of achievement.

CITY	POPULATION
Shanghai	14 348 535
Mumbai	11 978 450
Beijing	11 509 595
São Paulo	11 037 593
Moscow	10 536 005
Seoul	10 036 377
Delhi	9 879 172
Chongqing	9 691 901
Karachi	9 339 023
Mexico City	8 851 080
Jakarta	8 820 603
Guangzhou	8 524 826
Tokyo	8 489 653
Lima	8 472 935
New York	8 391 881
Wuhan	8 312 700
Tianjin	7 499 181
Cairo	7 248 671
Tehran	7 088 287
Shenzhen	7 008 831
Hong Kong Special Administrative Region of China	7 003 700
Dongguan	6 445 777
Rio de Janeiro	6 186 710
Shenyang	5 303 053
Lagos	5 195 247
Lahore	5 143 495
Santiago	5 015 680
Singapore	4 987 600
Saint Petersburg	4 591 065
Kolkata	4 572 876
Sydney	4 504 469
Xi'an	4 481 508
Aleppo	4 450 000
Chennai	4 343 645
Chengdu	4 333 541
Bangalore	4 301 326
Riyadh	4 087 152
Alexandria	4 030 582
Melbourne	3 995 537
Los Angeles	3 831 868
Hyderabad	3 637 483
Nanjing	3 624 234
Yokohama	3 579 628
Ahmedabad	3 520 085
Haerbin	3 481 504
Busan	3 471 154
Berlin	3 386 667
Dalian	3 245 191
Changchun	3 225 557
Madrid	3 213 271
Nairobi	3 138 369

COVERAGE AT THE HIGHEST LEVEL OF ACHIEVEMENT					COUNTRY
PROTECT PEOPLE FROM TOBACCO SMOKE	OFFER HELP TO QUIT TOBACCO USE	WARN ABOUT THE DANGERS OF TOBACCO	ENFORCE BANS ON TOBACCO ADVERTISING, PROMOTION AND SPONSORSHIP	RAISE TAXES ON TOBACCO	
					China
					India
					China
N	N	N	N		Brazil
					Russian Federation
	N				Republic of Korea
					India
					China
N					Pakistan
S		N			Mexico
S					Indonesia
					China
					Japan
N		N			Peru
S	N				United States of America
					China
					China
		N			Egypt
N	N	N	N		Iran (Islamic Republic of)
					China
C	C	C	C		China
					China
N	N	N	N		Brazil
					China
					Nigeria
N					Pakistan
		N		N	Chile
	N	N			Singapore
					Russian Federation
					India
S	N	N			Australia
					China
					Syrian Arab Republic
					India
					China
					India
					Saudi Arabia
		N			Egypt
S	N	N			Australia
	N				United States of America
					India
					China
					Japan
					India
					China
	N				Republic of Korea
					Germany
					China
					China
N			N	N	Spain
			N		Kenya

Table 4.1.0

Highest level of achievement in selected tobacco control measures in the 100 biggest cities in the world (continued)

N	City's population covered by national legislation or policy at the highest level of achievement
S	City's population covered by state-level legislation or policy at the highest level of achievement
C	City's population covered by city-level legislation or policy at the highest level of achievement

Notes: An empty cell indicates that the population in the respective city is not covered by the measure at the highest level of achievement. Refer to Technical Note I for definitions of highest level of achievement.

SYMBOLS LEGEND

☆	Separate, completely enclosed smoking rooms are allowed if they are separately ventilated to the outside and kept under negative air pressure in relation to the surrounding areas. Given the difficulty of meeting the very strict requirements delineated for such rooms, they appear to be a practical impossibility but no reliable empirical evidence is presently available to ascertain whether they have been constructed.
⊙	Policy adopted but not implemented by 31 December 2012.
–	Data not reported.

CITY	POPULATION
Kabul	3 052 000
Kunming	3 035 406
Ho Chi Minh	3 015 743
Jinan	2 999 934
Salvador	2 998 056
Casablanca	2 995 000
Guiyang	2 985 105
Chicago	2 851 268
Zibo	2 817 479
Jiddah	2 801 481
Rome	2 734 072
Kiev	2 724 224
Qingdao	2 720 972
Addis Ababa	2 646 000
Incheon	2 645 189
Osaka	2 628 811
Surabaya	2 611 506
Brasília	2 606 885
Zhengzhou	2 589 387
Pyongyang	2 581 076
Giza	2 572 581
Taiyuan	2 558 382
Kanpur	2 551 337
Pune	2 538 473
Damascus Rural (Rif Dimashq)	2 529 000
Fortaleza	2 505 552
Chaoyang	2 470 812
Belo Horizonte	2 452 617
Hangzhou	2 451 319
Daegu	2 443 994
Surat	2 433 835
Mashhad	2 427 316
Zhongshan	2 363 322
Jaipur	2 322 575
Bandung	2 288 570
Houston	2 257 926
Guayaquil	2 253 987
Nagoya	2 215 062
Lucknow	2 185 927
Quezon City	2 173 831
Kano	2 166 554
La Habana	2 145 063
Tashkent	2 137 218
Nanhai	2 133 741
Paris	2 125 851
Fuzhou	2 124 435
Changsha	2 122 873
Medan	2 097 610
Baku	2 052 322

COVERAGE AT THE HIGHEST LEVEL OF ACHIEVEMENT					COUNTRY
PROTECT PEOPLE FROM TOBACCO SMOKE	OFFER HELP TO QUIT TOBACCO USE	WARN ABOUT THE DANGERS OF TOBACCO	ENFORCE BANS ON TOBACCO ADVERTISING, PROMOTION AND SPONSORSHIP	RAISE TAXES ON TOBACCO	
					Afghanistan
					China
			N ⊙		Viet Nam
					China
N	N	N	N		Brazil
					Morocco
					China
S	N				United States of America
					China
					Saudi Arabia
☆				N	Italy
		N			Ukraine
					China
					Ethiopia
	N				Republic of Korea
					Japan
					Indonesia
N	N	N	N		Brazil
					China
–	–	–	–	–	Democratic People's Republic of Korea
		N			Egypt
					China
					India
					India
					Syrian Arab Republic
N	N	N	N		Brazil
					China
N	N	N	N		Brazil
					China
	N				Republic of Korea
					India
N	N	N	N		Iran (Islamic Republic of)
					China
					India
					Indonesia
C	N				United States of America
N and C		N			Ecuador
					Japan
					India
					Philippines
					Nigeria
				N	Cuba
					Uzbekistan
					China
☆	N			N	France
					China
					China
					Indonesia
					Azerbaijan

APPENDIX V: STATUS OF THE WHO FRAMEWORK CONVENTION ON TOBACCO CONTROL

Appendix V shows the status of the WHO Framework Convention on Tobacco Control (WHO FCTC). Ratification is the international act by which countries that have already signed a convention formally state their consent to be bound by it. Accession is the international act by which countries that have not signed a treaty/convention formally state their consent to be bound by it. Acceptance and approval are the legal equivalent of ratification. Signature of a convention indicates that a country is not legally bound by the treaty but is committed not to undermine its provisions.

The WHO FCTC entered into force on 27 February 2005, on the 90th day after the deposit of the 40th instrument of ratification in the United Nations headquarters in New York, the depository of the treaty. The treaty remains open for ratification, acceptance, approval, formal confirmation and accession indefinitely for States and eligible regional economic integration organizations wishing to become Parties to it.

Table 5.1.0

Status of the WHO Framework Convention on Tobacco Control, as of 2 May 2013

* Ratification is the international act by which countries that have already signed a treaty or convention formally state their consent to be bound by it.

[a] Accession is the international act by which countries that have not signed a treaty/convention formally state their consent to be bound by it.

[A] Acceptance is the international act, similar to ratification, by which countries that have already signed a treaty/convention formally state their consent to be bound by it.

[AA] Approval is the international act, similar to ratification, by which countries that have already signed a treaty/convention formally state their consent to be bound by it.

[c] Formal confirmation is the international act corresponding to ratification by a State, whereby an international organization (in the case of the WHO FCTC, competent regional economic integration organizations) formally state their consent to be bound by a treaty/convention.

[d] Succession is the international act, however phrased or named, by which successor States formally state their consent to be bound by treaties/conventions originally entered into by their predecessor State.

COUNTRY	DATE OF SIGNATURE	DATE OF RATIFICATION* (OR LEGAL EQUIVALENT)
Afghanistan	29 June 2004	13 August 2010
Albania	29 June 2004	26 April 2006
Algeria	20 June 2003	30 June 2006
Andorra		
Angola	29 June 2004	20 September 2007
Antigua and Barbuda	28 June 2004	5 June 2006
Argentina	25 September 2003	
Armenia		29 November 2004 [a]
Australia	5 December 2003	27 October 2004
Austria	28 August 2003	15 September 2005
Azerbaijan		1 November 2005 [a]
Bahamas	29 June 2004	3 November 2009
Bahrain		20 March 2007 [a]
Bangladesh	16 June 2003	14 June 2004
Barbados	28 June 2004	3 November 2005
Belarus	17 June 2004	8 September 2005
Belgium	22 January 2004	1 November 2005
Belize	26 September 2003	15 December 2005
Benin	18 June 2004	3 November 2005
Bhutan	9 December 2003	23 August 2004
Bolivia (Plurinational State of)	27 February 2004	15 September 2005
Bosnia and Herzegovina		10 July 2009
Botswana	16 June 2003	31 January 2005
Brazil	16 June 2003	3 November 2005
Brunei Darussalam	3 June 2004	3 June 2004
Bulgaria	22 December 2003	7 November 2005
Burkina Faso	22 December 2003	31 July 2006
Burundi	16 June 2003	22 November 2005
Cambodia	25 May 2004	15 November 2005
Cameroon	13 May 2004	3 February 2006
Canada	15 July 2003	26 November 2004
Cape Verde	17 February 2004	4 October 2005
Central African Republic	29 December 2003	7 November 2005
Chad	22 June 2004	30 January 2006
Chile	25 September 2003	13 June 2005
China	10 November 2003	11 October 2005
Colombia		10 April 2008 [a]
Comoros	27 February 2004	24 January 2006
Congo	23 March 2004	6 February 2007
Cook Islands	14 May 2004	14 May 2004
Costa Rica	3 July 2003	21 August 2008
Côte d'Ivoire	24 July 2003	13 August 2010
Croatia	2 June 2004	14 July 2008
Cuba	29 June 2004	
Cyprus	24 May 2004	26 October 2005
Czech Republic	16 June 2003	1 June 2012
Democratic People's Republic of Korea	17 June 2003	27 April 2005
Democratic Republic of the Congo	28 June 2004	28 October 2005
Denmark	16 June 2003	16 December 2004
Djibouti	13 May 2004	31 July 2005
Dominica	29 June 2004	24 July 2006

COUNTRY	DATE OF SIGNATURE	DATE OF RATIFICATION* (OR LEGAL EQUIVALENT)
Dominican Republic		
Ecuador	22 March 2004	25 July 2006
Egypt	17 June 2003	25 February 2005
El Salvador	18 March 2004	
Equatorial Guinea		17 September 2005 [a]
Eritrea		
Estonia	8 June 2004	27 July 2005
Ethiopia	25 February 2004	
European Community	16 June 2003	30 June 2005 [c]
Fiji	3 October 2003	3 October 2003
Finland	16 June 2003	24 January 2005
France	16 June 2003	19 October 2004 [AA]
Gabon	22 August 2003	20 February 2009
Gambia	16 June 2003	18 September 2007
Georgia	20 February 2004	14 February 2006
Germany	24 October 2003	16 December 2004
Ghana	20 June 2003	29 November 2004
Greece	16 June 2003	27 January 2006
Grenada	29 June 2004	14 August 2007
Guatemala	25 September 2003	16 November 2005
Guinea	1 April 2004	7 November 2007
Guinea-Bissau		7 November 2008 [a]
Guyana		15 September 2005 [a]
Haiti	23 July 2003	
Honduras	18 June 2004	16 February 2005
Hungary	16 June 2003	7 April 2004
Iceland	16 June 2003	14 June 2004
India	10 September 2003	5 February 2004
Indonesia		
Iran (Islamic Republic of)	16 June 2003	6 November 2005
Iraq	29 June 2004	17 March 2008
Ireland	16 September 2003	7 November 2005
Israel	20 June 2003	24 August 2005
Italy	16 June 2003	2 July 2008
Jamaica	24 September 2003	7 July 2005
Japan	9 March 2004	8 June 2004 [A]
Jordan	28 May 2004	19 August 2004
Kazakhstan	21 June 2004	22 January 2007
Kenya	25 June 2004	25 June 2004
Kiribati	27 April 2004	15 September 2005
Kuwait	16 June 2003	12 May 2006
Kyrgyzstan	18 February 2004	25 May 2006
Lao People's Democratic Republic	29 June 2004	6 September 2006
Latvia	10 May 2004	10 February 2005
Lebanon	4 March 2004	7 December 2005
Lesotho	23 June 2004	14 January 2005
Liberia	25 June 2004	15 September 2009
Libya	18 June 2004	7 June 2005
Lithuania	22 September 2003	16 December 2004
Luxembourg	16 June 2003	30 June 2005
Madagascar	24 September 2003	22 September 2004

Table 5.1.0
Status of the WHO Framework Convention on Tobacco Control, as at 2 May 2013 (continued)

* Ratification is the international act by which countries that have already signed a treaty or convention formally state their consent to be bound by it.
[a] Accession is the international act by which countries that have not signed a treaty/convention formally state their consent to be bound by it.
[A] Acceptance is the international act, similar to ratification, by which countries that have already signed a treaty/convention formally state their consent to be bound by it.
[AA] Approval is the international act, similar to ratification, by which countries that have already signed a treaty/convention formally state their consent to be bound by it.
[c] Formal confirmation is the international act corresponding to ratification by a State, whereby an international organization (in the case of the WHO FCTC, competent regional economic integration organizations) formally state their consent to be bound by a treaty/convention.
[d] Succession is the international act, however phrased or named, by which successor States formally state their consent to be bound by treaties/conventions originally entered into by their predecessor State.

COUNTRY	DATE OF SIGNATURE	DATE OF RATIFICATION* (OR LEGAL EQUIVALENT)
Malawi		
Malaysia	23 September 2003	16 September 2005
Maldives	17 May 2004	20 May 2004
Mali	23 September 2003	19 October 2005
Malta	16 June 2003	24 September 2003
Marshall Islands	16 June 2003	8 December 2004
Mauritania	24 June 2004	28 October 2005
Mauritius	17 June 2003	17 May 2004
Mexico	12 August 2003	28 May 2004
Micronesia (Federated States of)	28 June 2004	18 March 2005
Monaco		
Mongolia	16 June 2003	27 January 2004
Montenegro		23 October 2006 [d]
Morocco	16 April 2004	
Mozambique	18 June 2003	
Myanmar	23 October 2003	21 April 2004
Namibia	29 January 2004	7 November 2005
Nauru		29 June 2004 [a]
Nepal	3 December 2003	7 November 2006
Netherlands	16 June 2003	27 January 2005 [A]
New Zealand	16 June 2003	27 January 2004
Nicaragua	7 June 2004	9 April 2008
Niger	28 June 2004	25 August 2005
Nigeria	28 June 2004	20 October 2005
Niue	18 June 2004	3 June 2005
Norway	16 June 2003	16 June 2003 [AA]
Oman		9 March 2005 [a]
Pakistan	18 May 2004	3 November 2004
Palau	16 June 2003	12 February 2004
Panama	26 September 2003	16 August 2004
Papua New Guinea	22 June 2004	25 May 2006
Paraguay	16 June 2003	26 September 2006
Peru	21 April 2004	30 November 2004
Philippines	23 September 2003	6 June 2005
Poland	14 June 2004	15 September 2006
Portugal	9 January 2004	8 November 2005 [AA]
Qatar	17 June 2003	23 July 2004
Republic of Korea	21 July 2003	16 May 2005
Republic of Moldova	29 June 2004	3 February 2009 [a]
Romania	25 June 2004	27 January 2006
Russian Federation		3 June 2008 [a]
Rwanda	2 June 2004	19 October 2005
Saint Kitts and Nevis	29 June 2004	21 June 2011
Saint Lucia	29 June 2004	7 November 2005
Saint Vincent and the Grenadines	14 June 2004	29 October 2010
Samoa	25 September 2003	3 November 2005
San Marino	26 September 2003	7 July 2004
Sao Tome and Principe	18 June 2004	12 April 2006
Saudi Arabia	24 June 2004	9 May 2005
Senegal	19 June 2003	27 January 2005
Serbia	28 June 2004	8 February 2006

COUNTRY	DATE OF SIGNATURE	DATE OF RATIFICATION* (OR LEGAL EQUIVALENT)
Seychelles	11 September 2003	12 November 2003
Sierra Leone		22 May 2009
Singapore	29 December 2003	14 May 2004
Slovakia	19 December 2003	4 May 2004
Slovenia	25 September 2003	15 March 2005
Solomon Islands	18 June 2004	10 August 2004
Somalia		
South Africa	16 June 2003	19 April 2005
Spain	16 June 2003	11 January 2005
Sri Lanka	23 September 2003	11 November 2003
Sudan	10 June 2004	31 October 2005
Suriname	24 June 2004	16 December 2008
Swaziland	29 June 2004	13 January 2006
Sweden	16 June 2003	7 July 2005
Switzerland	25 June 2004	
Syrian Arab Republic	11 July 2003	22 November 2004
Tajikistan		
Thailand	20 June 2003	8 November 2004
The former Yugoslav Republic of Macedonia		30 June 2006 [a]
Timor-Leste	25 May 2004	22 December 2004
Togo	12 May 2004	15 November 2005
Tonga	25 September 2003	8 April 2005
Trinidad and Tobago	27 August 2003	19 August 2004
Tunisia	22 August 2003	7 June 2010
Turkey	28 April 2004	31 December 2004
Turkmenistan		13 May 2011
Tuvalu	10 June 2004	26 September 2005
Uganda	5 March 2004	20 June 2007
Ukraine	25 June 2004	6 June 2006
United Arab Emirates	24 June 2004	7 November 2005
United Kingdom of Great Britain and Northern Ireland	16 June 2003	16 December 2004
United Republic of Tanzania	27 January 2004	30 April 2007
United States of America	10 May 2004	
Uruguay	19 June 2003	9 September 2004
Uzbekistan		15 May 2012
Vanuatu	22 April 2004	16 September 2005
Venezuela (Bolivarian Republic of)	22 September 2003	27 June 2006
Viet Nam	3 September 2003	17 December 2004
Yemen	20 June 2003	22 February 2007
Zambia		23 May 2008 [a]
Zimbabwe		

Source: WHO Tobacco Free Initiative web site (http://www.who.int/fctc/signatories_parties/en/index.html, accessed 2 May 2013).

Though not a Member State of WHO, as a Member State of the United Nations, Liechtenstein is also eligible to become Party to the WHO FCTC, though it has taken no action to do so.

On submitting instruments to become Party to the WHO FCTC, some Parties have included notes and/or declarations. All notes can be viewed at http://www.who.int/fctc/signatories_parties/en/index.html. All declarations can be viewed at http://www.who.int/fctc/declarations/en/index.html.

Acknowledgements

The World Health Organization gratefully acknowledges the contributions made to this report by the colleagues in WHO country and regional offices that helped compile the data, and especially the following individuals:

WHO African Region:
Deowan Mohee, Ezra Ogwell Ouma, Nivo Ramanandraibe.

WHO Region of the Americas:
Adriana Blanco, Roberta Caixeta, Chris Childs, Rosa Sandoval.

WHO South-East Asia Region:
Nyo Nyo Kyaing, Sonam Rinchen, Dhirendra N Sinha, Barbara Zolty.

WHO European Region:
Céline Brassart, Tiffany Fabro, Rula Khoury, Kristina Mauer-Stender, Liza Villas.

WHO Eastern Mediterranean Region:
Nisreen Abdulatif, Fatimah El-Awa, Heba Fouad, Inas Hamad, Aya Mostafa Kamal Eldin, Farrukh Qureshi.

WHO Western Pacific Region:
Mina Kashiwabara, Susy Mercado, James Rarick.

WHO Headquarters Geneva:
Virginia Arnold, Diana Baranga, Lubna Bhatti, Vinayak Prasad, Luminita Sanda, Gemma Vestal.

Kerstin Schotte coordinated the production of this report.

Administrative support was provided by: Zahra Ali Piazza, Miriamjoy Aryee-Quansah, Gareth Burns, Luis Madge, Carolyn Patten, Elizabeth Tecson, Rosane Serrao and Jennifer Volonnino.

Armando Peruga was responsible for the country legislation assessment and analysis performed by Marine Perraudin with support from Emma Bagard, Lara Carreno Ibanez, Hibberd Kline and Mayank Verma.

Data management, data analysis and creation of tables, graphs and appendices were performed by Alison Commar. The prevalence estimates were calculated by Alison Commar and Edouard Tursan d'Espaignet, with support from Sameer Pujari.

Data on tobacco cessation were updated by Dongbo Fu. Martin Raw provided us with additional information on cessation services.

Financial and economic review and analyis, including tobacco taxation and prices, were provided by Hussain Ghulam, Mark Goodchild, Deliana Kostova, Nigar Nargis, Anne-Marie Perucic, Alejandro Ramos, Chonlathan Visaruthvong and Ayda Yurekli. Tax and price data were collected with support from officials from ministries of finance and ministries of health, and by the Consortium pour la Recherche Economique et Sociale (CRES), Luk Joossens, Konstantin Krasovsky, Aleksandra Makaj, Awandha Mamahit and Paula Toledo.

We thank Jennifer Ellis and Kelly Henning of the Bloomberg Initiative to Reduce Tobacco Use for their collaboration.

Melanie Wakefield, Gerard Hastings, Kathryn Angus, Megan Bayly, Rebecca Bavinger, David Ham and Rajeev Cherukupalli, among others, provided invaluable feedback and comments, thank you very much. Many thanks also go to Tiffany Fabro for her thorough review of the references used in this report.

Special thanks also to Colin Mathers and Gretchen Stevens, and to the team of the Office on Smoking and Health of the US Centers for Disease Control and Prevention (CDC) as well as to the Institute for Global Tobacco Control at the Johns Hopkins Bloomberg School of Public Health.

We would like to thank World Lung Foundation for their collaboration in collecting the data on anti-tobacco mass media campaigns, specifically: Alexey Kotov, Matthew Kusen and Stephan Rabimov. We would also like to thank Tom Carroll, Nandita Murukutla, Rebecca Perl, Irina Morozova, Claudia Cedillo, Jorge Alday, Stephen Hamill, Winnie Chen, Chun-Yu Huang, Yvette Chang, Sam Kolinsky, Vaishakhi Malik, Trish Cotter, Tahir Turk and Sandra Mullin.

Special thanks also to the Campaign for Tobacco Free Kids (CTFK) and especially to Monique Muggli, Kaitlin Donley, Liz Candler, Jo Birckmayer, Emma Green and Maria Carmona for our constructive exchange of tobacco control information and legislation.

The screening for the anti-tobacco mass media data collection was performed by Nidhi Arora, Bernat Galan Marin, Valerie Gebera, Hannah Harris Smith, Chisato Ito, Hibberd Kline, Awandha Mamahit, Paula Toledo, Anna Vasilyeva, Mayank Verma and Xiao Liang Wang.

We thank the team from Alboum for the quality and speed with which we received the translations of legislation.

Drew Blakeman acted as principal drafter of this report with support from Katherine DeLand. Douglas Bettcher and Armando Peruga reviewed the full report and provided final comments. Special thanks are due to our copyeditor and proofreader Angela Burton and our designer Jean-Claude Fattier for their efficiency in helping to get this report published in time.

Production of this WHO document has been supported by a grant from the World Lung Foundation with financial support from Bloomberg Philanthropies. The contents of this document are the sole responsibility of WHO and should not be regarded as reflecting the positions of the World Lung Foundation.

Photographs and illustrations

© **World Health Organization**
Page 11
Page 16 – Photographer: Sanjit Das
Page 19
Page 43 – Photographer: Anna Kari
Page 54
Page 58
Page 62 – WHO Eastern Mediterranean Region
Page 66 – Photographer: Christopher Black
Page 70 – Photographer: Christopher Black
Page 73
Page 75 – Photographer: Olivier Asselin
Page 76 – WHO country office Ghana
Page 85 – Photographer: Christopher Black
Page 86/87 – Photographer: Sanjit Das
Page 106 – Photographer: Rod Curtis
Page 120 – Photographer: Chadin Tephaval

© **The World Bank**
Page 12 – Photographer: Curt Carnemark
Page 14 – Photographer: Scott Wallace
Page 24 – Photographer: Hidajet Delic-Degi
Page 26 – Photographer: Scott Wallace
Page 35 – Photographer: Julio Etchart
Page 36 – Photographer: Curt Carnemark
Page 38 – Photographer: Curt Carnemark
Page 41 – Photographer: Curt Carnemark
Page 83 – Photographer: Hidajet Delic-Degi
Page 90 – Photographer: Curt Carnemark
Page 174 – Photographer: Curt Carnemark
Page 188 – Photographer: Tran Thi Hoa
Page 194 – Photographer: Curt Carnemark
Page 200 – Photographer: Curt Carnemark

© **Keystone**
Page 18 – Photographer: Everett Kennedy Brown
Page 22 – Photographer: Liba Taylor
Page 28 – Photographer: Frans Lanting
Page 33 – Keystone/STR

Page 30 – © Directorate of Health, Norway
Page 47 – © F5 Görsel Sanatlar Merkezi, Tic. Ltd. Sti, Turkey
Page 50 – © World Health Organization/Centers for Disease Control and Prevention (CDC)
Page 53 – © Heba Fouad
Page 53 – © Ministerio de Salud and Instituto Conmemorativo Gorgas (MINSA – ICGES), Panama
Page 54 – © Union of European Football Associations (UEFA)
Page 57 – © Harbin Health Bureau, China
Page 57 – © IndyACT, Lebanon
Page 61 – © National Quitline, Thailand
Page 65 – © Office National de Lutte Antitabac, Madagascar
Page 65 – © Commonwealth of Australia
Page 69 – © Quit Victoria, Australia
Page 77 – © Ministry of Health and Medical Education, Islamic Republic of Iran

Design by **Estúdio Infinito**
Layout by **Jean-Claude Fattier**
Printed by **Imprimerie Centrale**

The *WHO Report on the Global Tobacco Epidemic, 2013* was made possible by funding from Bloomberg Philanthropies